THE ISLAMIC CHALLENGE
Politics and Religion in Western Europe

The Islamic Challenge

Politics and Religion in Western Europe

JYTTE KLAUSEN

OXFORD

UNIVERSITY PRESS

OXFORD

UNIVERSITY PRESS

Great Clarendon Street, Oxford OX2 6DP

Oxford University Press is a department of the University of Oxford.
It furthers the University's objective of excellence in research, scholarship,
and education by publishing worldwide in

Oxford New York

Auckland Cape Town Dar es Salaam Hong Kong Karachi
Kuala Lumpur Madrid Melbourne Mexico City Nairobi
New Delhi Shanghai Taipei Toronto

With offices in

Argentina Austria Brazil Chile Czech Republic France Greece
Guatemala Hungary Italy Japan Poland Portugal Singapore
South Korea Switzerland Thailand Turkey Ukraine Vietnam

Oxford is a registered trade mark of Oxford University Press
in the UK and in certain other countries

Published in the United States by
Oxford University Press Inc., New York

British Library Cataloguing in Publication Data
Data available

Library of Congress Cataloging in Publication Data
Data available

Typeset by SPI Publisher Services, Pondicherry, India
Printed in Great Britain by
Ashford Colour Press Ltd., Gosport, Hampshire

ISBN 978-0-19-928992-9 (Hbk.)
978-0-19-923198-0 (Pbk.)

1 3 5 7 9 10 8 6 4 2

Contents

Foreword to paperback edition

'If it is not a clash of civilization, what is it then?' wrote a skeptical reviewer of my book. People who are inclined to believe the thesis can find plenty of evidence to cite in support. Since the publication of the first edition, a number of Jihadist terrorist plots in Europe and the USA have come to light. There were worldwide protests against the twelve cartoons depicting Prophet Muhammad published by the Danish newspaper *Jyllands-Posten*. I still do not think that we are dealing with a cultural war between Muslims and the West.

New evidence from survey analysis suggests that the intuitive appeal of the 'clash' thesis is unfounded. The Pew Foundation and the Gallup organization recently devoted significant resources to the difficult task of doing surveys of the opinions of European Muslims, who because they are a minority population—about 3–4 percent of the general population—are not picked up in sufficient numbers by conventional survey methods. Their surveys asked the same questions in several countries, and therefore allow comparisons to be drawn between Muslims living in France and Britain, for example, and between the views of European Muslims and those of Muslims in the Islamic countries.

Both Pew and Gallup found wide areas of agreement between Muslims and non-Muslims in Europe. They also identified the particular issues whereupon disagreement prevails, above all issues relating to Islam. But that does not mean that Muslims disagree with basic European values. Rather, they are more likely to believe that Muslims are not given an equal opportunity to benefit from values such as religious toleration, equality before the law, and the right to personal dignity. The surveys confirm that the pro-integration and pro-democracy values and policy preferences, which I found among Muslim elites, are widely shared by European Muslims. Finally, they pinpoint the minority of European Muslims who subscribe to a radical Islamic political ideology.

The Danish cartoon controversy is instructive. If it does not represent a clash of civilizations, there is certainly an element of cultural misunderstanding involved. Humor does not travel well, and Danish humor is rather idiosyncratic. Some of the cartoons referred to Danish expressions and to particular well-known Danes that non-Danes would never pick up. Few outside Denmark noticed that some of the cartoons ridiculed the editors of the newspaper which published them. But the reaction was also misinterpreted. Most European

Muslims were not particularly upset by the paper's decision to depict the Prophet. They objected rather to what they saw as defamatory, blasphemous, 'Islamophobic', and racist representations.

There is another lesson to be drawn from this episode. The cartoons were published on September 30, 2005, but the international protests did not start until months later. A demonstration in Islamabad in mid November, led by the youth organization of the Jamaat-e-Islami, an Islamist party, presented an early warning sign of the global politicization of the conflict, but this was not appreciated for several months. On Friday, February 3, 2006, just in time for planned weekend demonstrations across Europe and the Middle East, Sheikh Yusuf al-Qaradawi, who lives in Qatar and is associated with the Muslim Brotherhood, said:

> The *ummah* [the Muslim nation] must rage in anger [over the cartoons]. It is told that Imam Al-Shafi'i said: "Whoever was angered and did not rage is a jackass." We are not a nation of jackasses. We are not jackasses for riding, but lions that roar. We are lions that zealously protect their dens, and avenge affronts to their sanctities. We are not a nation of jackasses. We are a nation that should rage for the sake of Allah, His Prophet, and His book. We are the nation of Muhammad, and we must never accept the degradation of our religion.

The sermon was broadcast by Al-Jazeera and Qatar TV, stations widely watched in Europe and elsewhere, and on IslamOnline, an Internet site run by al-Qaradawi. By the weekend, the Danish consulates in Beirut and Damascus were burned down. Worse was to follow. Six weeks later, when protests that spread from Europe to the Middle East, Africa, and Asia finally petered out, 250 people had died in riots, over half in Nigeria when demonstrations turned into violent clashes between Christians and Muslims. Watching the violent anger grow, the Danes and many others saw evidence that the 'clash of civilization' is a reality. European Muslims did not like the cartoons, but neither did they like the reaction in the Islamic countries.

In fact, the episode provides a lesson in globalization. Europe and the Islamic countries are united in a shared political cycle, a feedback loop, structured by cross-national contacts between diaspora communities and the 'home countries', political networks, and also by Internet and cell phones. Almost 80 percent of the individuals included in a thirteen-country public opinion survey conducted by the Pew Global Attitudes Project in 2006 had heard about the cartoons, a number that rose to 90 percent in the four European countries surveyed (France, Great Britain, Germany, and Spain) and in Jordan and Egypt. Each side thought the other was responsible. European Muslims thought Western arrogance was at fault; 'Westerners' thought that Muslims were at fault. (The unfortunate term is Pew's. Obviously, European Muslims are also 'Western'.)[1]

A more detailed reading of the polls tells a different story, however. The conflict was not so much about core values as about how to handle conflicts between shared values. Free speech may be valued, but it does not necessarily trump other values, such as respect for different beliefs. Christians and Jews are, perhaps for different reasons, also sensitive to blasphemy and hate speech issues. Of British Muslims 92 percent said they could understand that Muslims were offended by the Danish cartoons, but 52 percent of non-Muslim Britons also said they could understand why Muslims took offense, according to the Pew survey. A survey conducted by PolicyExchange, a liberal think tank, found British Muslims to be moderately supportive of free speech. Almost 37 percent of British Muslims agreed that 'one of the benefits of modern society is the freedom to criticize other people's religious or political views, even when it causes offense'. Interestingly, the general population was even less inclined to agree with this proposition (29 percent). The result should not surprise us. Muslims are a minority in Europe, and they often feel the weight of majority opinion. The researchers also found that most Muslim respondents readily admitted they did not like the cartoons but also thought that Muslims 'behaved badly'.[2]

What about support for democratic institutions? The 'clash of civilizations' argument presumes that Muslims are averse to elections and democratic institutions because Islamic religious law prohibits secular law-making. Gallup asked Muslims and non-Muslims in Berlin and Paris to say if they had confidence in various government institutions, and found that on balance Muslims are more supportive of elections, the judicial system, and even the media, than non-Muslims are. Almost 73 percent of Muslims in London said they were supportive of elections compared with 60 percent of non-Muslims. Only the military had greater support among non-Muslims than among Muslims. London Muslims (78 percent) were even more supportive of the police than the general public (69 percent). This is a bit of a surprise in view of frequent complaints by British Muslim lobby groups about 'Islamophobic' policing. The police also had majority support among Muslims in Paris and Berlin, although Muslims in those two cites were less supportive than the general public.[3]

Gallup also found little difference between Muslims and non-Muslims about what Muslims need to do to integrate. Finding a job, learning the language, getting a better education, and celebrating national holidays all elicited scant differences between Muslims and non-Muslims, who overwhelmingly agreed that those were the things to do. Disagreement existed only when it came to political participation—Muslims thought they should participate, non-Muslims thought they should not—and matters of religious observation. Non-Muslims readily agreed that Muslim women should take off the headscarf and remove the face veil in order to integrate. Muslims disagreed, although 44 percent of Berlin Muslims agreed that the face veil should be removed. (They had no problem with the headscarf.) In all the above issues, survey research shows that large majorities of Europe's Muslim populations see eye to eye with the elite interviewed for this book on matters of integration and religious toleration. Value disagreements with the majority of society are on matters of religious toleration and the room for Islam in Europe.

The book was completed shortly before four suicide bombers killed 52 people in four separate bomb attacks on London trains and a bus on July 7, 2005. Three weeks later another attack was attempted, but it fortunately failed to cause the intended harm. Commentators at the time tended to conclude, as did two official inquiries, that this is what young Muslim men do when they get angry and alienated. It was a misreading of the facts. As it later turned out, the two sets of terrorists belonged to the same extremist network and their attacks were carefully planned and coordinated over a long period of time. They were not spontaneous eruptions of anger, and we have come to see political ideology rather than social alienation as the key motivation for young men to join the Jihad. There have since been some 200 more arrests on terrorism charges in England alone, and terrifying plots have been unraveled in other countries. The question must therefore be asked: does Europe harbor a homegrown 'fifth column' of Jihadists?

A poll carried out in early February 2006 found that as many as 20 percent of British Muslims felt sympathy with the 'feelings and motives' of the July bombers; 1 percent felt the attacks were 'right'.[4] Counterterrorism officials warned about the existence of a 'tacit circle of support' for terrorism in Britain.[5] Newspapers speculated that there might be 16,000 potential terrorists in Britain. The number was extrapolated from the 2001 Census, which identified 1.6 million Muslims living in Britain. In fact, the census is outdated and underestimates the current number of Muslims living in Britain by about 500,000; so if 1 percent are potential terrorists, the risk may be even greater. However, the argument is fallacious. Telling a pollster that the bombers were 'right' does not mean that one wants to join them.

It is nonetheless appropriate to be concerned about denial and the existence of tacit support for terrorism in the British Muslim community. Surveys show that British Muslims are more supportive of radical Islamists than are Muslims elsewhere in Europe. However, they also reveal that the supporters of violent Jihad are isolated in a sea of disapproval. A second survey, from June 2006, found that 16 percent of British Muslims thought that the bombers' cause was just; 7 percent said that suicide attacks on British civilians could be justified under some circumstances, a proportion that rose to 16 percent if the targets were military.[6] Yet this survey also revealed Muslims to be deeply divided on questions related to the policing of terrorism. Almost 56 percent said the police was doing too little to combat extremism among Muslims, compared to 49 percent of the general population; among Muslims 49 percent said that the government was right to keep an eye on what was said in mosques, but 46 percent disagreed.

The same survey hinted at the extent of denial among British Muslims, in comparison with Muslims in some other European countries. Three-quarters of the British public anticipated more suicide attacks. Nearly half of British Muslim respondents thought that was unlikely. More plots have in fact been subsequently uncovered. Muslims also underestimated the degree of support for the Jihadists in their midst. Two-thirds thought that only a tiny minority of British Muslims sympathized with the July bombers. However, 16–20 percent is not a tiny minority. The Pew survey cited earlier also looked for support for suicide bombings among Muslims in all four European countries. Around 16 percent of respondents said that they were 'sometimes' acceptable. The exception was Germany, where only 7 percent held this view.

But once again, it is by no means evident that Muslim opinion is out of line with general European beliefs, in this case with views about political violence. In April 2007, the Gallup World Poll asked both Muslims and non-Muslims if violence for a noble cause can be morally justified. They found that 81 percent of British Muslims thought that it is not justified and 88 percent said that attacks on civilians were not justifiable. The general public was more willing to entertain the idea that a noble cause could justify violence. Nearly 30 percent said that political violence could be justified, although 92 percent believed that attacks on civilians were unacceptable.[7]

The results of the different surveys all point to the same conclusion. A significant but small minority of Muslims support the Jihadist cause. Gallup asked the question differently but found the same division: roughly one-fifth of Muslims condone violence for Jihadist causes outright or with some reservations, and four-fifths unequivocally reject it. British Muslims are on balance more inclined to express support for Jihadist movements than are Muslims in other countries, and they are also more likely to engage in wishful thinking or straight-out denial that it is a 'Muslim problem'. At the same time, perhaps the most important argument against the 'clash' theory is that the Muslim terrorist movement has very little support in European Muslim communities.

It is also the case that Jihadist extremism is by no means the only source of terrorist sympathies and actions in contemporary Europe. In some countries other terrorists outnumber the Jihadis. Nicolas Sarkozy, President of France, who was previously Minister of the Interior, said on January 11, 2007, that 317 individuals were detained in connection with terrorism and terrorism-related charges in 2006.[8] Of these, 54 remained in custody; 150 were detained in connection with terrorism in Corsica, 27 in connection with terrorism in Basque, and 140 (44 percent) in connection with Islamism. In an article praising the French use of 'preemptive arrests' as a primary counter-terrorism instrument, Jean Chichizola, a journalist for *Le Figaro*, cited the French arrest statistics since September 11, 2001. Out of about 400 arrests in relation to Islamist terrorism, just over 150 (40 percent) resulted in indict-ments or imprisonment of the suspects.[9] The article also cited the French security agency for estimating that there are about 500 'hard core' targets of surveillance in France, out of a general population of extremists estimated at 5,000. This represents 0.1 percent of a total Muslim population estimated at 5 million. These numbers are worrying; however, they do not suggest that Europe is faced with a massive homegrown Muslim insurgency.

Jihadi recruitment has been less successful elsewhere in Europe. The Dutch National Counter-Terrorism Coordinator (NCTB) estimated in quarterly reports from October and December 2006 that the risk of an Islamist attack had decreased in the preceding three months, although it also warned about increased radicalization of far-right youth groups, naming the Lonsdale group and the international *Blood and Honor* group, a member of the neo-Nazi ZOG movement that includes the American Aryan Nation. (ZOG stands for 'Zionist Occupation Government', which in the conspiracy theories of the movement is a reference to the US government.)[10] Danish and German counterterrorism agencies and prosecutors, in contrast, found evidence of increased domestic Jihadist activity and are expecting more terrorism cases to follow. They have not explained their reasons for these expectations. The Jihadists aim for massive civilian casualties, and even if some of the plots revealed have been fantastical—one British plot involved putting 'dirty bombs' in limousines driving around London—government officials have reason to be particularly focused on the Jihadi radical networks. It is none-theless a mistake to argue, as some people do, that 'not all Muslims are terrorists but all terrorists are Muslims'. Jihadi terrorism is a deadly variant on a familiar and all too Western problem.

The theory of the 'clash of civilization' has become a meta-narrative for any conflict or disagreement involving Muslims, be it schoolgirls' headscarves, terrorism, or Muslims insisting that they have rights, too. Yet there has been a quiet transformation of European politics that contradicts assumptions about the widening gap between Muslims and non-Muslims. Wolfgang Schäuble, a Christian Democrat and the German interior minister, invited representatives of national Muslim associations to meet in September 2006 to start hammer-ing out an agreement that will allow German Muslims to receive official recognition as a German faith. A new generation of Muslim parliamentarians is stepping into public view. Danish conservatives have defected to a new party formed by a Muslim immigrant, Naser Khader, because they despaired of the dominance of the xenophobic and rabid anti-Muslim Danish People's Party. The Netherlands has a Muslim woman, Nebahat Albayrek, as justice minister. Nyamko Sabuni, the first black and Muslim to enter into a government position, is minister of integration and gender equality in Sweden. Rachida Dati, a self-made businesswoman and a Muslim of North African origin, was made minister of justice in Nicolas Sarkozy's new government.

This book focuses on the views of a new generation of Muslim leaders in Europe. They do not all say the same thing, but theirs is a very European discourse.

Boston, May 2007

NOTES

[1] Pew Global Attitudes Project, *Europe's Muslims More Moderate: The Great Divide—How Westerners and Muslims View Each Other*. Released June 22, 2006.
[2] PolicyExchange, *Living Apart Together: British Muslims and the Paradox of Multiculturalism*. Munira Mirza, Abi Senthilkumaran, and Zein Ja'far. London, 2007.
[3] Gallup World Poll, *Muslims in Europe: Berlin, London, Paris—Bridges and Gaps in Public Opinion*. Zsolt Nyiri. Released April 2007.
[4] *Sunday Telegraph*, February 19, 2006.
[5] Shamit Saggar, 'The One Per Cent World: Managing the Myth of Muslim Religious Extremism', *The Political Quarterly* 77 (3) 2006: 314–27.
[6] Populus Muslim 7/7 Poll, June 2006.
[7] Gallup World Poll, *Beyond Multiculturalism vs. Assimilation*, Special Report by Dalia Mogahed. Released April 2007.
[8] *AFP*, January 11, 2007
[9] *Le Figaro*, September 27, 2006.
[10] *NRC Handelsblad*, October 16, 2006, and December 14, 2006.

Acknowledgements

I could not have completed this book without the goodwill of the people who funded me, my employer, Brandeis University, and my family and friends. My family earns my gratitude for their unwavering encouragement. I am grateful in particular to the following colleagues and friends, who have helped and encouraged me: Erik Albæk, Steven Burg, Michael Bommes, Desmond King, Adam Kuper, Claus Offe, and Bhikhu Parekh. I am indebted to Fiyaz Mughal for educating me in British politics and to Mohamed Alibhai for tutoring me in Islam.

My research assistants, Andre Amtoft, Martin Steinwand, Maria-Soledad Amador-Cuadro, Marianne van Steekelenburg, and Anna Böhning, helped me organize my research and interviews, and put up with my occasional confusion and desperation, and rewarded me by becoming engaged and insightful advocates for the research and the book. In Paris and Lyon, I am thankful to Moussa Khedimellah, Hakim El Ghissassi, and Redouane Abouddahab for their generosity and assistance. I am grateful to Levent Ermek for taking care of me in Rotterdam. Michael Blume and Riem Spielhaus generously helped me out in Stuttgart and Berlin.

I owe special thanks to my hosts. In Copenhagen, Peter Abrahamson and the Institute of Sociology at the University of Copenhagen provided a home throughout the project. My thanks go to Trine-Louise Andersen for administrating my grant. I am thankful to my friend, Lotta Hedberg, and to Kay Glans, the editor of Axess, and the Axel and Margaret Ax:son Johnson Foundation, for space and help in Stockholm, and to Gerhard Baumann, Jan Rath, and the Institute for Migration and Ethnic Studies for assistance in Amsterdam. Nuffield College, at Oxford University, housed me as a British Academy Visiting Professor. Anna Coote was wonderfully kind to put me up many times at short notice.

A semester spent at the American Academy in Berlin enabled me to finish the manuscript. Gary Smith and the Academy's staff earned my deep appreciation for their extraordinary hospitality and efficient help. They helped deliver the manuscript on time, but like all midwives they cannot be blamed for how it turned out.

The Danish Social Science Research Council provided generous funding for my research. I am grateful to the Council and to the British Academy, the American Academy in Berlin, the United States Institute of Peace, and

Brandeis University for funding my leaves from teaching and for additional grants in support of the research. Finally, I want to thank my husband, Alan Wolfe, for his patience and support and also I want to thank Dominic Byatt and the OUP staff for making it a pleasure to produce this book.

JK

Introduction: Islam in Europe

The voices in this book belong to parliamentarians, city councilors, doctors and engineers, a few professors, lawyers and social workers, owners of small businesses, translators, and community activists. They are also all Muslims who have decided to become engaged in political and civic organizations. They are Europe's new Muslim political elite. And for that reason, they are in the special role of constantly having to explain themselves, mostly in order to say who they are *not*. They are not fundamentalists, not terrorists, and they mostly do not support the introduction of Islamic religious law in Europe, and they definitely do not support applying it to Christians. This book is about who these people are, and what they want.

Without the willingness of these 300 people to explain themselves yet once more, for my benefit, and to do so at great length, and under the pressure of what may have seemed undiplomatic questioning, this book would not have been possible. Many people invited me to their offices or homes. Others I met with in mosques or coffee bars, or in the temporary offices I borrowed from academic friends across Western Europe. Often what was supposed to be a thirty-minute interview went on for much longer. The leaders chosen for interviews were from Sweden, Denmark, the Netherlands, Great Britain, France, and Germany.

I learned to find my way in every one of the legislatures in six countries. I had tea in the House of Lords and a beer in the Dutch Tweede Kamer. I saw the empty hall of the Swedish Riksdagen—'the most boring place in Stockholm,' the young member told me, as she showed me around—and squeezed into an office the size of a large broom closet in the cramped French Sénat. The posh new offices of the German Bundestag seemed like the parliamentarian's dream until I learned that you had to petition the architect for permission to change the trash can or bring in a new chair.

I was treated to coffee and cake, home-cooked dinners, and great hospitality. 'You are the first one to come and talk to us,' I was often told. 'Thank you for coming.' Once I was scolded, and another time I was asked to leave because my presence was considered offensive. That was it. Two incidents. Even when my presence was clearly unusual, I was treated graciously and made to feel welcome.

My respondents were very largely moderate Muslims, but I did also meet some radicals. An interview with someone who presented himself as a 'moderate,' but who I later discovered to be a member of Hamas, triggered my memories of the occasional dishonesty of the 'old' New Left. (Also known as the Islamic Resistance Movement, Hamas is a political group with a terrorist wing based in the Gaza Strip and West Bank.) On another occasion, when I attended Friday prayers and heard the khutbah, the Friday sermon, being delivered in a converted nineteenth-century red brick factory building close to where, thirty years earlier, I had enjoyed a hot summer and free housing in a Copenhagen neighborhood taken over by squatters, I found myself the only woman among five hundred men at the service. The sermon was delivered in Arabic and English, and translation to imperfect Danish was available over a closed-circuit system. I did not like what I heard. But it was not until I met with the 'Sheikh,' as he wanted to be addressed, that I became uncomfortable.

When I asked what should be done about radical imams, the Sheikh angrily denounced the failure of Western democracy. Islam has a chance at a new start in Europe, if only Europeans would live up to the human rights they preach, he said, starting on what promised to be a diatribe. The situation was diffused by the providential appearance of André, my research assistant, and next the Sheikh was giving me photocopies of a recent consumer survey he had made of the mosque members. The survey aimed to find out what the attendees at Friday prayers wanted from the waqf. (A waqf is an Islamic charity, but in this case the term was used to describe the mosque community and its leader.) Should the Sheikh participate more in the media debates? (Yes) Should the khutbah address political issues of concern to Muslims? (Yes) Administered in Arabic, Danish, and English, it would have been the envy of an American Evangelical preacher aiming to hone his skills and enlarge his flock. The current European panic about radical clerics is fueled by stories like this one, but missing from the newspaper accounts is that most Muslims are as discomfited by this kind of manipulative politicization of Islam as I was.

Western European governments currently find themselves in a dilemma. They are coming to realize that they must find ways to fund and support the development of an independent Islam in Europe. At the same time, they are faced with the leakage of voters to xenophobic parties. This dilemma accounts for some of the strange signals coming out of Europe. New German legislation to ease access to naturalization for immigrants has relaxed the historical ties between descent and German citizenship, yet some German states have banned the headscarf and mandated the crucifix in public schools, declaring that Germany is a 'Judeo-Christian' state. France banned girls from wearing the headscarf at school and is moving towards even wider application of a headscarf ban, while at the same time announcing the creation of a foundation to fund 'French Islam.' The British government passes antiterrorist laws that target Muslims while promising to allow shariah law to be used in courts.

In this volatile and contradictory environment, Muslims are building representative institutions and mastering the skills of democratic negotiation. This book cannot do justice to the diversity of responses and to the nuances of the new European politics of Islam, but it does, I hope, sketch the main contours of the emerging institutions, debates, adaptations, and confrontations, while noting some of the complexities and indicating the main cross-national differences.

CULTURE WAR OR RELIGIOUS TOLERATION?

'Europe has become a battlefield,' according to Gilles Kepel. Samuel P. Huntington says it is facing a 'clash of civilizations' and 'cultural war,' a new 'Kulturkampf.'[1] Helmut Schmidt, the former Chancellor of Germany, argues that a peaceful accommodation between Islam and Christianity is possible only in authoritarian states.[2]

These apocalyptic pronouncements are not only counterproductive. They are dangerously misleading. I shall argue that the question of Islam in Europe is not a matter of global war and peace. Rather, it raises a more familiar set of domestic policy issues about the relations between church and state, and on occasion even prosaic questions about government regulation and equitable policy enforcement. My central thesis is that Muslims are simply a new interest group and a new constituency, and that the European political systems will change as the processes of representation, challenge, and co-optation take place. There is a clash of values, but perhaps the most important is that between two old European parties, secularists and conservatives, as each struggles to come to terms with religious pluralism. The conflict does raise large questions, but these have to do with long-standing European preoccupations with state neutrality in religious matters and the place of Christianity in the construction of European public identity.

Europe's Muslim political leaders are not aiming to overthrow liberal democracy and to replace secular law with Islamic religious law, the shariah. Most are rather looking for ways to build institutions that will allow Muslims to practice their religion in a way that is compatible with social integration. To be sure, there is not one Muslim position on how Islam should develop in Europe but many views. However, there is general agreement that immigrants must be integrated into the wider society. There is also a widespread feeling that Europe's Muslims should not rely on foreign Islamic funding of local institutions but be able to practice their faith in mosques built with local funding and with the assistance of imams certified and educated at European universities and seminaries.

FOREIGN AFFAIRS

Huntington predicted a historic and decisive global confrontation between 'Islam' and 'the West,' and he represented problems with Islamic minorities in Western countries as local skirmishes in this international struggle, a struggle that was at bottom one of values, symbols, and identity.

From the September 11, 2001, attacks on the World Trade Center and the Pentagon to the March 11, 2004 to the Madrid train bombings and the July 7, 2005, bombings in London, events seem to confirm this view that the West has to rise to the defense of liberalism and Christianity against the threat posed by Muslims in their midst. The murder, in November 2004, of a Dutch filmmaker, Theo van Gogh, on the streets of Amsterdam by Mohammed Bouyeri, a Dutch-Moroccan who was linked to Hizbollah, an Islamic terrorist group, elicited strong reactions against Muslims across northern Europe. In the weeks following the murder, over twenty religious elementary schools, mosques, and churches were burned down in Holland by self-appointed Christian crusaders and Islamic jihadists. Editorials in the papers and on TV asked—and mostly took the answers for granted—'could it happen here?' and 'what went wrong?'

Huntington's thesis rests on two postulates. The first is that religion is the predominant source of identity and value orientation for Muslims. 'Liberal' and 'Muslim' values are irreconcilable. The religious Muslim cannot separate public law and private religion. Only individuals who renounce key parts of Islam can be trusted as interlocutors in democratic societies. The second postulate is that Islam and Christianity are competing for global control. Islam is represented as monolithic and intent on world domination. As the Princeton historian, Bernard Lewis, put it, 'in any encounter between Islam and unbelief, Islam must dominate.'[3] From this perspective, a Muslim schoolgirl's headscarf is imbued with symbolic significance beyond the individual girl's reasons for wearing the scarf.

However, domestic conflict over the integration of Islam in European countries has little to do with foreign policy. Muslims in Great Britain and the USA—the two allies in the war in Iraq—find fewer obstacles to the development of faith institutions than do Muslims in France and Germany, the two leading European antiwar countries. Rather, domestic conflicts have local causes, rooted in the particular histories of modern European states. One of the key factors, usually neglected in these debates, is the legacy of the 'stability pacts' that were made between the majority churches and European states in the course of twentieth-century adjustments to universal suffrage and constitutional reforms. The accommodation of Islam necessitates a rethinking of those pacts and obliges national churches to reconsider their own position on matters of proselytizing, interreligious relations, and even questions of theology and liturgy.

Until very recently, European governments have been reluctant to formulate policies for the integration of Muslim minorities. Muslims interpret this neglect as yet another form of discrimination, an extension of the discrimination experienced in daily life, in employment, education, and the provision of social services. Yet governments are now beginning to grapple with the issues. Some of their initial measures provoked fresh conflicts, notably bans on wearing the hijab, the Islamic headscarf, by female Muslim students and teachers; policies curtailing ritual slaughter; and immigration controls on imams. These policies are often perceived to be discriminatory, but they are sometimes supported also by Muslim leaders. There is little disagreement that radical clerics should be kept out, although the general view is that Muslims have democratic rights to say stupid things too. Most Muslims think the headscarf should be tolerated, but many think it is a bad idea to wear it. However, few governments have institutionalized democratic consultative mechanisms with Muslims, or come to terms with the fact that they are dealing with a diverse religious constituency that cannot be represented by a single head of a national 'church' as is the European custom.

WHY ARE THERE SUDDENLY PROBLEMS?

For decades, Europeans paid little attention to the modest prayer halls and mosques that sprang up in their cities. Benign neglect was the preferred official response to the growing presence of Muslim immigrants. A Dutch anthropologist, Jan Rath, and his collaborators found that the first reference to Muslims in Dutch government sources was a Memorandum on Foreign Workers from 1970, which referred obliquely to the need to provide 'pastoral care' for foreign workers.[4]

The lack of public policy involvement has both historical and political roots. When Muslims first began to come to Europe in the 1950s and 1960s, they were not expected to stay. They were mostly labor migrants, and often single men, who themselves expected to return with savings to the families they had left at home. Ironically, it was the collective recognition by Europe's Muslims that they were 'here to stay' that triggered conflict. Once Muslims demanded integration it became evident how much Europeans and their governments would have to change in order to accommodate them.

There are probably about 15 million Muslims living in Western Europe, but the exact number is in doubt. The count is subject to inflation, in part because Muslim leaders and populist politicians like to exaggerate the number to press their causes, but also because few reliable statistics exist. Most European countries do not include questions on religious affiliation in their census. Commonly, the size of the Muslim population is therefore extrapolated from immigration statistics. For example, if there are 2.4 million Turkish-origin residents in Germany, and 98 percent of the Turkish population is Muslim, there are 2.3 million Turkish-origin Muslims in Germany.[5] And if two-thirds of the population of Turkey are Sunni and one-third Shia, German Turks are assumed to be divided similarly. It is routinely said that there are 5 million Muslims in France. An official report, by the Haut Conseil à l'Intégration from November 2000 embraced a slightly lower estimate of 4.1 million.[6] Patrick Simon, a French demographer, regards that number as inflated. Using the method just described, he considers 2.6 million, or at most 3 million, to be a more accurate estimate.[7] However, this method may also exaggerate the size of the Muslim population, since allowance is not made for assimilation through intermarriage or the acculturation of descendants, and it obviously confounds religious affiliation with country of origin. (Nor, on the other hand, does it allow for conversions to Islam.)

In Great Britain the census of 2001 did ask respondents to state their religion, and reported a Muslim population of 1.5 million, or 3 percent of the total population.[8] But official estimates do not include illegal immigrants, who in recent years have arrived primarily from predominantly Muslim countries, such as Albania, Algeria, Morocco, and Nigeria. In Spain alone, the influx of illegal migrants from North Africa has been guessed at 4 million in the last decade. In Germany, estimates for the illegal population range from 0.6 to 1.5 million people, of whom Muslims represent an unknown proportion.

Public reactions in Western Europe to the growing presence of adherents of an unfamiliar religion have been remarkably similar. From Protestant Scandinavia to pluralist Holland and Catholic France, controversies have broken out over religious holiday schedules, accommodations for prayers, the wearing of Muslim dress in the workplace, the provision of building permits for mosques, the public ownership of all available cemeteries, concerns about animal rights that disallow ritual slaughter, issues of pastoral care for Muslims in prisons and social services, the teaching of religion in public schools, and divorce law and other family law issues.

At the same time, there has been a growing suspicion about Muslims' loyalty to Western values. The issue was first dramatized in 1989. Ayatollah Khomeini pronounced a death sentence in absentia against Salman Rushdie for the blasphemous descriptions of the prophet Muhammad in his novel,

Satanic Verses.[9] Book-burning demonstrations in the English towns of Bradford and Oldham and violent demonstrations across the Islamic world invited comparison to fascist bonfires of banned books in the 1930s.[10]

A decade later, there were fears that terrorist networks were embedding themselves in little known mosques throughout Europe. Mohammed Atta, one of the 9/11 terrorists, attended the al-Quds mosque in Hamburg. When the German police found a tape featuring the imam of the mosque, a man of Moroccan origin known only by his last name, al-Fazizi, raging that 'Christians and Jews should have their throats slit,' seven men from the mosque were arrested on terrorism charges.[11] It was discovered that a thirty-seven-year-old Swedish Muslim, who was convicted of possessing weapons and suspected of planning terrorism, had links to the Finsbury Park mosque in London and its fiery preacher, Abu Hamza.[12] The shoe-bomber, Richard Reid, and the suspected twentieth 9/11 hijacker, Zacarias Moussaoui, were also linked to the Finsbury Park mosque. Abu Hamza became an emblematic figure for those who feared that a new jihad was being prepared in Europe, as was the 'Kalif aus Köln,' Metin Kaplan, who was extradited to face murder charges in Turkey in October 2004.[13] However, the overwhelming majority of European Muslims are as repelled by the ranting of these clerics as are Christians.

The Muslim mainstream is better represented by civic and political figures who have been elected to public office by voters and parties that draw support from all voters and by leaders of Muslim national and community organizations. That is why it is their views and policy choices that are the focus of this study. European Muslims are necessary partners in the negotiation of accommodation with Islam, and the Muslim political and civic leaders will play a critical role in that process. Democracies are tested by their capacity to respond to the claims and needs of new social groups and by their capacity to integrate new elites representing those claims. The prospects for the accommodation of Islam rest in part on the ability of governments to come up with solutions, and in part on the Muslim elite's involvement in the resolution of conflict.[14]

What does Europe's Muslim political elite want from governments? Europe's Muslim civic and political leaders are engineers, doctors, social workers, lawyers, and professionals, or business owners. It struck me when I started this book that people who have in one way or another chosen to live in Europe and indicate their acceptance of European norms and institutions by engaging in civic and political life are unlikely to share the views of the West attributed to them by the 'clash of civilizations' thesis. But how committed to liberal values are Muslim leaders? And how do we then explain the escalation of conflict over the accommodation of Islam? These are the questions that this book seeks to answer.

LIBERAL AND ILLIBERAL CHRISTIANS

It is not possible to discuss the 'clash of practices' set off by Muslims' claims for recognition without also discussing the reaction of the Christian churches.[15] There is a popular fallacy that public life in Europe is secular. On the contrary, European states have given privileges to the Christian churches for centuries, from public funding for religious schools to tax support, to the maintenance of church real estate and clerical salaries. Most Europeans are accustomed to relying on the state for the public provision of pastoral needs, from cemeteries to churches and the training of clergy. The bias of current policies has become perceptible only with the increased visibility of the different customs of the immigrant religions.

However, Muslim leaders are generally reluctant to press too hard for equal treatment on all fronts. The German Greens were the first to suggest that an Islamic holiday—Eid al-Fitr, the end of Ramadan—should be added to the long list of official German holidays, but the other parties responded with derision.[16] Few Muslim leaders who I spoke to think that holiday equity is a cause worth fighting for. Granting Muslims employment protection to take the day off as a personal holiday is sufficient. It is not productive for Christian–Muslim relations in the current situation to suggest that Christians should take off Islamic holidays. As a Dutch Muslim parliamentarian said to me when I suggested that the Netherlands needed to beef up antidiscrimination law in the face of unequivocal evidence of widespread employment discrimination against well-educated immigrants, 'any suggestion that Muslims are victims of discrimination is not helpful right now, when Christians think that Muslims already take far too much.'[17]

The issue is a good example of the urgent need for a wide-ranging public debate about the implications of state neutrality and how equitable treatment of different religions is possible. The main concerns of Muslim leaders are, however, rather with what is seen as the persistent mischaracterization of Islam by the media and politicians, the absence of public policy initiatives to support Islamic religious organizations, and the lack of public recognition that Muslims are Europeans too.

EUROPE'S NEW RELIGIOUS REVIVAL?

Is Europe becoming the center for an Islamic revival? Gilles Kepel and Tariq Ramadan both think so. Kepel sees the new Muslim associations in Europe as vehicles for the global spread of Islam. Fouad Ajami has expressed a similar view, foreseeing even more alarming consequences.[18] Ramadan, however, argues that a revitalization of Islam can take place in Europe, because European Muslims are free to develop an Islam that is a 'pure faith,' freed from the ethnicized doctrines and rituals that characterize practices in the Islamic world.[19]

There *is* a movement of religious reform and revival, but it lacks the coherence attributed to it by either Kepel or Ajami, or hoped for by Ramadan. Its means are Koran study circles and collective Koran translation projects. It attracts converts and native-born young Muslims, who say they crave spirituality. Some groups even welcome women and gays on equal terms, and allow women to lead men in prayers. The traditionalist-minded are the clear majority, but even they generally accept that Islam must be reformed and that women's position is an issue that has to be addressed. Ijtihad, the practice of using reason to reinterpret the meaning and application of religious law, has become the rallying cry for self-styled moderate and progressive Muslims, who want to bridge faith with integrated lifestyles and professional occupations.

The Islamic countries have made efforts to control Europe's Muslims, in part through the provision of imams with traditionalist views and also by financing the construction of mosques in Europe's main cities. Local mosque communities have recruited imams from a madrasa 'back home' known to the mosque elders. In other cases, donors from Saudi Arabia, Libya, or Pakistan have sent imams along with their contributions. The Diyanet, a section of the Turkish Foreign Ministry, has about 1,200 imams stationed in Europe according to agreements made with national governments. These imams are educated and do not agitate for Islamist causes, but they rarely master European languages and are increasingly seen as inadequate spiritual leaders by the young professionals who are taking over mosque managements.

Foreign funding—whether private or government-controlled—is now regarded as undesirable, and foreign imams are unable to communicate easily with the younger generation. However, European states are doing little to fill the vacuum. The French government has taken initiatives to work with Muslim councils to develop imam training programs that would supply 'home-grown' imams. The Dutch government now requires all imams to sit through an acculturation program, which teaches the imams the language and aspects of Dutch law pertinent to their duties. The University of Amsterdam has started a program that leads to a certificate in Islamic chaplaincy. Denmark has stopped issuing visas for foreign imams, whom it describes as 'Islamic missionaries.' Sweden and Spain have provided modest funds for mosque construction, and taken steps to integrate Islam within a common policy for minority faiths. Belgium and Sweden have found ways to provide direct or indirect salaries for some imams. But these are small initiatives, and in general it remains the case that European governments are loath to be seen to be encouraging Islam, and some established political parties query the legitimacy of the religious needs of European Muslims. 'This is not an Islamic country, it is a Christian country,' says Wolfgang Bosbach, the spokesperson for domestic affairs for the German Christian Democratic party, 'and we should not be forced to accommodate Islam.'[20] That is an extreme position, but even among those who are willing to contemplate some form of accommodation, or integration, or assimilation, the goals are by no means agreed.

The term integration implies a process of give and take on both sides. Assimilation suggests that the immigrants must do the adjusting. If the aim is coexistence or simply toleration of immigrant religions and faith practices, the burden of adjustment is in practice on European society. Some Muslim politicians—native-born or of immigrant origin—argue for a bare minimum of basic agreement on principles for conflict resolution and constitutional values. Others are more concerned with the depth of social ties and cohesion, and focus on the importance of value commitments as a resource for the community and a prerequisite for social solidarity. Interestingly, most people I spoke to reject the minimum solution, which might be described as a 'separate spheres' arrangement or multiculturalism. Their reasons varied, but Muslims often worried that such policies deprive them of equal status and perpetrate inequitable treatment by local authorities, police, and national policymakers. Others noted simply that multiculturalism is politically un-acceptable in European societies.

The threshold for what constitutes 'integration' may be set high or low, but in practice few people disagree that it means that adjustments have to be made by both Muslims and the majority. A Dutch Muslim parliamentarian elected from the Christian Democratic party was forthright about the need for change in the Muslim community. He mentioned the lack of women in leadership positions in Muslim organizations. It is not wrong to discuss segregation, he said, referring to a contentious Dutch debate over 'parallel societies', but Muslims are entitled to respect. The limit is reached when politicians begin to describe Islam as 'a backward religion.'[21] This threshold has been passed in Dutch public debate many times since the interview.

A dialogue on how to accomplish integration requires that policymakers accept that Muslims are partners in the determination of policy and that current national frameworks must change. Neither premise is widely accepted by Europeans today.

ABOUT THIS BOOK

The interviews were carried out between September 2003 and February 2005. A large part of Europe's Muslim minority lives in the six countries discussed here, and all six have experienced controversy over the presence of Islam. They are also different with respect to church-state policies and the majority religions.

Sweden and Denmark are overwhelmingly Protestant countries. France is predominantly Roman Catholic. Germany has two recognized major religions (Protestantism and Catholicism). Less than half the British population belongs to the Church of England. Britain is divided for religious purposes into four countries, with an established church in England, the Anglican Church, or the Church of England, a national church in Scotland with few privileges, the Presbyterian Church, and no established church in Wales or Northern Ireland. Only the Church of England has automatic representation in the House of Lords, which nevertheless represents also Wales, Scotland, and Northern Ireland. The Netherlands is the only state in this group with a long history of religious pluralism, but even here the separation of church and state dates back only to 1983.

I asked the leaders about their views of Islam, of the nature and sources of Muslims' problems in Europe, and about policies for Islam and for Muslims. When I speak about Islam, I am referring to the religion and to the faith's institutions. Muslims are people who are either practicing the faith or individuals whose family background is Muslim. Their views of the issues and conflicts over Muslims' position in Europe and the difficulties associated with the integration of Islam are described in what follows.

I use the label 'Muslim' to describe faith and heritage in the same way one would use 'Christian' or 'Jewish.' It is a flexible description, and I did not make any prior assumptions about how important faith was to the participants in the study. (It was one of the questions asked.) These countries all have relatively large Muslim minorities, and have taken different approaches to the organization of church-state affairs. The methodology used to select the leaders and the thoughts behind the interview questions and procedures are described in detail in the Appendix.

My aim was not to produce a survey but to understand the range of views and to identify areas of overlapping concern and preferences with respect to solutions. Still, the present study should be read as a political anthropology of Muslim leaders rather than an opinion survey. Among the questions I asked these Muslim leaders are what they think it will take to integrate Islam in Europe, and how bad they think things are. I also asked what changes Muslims must make to adjust to European norms. Finally, I explored their views on the main problems that Muslims face in Europe. One-third of the interviews were face-to-face, personal interviews, and the rest were made by e-mail, fax, or phone using a standard questionnaire. The total number of interviews was just over three hundred.

The people who are cited in this book are mostly quoted anonymously or, when that seemed awkward for the narrative, I assigned fictitious names (in the form of a single first name). When I cite people using their real names, the statement is either already in the public record, in which case I cite from the source or, alternatively, I received permission to attribute the quotes. These conventions are in accordance with policies on research with human subjects. The informed reader will sometimes be able to guess the identity of individuals cited anonymously. There are only two French Muslim senators, for example, and both are women, but even in cases such as these I thought it best to stick to my citation policy.

Readers should bear in mind that while questions of the 'representativeness' of a particular study are frequently raised, we have no way of assessing what that means if we have to guess the size of the population from which we would like to draw a sample. I portray the actual views of a high proportion of European Muslim leaders. By my estimate there are between 1,500 and 2,000 individuals, in the six countries included in this study, who meet my definition of an elected or appointed leader in a national or regional civic or political organization, who is of Muslim faith or background. But there is no directory of 'Who's Who in European Islam' from which I could have picked a random sample, and I opted instead to talk to as many people as I could locate in the parliaments, main city councils, and political parties who are Muslims. I also interviewed leaders and spokesmen from civic associations, advocacy groups, and local and national umbrella organizations of mosque councils and interfaith groups, and also some of Europe's leading imams and Islamic scholars. They were requested not to speak for their organization but for themselves. On a few occasions, I interviewed Christian religious leaders and non-Muslim policymakers engaged in questions related to the integration of Islam.

In the following chapters I first describe Europe's new Muslim elite. A common misperception is that today's national Muslim associations are direct descendants in new clothing of an earlier generation of exile organizations from the Islamic countries. Muslim organizations that link faith with political advocacy are often described as the offspring of the 'Muslim Brotherhood,' but the label lumps together groups and individuals who have little in common. As Kepel notes, the Brotherhood's political philosophy is widely condemned by European Muslims.[22]

Another inaccurate assumption is that today's leaders are the native-born descendants of the first cohorts of labor migrants. The new Muslim associations are different from the old organizations that were created to cater to émigrés and migrant workers, who often had left their families behind. Most of today's leaders are foreign-born recent immigrants, and many are refugees. In Chapters 2 and 3, I describe their views of key policy issues and how they would like to see Islam integrated in Europe. A minority does not think Islam can or should be integrated, either because they fear assimilation or because they think Islam cannot be 'fixed'. Chapter 4 describes three instances where policymakers have failed to find solutions to the problems Muslims face with respect to the exercise of their faith. They are the failure to create cemeteries where Muslims can be buried following religious prescriptions, the obstacles to ritual slaughter and halal certification, and the near-collapse of efforts to create recognized degree programs for imams. In Chapter 5, I describe the barriers to state neutrality in religious matters posed by the existing church-state arrangements and discuss the conflicts within the Christian churches over an 'Abrahamic' approach to interreligious dialogue between the three monotheistic faiths, Christianity, Judaism, and Islam. Finally, Chapter 6 turns to a discussion of multiculturalism and the sexual politics of Islam in Europe.

NOTES

1. Gilles Kepel, *The War for Muslim Minds: Islam and the West* (Cambridge, MA: Harvard University Press, 2004), 241. Samuel P. Huntington first launched the argument that Islam and Christianity represented irreconcilable worldviews in an essay, 'The Clash of Civilizations?,' published in *Foreign Affairs*, in 1993. He developed the argument in subsequent books, *The Clash of Civilizations and the Remaking of World Order* (New York: Simon and Schuster, 1996) and *Who Are We? The Challenges to America's National Identity* (New York: Simon and Schuster, 2004). The term 'cultural war,' or in German, *Kulturkampf*, was originally used to describe the struggle between liberals and conservatives over the German constitution in the Bismarckian period from 1871 to 1891. It was also used by the Nazis to describe the struggle against socialists and secular liberals until Hitler's assumption of power in 1933.
2. Quoted in *Hamburger Abendblatt* (November 24, 2004).
3. Bernard Lewis, *Islam and the West* (New York: Oxford University Press, 1993), 4 and 53.
4. Jan Rath, Rinus Pennix, Kees Groenendijk, Astrid Meyer, *Western Europe and Its Islam* (Leiden: Brill, 2001), 29.

5. Catholics, Protestants, and Jews have an opportunity to be officially counted, as the German tax return forms instruct you to check off your faith for the purpose of allocating revenues to the recognized faiths. Islam is not a recognized faith, and Muslims are not similarly counted.

6. Haut Conseil à l'Intégration, *L'Islam dans la République*, Paris (November 26, 2000).

7. Personal interview with Patrick Simon, INEED (May 25, 2004), Interview 87.

8. *Census 2001*, Office for National Statistics, London. (www.statistics.gov.uk/census2001)

9. On February 15, 1989, the *New York Times* reported that '[t]he Teheran radio quoted Ayatollah Khomeini as asking "all the Muslims to execute them," referring to Mr Rushdie, ..., and the publishers of the book, Viking Penguin, "wherever they find them." He said that anyone killed carrying out his order would be considered a martyr.'

10. Salman Rushdie, 'The Book Burning,' *New York Review of Books*, 36 (3) (March 2, 1989). The *Guardian* provided an overview of events on February 19, 1989; available at http://observer.guardian.co.uk/race/story/0,11255,603760,00.html

11. 'Imam at German Mosque Preached Hate to 9/11 Pilots,' *New York Times* (July 16, 2002).

12. *Dagens Nyheter* (November 17, 2003).

13. Under British law, Abu Hamza can be extradited only if the United States agrees not to seek the death penalty. At the time of writing, Abu Hamza is held in Belmarsh prison in London on murder charges.

14. For a survey of the literature, see John Higley and Michael G. Burton, 'The Elite Variable in Democratic Transitions and Breakdowns', *American Sociological Review*, 54 (1) (1989), 17–32.

15. I borrow the term 'clash of practices' from Bhikhu Parekh, 'Comments.' In *The Spiritual and Cultural Dimension of Europe*, Reflection group initiated by the President of the European Commission and Coordinated by the Institute for Human Sciences, Vienna/Brussels (October 2004).

16. 'Grüne fordern gesetzlichen Feiertag für Muslime,' *Die Welt* (November 16, 2004), 1.

17. Interview 68, The Hague (November 27, 2003).

18. Fouad Ajami, 'The Moor's Last Laugh. Radical Islam Finds a Haven in Europe,' *Wall Street Journal* (March 22, 2004).

19. Tariq Ramadan, *Western Muslims and the Future of Islam* (New York: Oxford University Press, 2004), 225.

20. *Deutsche Welle* (April 21, 2004), www.dw-world.de. Article by Andreas Tzortzis.

21. Interview 74, The Hague (December 2, 2003).

22. Kepel, op. cit., 253–5. Islamist groups are easily found on the Internet, but the actual reach of the organizations is difficult to tell. See http://www.ummah.org.uk/ikhwan/index.html.

1

Europe's New Muslim Political Elite

Farah Karimi is an Iranian political refugee and a member of the Dutch lower house of parliament, the Tweede Kamer, elected in 1998, a decade after she came to the Netherlands, to represent a Green Party, Groen Links. As a student, she had taken part in the 1979 Iranian revolution but her hopes for a national democratic revolution were dashed when the new Islamic government began enforcing religious laws. Women were segregated from men at universities and in public. Wearing the hijab, the Islamic headscarf, which the female revolutionaries had put on as a protest against the Shah's forced Westernization, was made compulsory. Today, Karimi thinks that she was naive about religion when she joined the Islamic student movement. 'We thought Islam was good,' she says, 'because at least it was our own culture.'[1] Now, she worries about the conservatism of the Muslim community in the Netherlands and points out that the immigrant organizations are led by old men.

At the same time, Karimi despairs that Dutch politicians do not have the courage to explain to the public why it is necessary to finance certain unpopular policies. Public funding for Islamic schools or the education of imams is needed, she says, to prevent countries like Saudi Arabia and Turkey from having influence in the Muslim community. But the conditions for rational debate have deteriorated. She has seen a drastic shift in public attitudes toward Muslims, in particular through the experiences of her twenty-year-old son. 'They see me as a Muslim,' she says he tells her, 'so I have to be one.' Karimi thinks the current political climate in the Netherlands is 'stupid,' a word she uses deliberately, because the climate encourages extremism on all sides.

Fatih Alev was at the time of the interview the head of a Danish Muslim student organization. He serves as imam for a small congregation at an inner-city cultural center in Copenhagen. In our conversations, he describes himself as a hyphenated Dane. He was born in Denmark to Turkish labor immigrants and is university-educated. He approaches all people, men and women, in the easy egalitarian way that characterizes Danes. He preaches in Danish, and embraces his Danishness—with one notable exception. He thinks that Danes have lost their spirituality, and that this loss is a primary reason they have become so intolerant of immigrants. 'The Danish shelves for faith and spirituality are empty,' he says, 'they fill them instead with fear of the "strong" foreigner.'[2] His hope is that the presence of Muslim believers will challenge Danes to rethink their relationship to religion.

Alev invests much of his time in interfaith dialogue and groups involved with Islamic education and theological renewal. He advocates strengthened antidiscrimination policies, which he thinks will help Muslims acquire a measure of equality with Christians. He is scandalized, however, when I suggest that new European Union rules on discrimination may be interpreted to disallow religious organizations from discriminating against gays. He is also skeptical of the proposition that women can become imams, and insists that the Koran is explicit that women can lead only other women in prayer. Two young women from his student association disagree vocally in his presence. Of course women can be imams, they say.[3] Women's ability to lead men in prayers has become an issue of public controversy since this conversation took place.[4]

Islam is now the largest minority religion in Europe and there are more Muslims than Catholics in Protestant northern Europe and more Muslims than Protestants in the Catholic South. Europe's Muslims far outnumber European Jews. Yet, while there is constant debate on the place of Islam, few changes have been made to existing public policies on religion. Faced with Islam, some Europeans respond by reasserting the primacy of Christianity, while others assert the commitment to secularism as an essential European value.

Karimi and Alev, one a left-wing parliamentarian and the other an imam and a university student, are part of a growing new European Muslim elite. They are educated and talented young people who have risen to the top in political and civic organizations because of their engagement and abilities. Their accomplishments and moderation suggest that the current panic about the Islamicization of Europe is seriously ill-informed.

THE 'NEW LINE' AND THE SECOND GENERATION

N.B

Who are Europe's Muslim leaders? My most significant finding is that the current political leaders—elected representatives of Muslim background or leaders of Muslim associations and groups—are themselves immigrants. They are typically not descendants of earlier generations of labor migrants who have risen to the top in mainstream politics because of their acculturation to European norms and languages. Some have managed to do this, but the majority arrived as young adults to continue their studies at Europe's universities, or came as experienced political activists and, commonly, as political refugees.

A common assumption is that it is the native-born descendents of immigrants who lead the charge for political integration. However, that is not necessarily true of the new Muslim political elite in Europe. One reason is that the native-born descendants of immigrants do not have an automatic claim to citizenship, and suffer the same legal disabilities that hobbled the first generation.

The Muslim leaders often identify themselves with what was described to me as the 'new line' in European Muslim politics. When I asked what the difference is to the 'old line,' it was described as a focus on national politics, a new emphasis on Muslim unity irrespective of ethnic and religious differences, and certain expectations about professionalism and 'playing by the rules' of national political discourse. Further, the new associations mostly conduct business in the national language—Danish, Dutch, or German—rather than in the languages of the country of origin, as was normal in the old migrants' associations. The generational label turns out to have only metaphorical meaning.

Writing about immigrant communities, social scientists typically invoke what they see as a new reality of transnational modes of political engagement and social identity. Key terms are 'diasporic communities,' 'bricolage,' 'hybridity,' 'postnational' citizenship, and 'transnational public space.' An anthropologist, Pnina Werbner, describes the collective identity of Manchester Muslims as an 'imagined diaspora' and identifies a global myth of the transnational Islamic community—the ummah—as a central feature of a new British-Muslim-Pakistani self-understanding.[5] The diaspora is an exile community that retains the core ethnic, linguistic, and cultural identities of the country of origin. Diasporas get involved in politics through the experience of political exile or by relating to the politics of the country of origin.

Economic theories of migration draw attention rather to economic calculations. Cultural rootedness and engagement are 'transaction' costs. Migrants will rationally attempt to minimize territorially bounded affinities. Instead, they invest in the development of global kinship networks that facilitate migration in search of new economic opportunities.[6]

However, the emergence of broad national Muslim associations that claim to represent a de-ethnicized national community of Muslims to the governments and publics of Western European countries contradicts these expectations. The current efforts to represent Islam in Europe are strikingly *national.*

N.B.

Some obvious reasons suggest themselves. Concepts of 'transnational identity formation' or 'diasporic identities' make little sense in the case of members of national parties and city councilors, who have joined mainstream
political organizations and choose to participate in national politics. Even
when the ultimate goal is to change foreign policy, for example, in the
Palestine conflict, the means are national. Finally, the xenophobic perception
that it is not possible to be European *and* Muslim invites Muslims to prove
that it *is* possible to be both.

Muslim activists are not pleased when their efforts to ground Islam in
European soil is described as an example of 'cultural hybridity.' It has become
important to many Muslims to demonstrate the essential European-ness of
Islam. Hardly a debate or a meeting passes without someone invoking history,
and, as is often the case when history is mobilized to prove a point of
contemporary contention, a good deal of historical revisionism is involved.
The Córdoban caliphate (929–1236) and the continued presence of Islam in
southern Europe until the expulsion from Granada in1492, as well as the siege
of Vienna in 1529, are cited to prove the European provenance of Islam. The
examples of converts to Islam, old or new, are cited as further evidence that
the faith is not foreign to Europeans. It is obviously true that contact between
Christianity and Islam has been a constant feature of European (and Islamic)
political and cultural history, and it characterized the British, French, and
Dutch colonial empires. However, the fact remains that Islam grew in Europe
over the past five decades as a result of global migration movements. And now
the migrants want to belong. The animosity between Islam and Christianity
has ancient roots, but it is late twentieth-century policies with respect to
church-state relations and the accommodation of migrant populations that
are the direct causes of today's problems.

The early political activities of Muslim immigrants might more accurately
be described as transnational associationalism. A comparative study published in 1987, organized by the European Science Foundation, found that
associational structures among European immigrants were determined by the
length of stay of the immigrants and patterned on homeland political divisions. The recurrent themes of associational activities were the maintenance
of kinship links with the homeland, religious fellowship, and legal and
practical advice related to migration.[7]

Ethnic-origin associations with one foot in the country of origin and
another in the country of residence continue to play a role. One example is
the Türkischer Bund Berlin-Brandenburg (TBB), a workers' association
started twenty-five years ago for migrant workers that is now trying to branch
out to include North African migrants. Similar associations exist for Turkish
and North African workers in France and in the Netherlands. Many were

started in the late 1970s to serve the first waves of labor migrants. European countries commonly funded civic groups of a cultural or educational nature, including sports associations, but they did not fund religious associations. Funding practices were reflected in the names of associations, as in Anatolsk Kulturforening (Denmark) or Association Culturelle et Sportive Cappadoce (France). The 'cultural associations' are often storefront mosques, where cultural activities pay the rent for a place to worship on Friday. Only a few are large and vibrant multipurpose organizations like the TBB.

The concept of postnational citizenship became popular among scholars a decade ago, because it captured a perceived shift towards a more effective implementation of international human rights norms within national juris-dictions and the development, within the European Union (EU), of common rights that all EU citizens can claim in any member state.[8] Nonetheless, the pronouncements of the decline of the nation-state and the emergence of non–national 'citizenship' proved premature. European states tightened immigration rules and reduced the rights of non–nationals. They set up holding camps for asylum-seekers and the majority of welfare recipients of immigrant origin were assigned special reduced benefits. EU rights have been expanded, but they are mostly tied to employment and cross-border eco-nomic transactions between member states, and are not applicable to indi-viduals who do not carry EU passports. European Muslims are mostly of Turkish, North African, or South Asian origin, and fall into this category. The European Court of Justice (ECJ) has been willing to extend some employ-ment rights to third-country migrants, but again these rights are related to work and do not remedy problems stemming from the lack of civic and political rights.[9]

Muslim parliamentarians, councilors, and national and local civic leaders are, in consequence, integrationists, and have little time for left-wing ideas about global citizenship and transnational identities. By the same token, they are not the Islamist militants of conservative nightmares. Fouad Ajami, a respected Middle East expert, has painted a dark picture of the emergence of a new Muslim political presence in Europe. In his view, Europe's new Muslim groups are fronts for Islamic militants from the Muslim Brotherhood and other banned organizations. He argues that Islamic radicals who were ejected from the Muslim world found a new home in Europe because of humanitar-ian asylum policies. Buoyed by the growth of the Muslim population in Europe, the Islamic radicals have gained power and are influencing European governments. The radicals have succeeded in doing in Europe what they failed to do in the Arab world.[10] Niall Ferguson has similarly invoked the specter of a Muslim demographic explosion as a source of a widening gap between the USA and Europe.[11] There are cases that fit this description. Omar Bakri

N.B.

Mohammed, a London-based cleric and leader of a militant group, al-Muha-jiroun, was granted asylum in 1985 after he was deported from Saudi Arabia, for example. But Ajami and Ferguson neglect to mention that even by the most exaggerated counts, less than ten percent of the general population in France are Muslim and in England only 3.1 percent are Muslim. Moreover, less than half of these people have the right to vote (and far fewer exercise that right).

Ajami is right that Europe's new Muslim leaders are often refugees from the Islamic world but wrong about the political implications. Many are political refugees, and they express views and values that are shaped by this back-ground. Sometimes they are Islamic radicals, but most are refugees because they were dissidents and participated in democracy movements. When Muslim leaders invoke human rights discourse to explain their views, they draw upon past experience. Their present engagements are a continuation of previous political commitments. Human rights are a primary political belief system, in part because the old left–right cleavage system that has structured European politics is a poor fit for immigrants and the descendants of immigrants.

The responses of Europe's political parties to the Muslim presence is an additional factor behind Muslims' unease with the established parties. Anti-immigrant and anti-Muslim sentiments have spread across the political spectrum, from left to right. The left is more supportive of social rights for immigrants—or at least it has been so in the past—but left parties are often anticlerical, as in the case of the French socialists, and find religion a vexing issue. The right, albeit more friendly to religion, has declared its support for the defense of Christian values and voiced anti-Muslim sentiments. There are exceptions to this picture, most importantly the Dutch Christian Democrats and the British Conservatives on the right, and the British Labour Party and the French and German Greens on the left.

GETTING THROUGH THE EYE OF THE NEEDLE

Muslims are seriously underrepresented in European power elites. At the time of this writing, there are about fifteen million Muslims in Europe but fewer than thirty Muslim members of European national parliaments. Restrictive naturalization rules mean that political parties can continue to ignore Muslim voters at very little cost.

The proportion of Muslims who are citizens varies between European countries, largely as a function of different naturalization rules. Regulations that affect the ability of Muslims to vote and to become elected officials also vary. In most countries, only 10–25 percent of the Muslim population can vote. There are two exceptions, the Netherlands, where fifty percent of Turks and Moroccans hold Dutch citizenship, and Great Britain.[12] Large pockets of disenfranchised residents, in some cases a quarter or more of the local population, are developing in cities with large concentrations of immigrants and non–national descendants.

Noncitizens cannot stand for national or local political office, and they generally cannot participate in elections. Denmark and Sweden allow foreign nationals who fulfill certain residency requirements to vote in local elections. About one-third of the eligible non–national legal residents take advantage of this opportunity. Denmark has 3.5 million eligible voters but there are about 250,000 long-term non–national residents (7 percent) in Denmark who cannot vote in national elections. One estimate is that only half of Danish Muslims can vote in national elections. In Italy, less than ten percent of Muslims are eligible. In Germany, as few as 500,000 of 3.2 million resident Muslims are naturalized citizens of voting age.[13] In Great Britain, half or more of all Bangladeshis, Pakistanis, and Indians were born in the country and are citizens, and three-fourths described their national identity as English, British, Scottish, Welsh, or Irish.[14]

Naturalization rules vary widely from country to country but even where the door to naturalization is open, access is restricted by administrative rules that narrow the pool of applicants, for example by prohibiting them from receiving social benefits. Proof of a minimum of savings and of acculturation, or 'attachment,' is also required. Most countries now allow a narrow window for young people, between eighteen and twenty-three years of age, who have lived in the country for a specified period of time, usually between five and ten years, to claim citizenship under relaxed procedures. In France, the Pasqua laws from 1993 eliminated the previously existing guarantee that anyone born in France was entitled to French citizenship—the *jus soli* principle. Since a new German citizenship reform went into effect from January 1, 2000, the difference between French and German rules has narrowed. In Germany, the sticking point is proof of commitment to the values of the Constitution, the Basic Law, a requirement that is incompatible with membership in a number of German Muslim associations. John R. Bowen, an anthropologist, describes how French civil servants regard adherence to the daily prayer schedule—al-Salat—as self-evident substantiation of insufficient assimilation to French norms and grounds for disqualifying an applicant from obtaining French citizenship.[15] The self-sufficiency criterion means that anyone receiving public aid—including social assistance and housing aid—is disqualified. Dual citizenship is mostly disallowed, which poses a problem for many immigrants because they often lose inheritance rights if they forfeit the citizenship of their country of origin. Since the reforms, naturalization rates have dropped off in France and the German reform has not advanced naturalization rates with the speed supporters had anticipated.

Despite these obstacles, the number of Muslims in Europe's parliaments and city councils has grown in recent years. Currently, the only Muslim member of the French National Assembly is from an overseas territory. In September 2004, two women of Muslim origin, Bariza Khiari from the Socialist Party and Alima Boumediene Thierry from the Green Party, were elected to the French Senate. There were two Muslim MPs in the British House of Commons, Mohammad Sarwar and Khalid Mahmood, at the time of my interviews. The 2005 election added two more Muslims to the Commons, Sadiq Kahn and Shahid Malik. All four are from the Labour Party. There are seven Muslim members of the House of Lords, including one who is openly gay. Two Muslims, both women, are seated in the German Bundestag, one from the Green Party and one from the Social Democrats, the SPD. There are five members of the Swedish Riksdagen who are Muslim, and, since the February 2005 parliamentary elections, three in the Danish Folketing. There are seven Muslims in the Dutch Tweede Kamer, including two representing the Christian Democratic Party.

Hundreds of Muslims have been elected to city councils in the major European cities, and with every election more are added. In certain cities, Berlin and Rotterdam, for example, Muslim voters are becoming important and are beginning to influence city council elections. Nevertheless, it is only in Great Britain that Muslim voters have emerged as a distinct and significant voter bloc roughly comparable to the Cuban vote in the USA. However, here, as elsewhere in Europe, party discipline is strong, and representatives are not free to become spokesmen for special interests. As one parliamentarian's assistant explained to me as we were chatting about the member's policy priorities, 'discrimination and the position of Muslims are really difficult areas.'[16] For many Muslim politicians, who need the support of party colleagues to get ahead, Islam and discrimination amount to what in the USA is referred to a the third rail of politics, 'you touch it and your are dead.'

FOREIGN-BORN LEADERS TAKE THE LEAD

About 85–95 percent of the Muslim leaders who participated in this study were born abroad and came to Europe as young adults. The share of native-born leaders was higher in Great Britain and the Netherlands than elsewhere, undoubtedly a reflection of the earlier onset of mass migration to those countries. The high proportion of native-born French leaders—over half—reflects the relative youth of the French respondents who returned the questionnaires that Tables 1.1 and 1.2 are based upon. On the other hand, the rate of naturalization among the French participants appears to be surprisingly low considering their youth—the average age is thirty-two compared to 40–42 in the other countries—and high educational status.

A number of Muslim parliamentarians in Sweden and in the Netherlands arrived as political refugees, and within the span of a decade obtained citizenship and won election to national office. This group includes some of the most talented young members of the two parliaments, such as Farah Karimi and Ayaan Hirsi Ali in the Dutch Tweede Kamer and Mauricio Rojas, Rezene Tesfazion, and Nyamko Sabuni in the Riksdagen. Rojas is a Catholic and Tesfazion a Coptic Christian. Karimi and Sabuni describe themselves as culturally Muslim. Hirsi Ali, a Dutch-Somali legislator, describes herself as an ex-Muslim and is famous—or notorious—for calling the Prophet a 'pervert.' She has blamed the Prophet for the suppression of women in Muslim countries, and has argued that Islam 'cannot be trusted.'[17] She belongs to the VVD, the Liberal party, and received a record number of personal votes, 68,000, in the 2002 election. (The Dutch electoral system allows voters to vote for a party or an individual candidate.)

Elected office aside, citizenship is not a legal prerequisite for civic and political engagement, but it matters greatly in practice. The non–naturalized leaders, who constitute between one-tenth and one-quarter of the participants in the study, were found in civic associations and not in the political parties. Denmark and Germany, countries with particularly restrictive naturalization laws, had a larger proportion of non–naturalized leaders.

The barriers to representation are often lower in city councils. In Great Britain, two factors boosted Muslim participation in local government. One is

Table 1.1. Citizenship and origin by country

Country of residence	Citizen (%)	Native-born (%)
Denmark	90.9	12.1
Sweden	95.5	4.5
Netherlands	100.0	26.1
Germany	76.6	25.5
Great Britain	96.8	16.1
France	89.4	60.0

$n = 161$

Table 1.2. Personal importance of faith by political orientation

	Islam not important (%)	Islam sometimes important (%)	Islam very important (%)
Right	11.4	6.3	5.7
Center	31.4	53.1	64.8
Left	57.1	40.6	29.5
Subtotal	100.0	100.0	100.0
Total	35	35	95

$n = 165$

that local party committees are largely free to decide who gets to stand for elections. The other is the combination of decentralized local government and a high degree of residential segregation, which facilitates immigrant representation. The same factors are occasionally at play in other countries, and some areas have emerged as recruiting grounds for immigrant politicians. The Berlin city council has three Muslim members, one from the Greens and two from the PDS, a successor party of the former Communist Party of East Germany. Riza Baran, also from the Green Party, is president of the Friedrichshain-Kreuzberg district council. Rinkeby, a planned city of high–rises and public housing outside Stockholm, has thirteen immigrant-origin representatives out of twenty-two councilors, and eight (including the chairman) are Muslim. Tower Hamlets in the center of London is another urban community where the concentration of immigrant or immigrant-origin residents has changed the composition of local political leadership. About half of the fifty-one councilors are immigrant-origin and some fifteen are Muslim. Similar trends have changed municipal government in Rotterdam, Marseilles, and Birmingham. Demography and the boundaries of municipal government conspire in some cases to dissociate immigrants from urban politics, and in others to foster inclusion.

FAITH AND POLITICAL IDEOLOGY

It is commonly assumed that faith predisposes individuals to a conservative political stance. This is not the case for Muslims in Europe. Most Muslim leaders say that Islam is significant in their personal lives. Four out of five of the leaders said their faith was either 'very important' or 'somewhat important' to them. Over half of the leaders were strong believers. Within this group, one-third belonged to the left and two-thirds to the center. Religious centrists constituted the single largest subgroup. Contrary to the general belief that religious Muslims are right-wingers, I found only a handful of people who said both that they supported the right and that they were strongly religious. Half of the agnostics were on the left and the other half on the right, but then only one out of five leaders admitted that faith was not important in their personal lives.

In some cases, commitment to Islam is a response to perceived prejudices in general society, and I found this to apply both among nonpartisan leaders and within the left-wing political parties. Two women of Turkish origin who both held important party positions in their country's social democratic party, expressed identical feelings of rising impatience and belated self-discovery. 'When I hear them talk about "those people," meaning Muslims, I feel like standing up and saying "hello, I am one of those people," ' said one parliamentarian while pulling at her mini-skirt.[18] When I described to the other how I had just spoken to some left-wing feminists in the party, who were toying with the idea of putting forward legislation that would ban the headscarf (the French headscarf ban had just been proposed at that time), she looked quizzical at me and said, 'I did not used to think much about Islam; it was just something we do. But my mother wears the headscarf, and I do not see any reason to make her feel bad about that.'[19]

Party ideologies are not always a comfortable fit for Muslims. The dissonance is evident in a mismatch between self-described political orientation and partisan choice, at least compared to the standard left–right template for party placement. Muslims who belong to Christian democratic parties, a surprisingly large number, generally describe themselves as centrists rather than as belonging to the right. Similarly, some of the leaders who described themselves as centrists belonged to what are traditionally regarded as left-wing parties, including the Danish and Swedish social democratic parties and the British Labour Party, as well as the Green parties in France and Germany. An old friend, who is now a left-wing member of the Danish parliament, said to me when we met and discussed my research, 'those people do not think as we do about the histories of the parties and the importance of programs.'[20]

The increasingly anti-immigrant—and anti-Muslim in particular—stance of some of the left parties is another possible reason for the observed dissonance. The Danish Social Democrats and the French Socialists in particular have been stressing the importance of protecting national values and customs against Islamic dilution. In response, a number of centrist Muslim leaders in France and Germany have migrated to the Green parties. In Denmark, they are joining other small parties in the center or on the left. In Britain, the Liberal Democrats have benefited from Muslim defection from Labour. According to a special *Guardian*/ICM poll, one year after the start of the Iraq war Labour's share of the British Muslim vote had fallen by half, from 75 to 38 percent of all Muslim voters, since the 2001 general election. Six months later, a second poll found Labour's position to have deteriorated further.[21]

Partisan affiliations are not set in stone. One religiously conservative manager of a controversial German association of mosques hesitated when I asked which party Muslims like himself could best expect to work with in the future. 'Many people say the Greens,' he said. 'I am not so sure. Probably, the Christian Democrats are better.' His hesitation was understandable, since he and his association had just been subjected to yet another volley from the Christian Democrats about German commitments to 'occidental' and 'Christian' values.[22]

The more religious leaders tended to describe themselves as centrist, in part because many Muslim leaders, and particularly individuals who are associated with Muslim associations or mosque groups, are uneasy about the large political parties. The preponderance of centrists among the more religious leaders may reflect a deliberate decision on the part of the national Muslim civic associations to avoid becoming identified—and taken for granted—by the social democratic or Labour parties that historically have been able to count on immigrant voters.

On the other hand, Muslims who might be inclined to support conservative parties are made to feel unwelcome. One young German Muslim Christian Democrat told me that he had refrained from running for office again (he was formerly elected to a regional parliament). He and his friends within the CDU had also decided not to proceed with a plan to organize a large meeting of Muslim party members. 'What is the point?' he said. 'They will call us Islamist every time we do anything.'[23] The Dutch Christian Democratic party is more open to Muslims than its German counterpart, and the British Conservative Party has tried to woo Muslim voters by promising, among other things, to support the creation of more Muslim faith schools with public support. A small number of Muslims have even run successfully for local office representing the xenophobic French National Front and the Dutch Lijst Pim Fortuyn.

In European politics, faith has generally compelled people towards the right while the left has been resolutely anticlerical. French Muslims (and non-Muslim academics) complained bitterly about the Socialist Party's intolerance of religious expression, and tended to remark that you had to be committed to 'the holy principle of laïcité' to succeed in the party.[24] Abortion, gay rights, and bioethics are some of the issues where religious Muslims find common ground with other religious associations and lobbies. It is clear, nonetheless, that for many religious Muslims 'value conservatism' may be less salient than other issues, which are generally important for the left, in

N 3

particular antidiscrimination enforcement and social protection. The success of the Dutch Christian Democratic party in attracting support from Muslims suggests, on the other hand, that the right could do better among Muslims if it de-emphasized Christianity and instead spoke about faith and religious values in general.

Recruitment patterns are difficult to discern, except for the simple observation that Sweden and the Netherlands have more Muslim parliamentarians than the other countries. And Britain has a large number of Muslim—and other ethnic origin—politicians involved in local government, but ethnic minority representation lags behind in the House of Commons.

Party membership is a prerequisite for recruitment to political office. There are significant national differences in the propensity to join political parties across the countries. In Germany, half of the sample reported no party affiliation. Sweden had the highest rate of party membership with only one in five reporting no party affiliation. These variations may have many causes, from differences in party norms to the rate of noncitizenship status among Muslims in general. Ultimately, it is reasonable to expect that the number of Muslim voters will affect the willingness of the political parties to put up Muslim candidates for seats to which they are likely to be elected. But as the case of Ayaan Hirsi Ali suggests, it is possible for a Muslim to become a high-profile vote getter, in this case, curiously, by attracting the anti-Muslim vote.

The factors I have identified are certainly significant, but it is not possible to say which is the more significant for shaping Muslim political engagement. The number of Muslims who have won elected office in national and local government remains low, and there are many possible explanations, including fairly random ones such as when the last election was held.

THE QUEST FOR MUSLIM UNITY

The 9/11 terrorist attacks became a catalyst for anti-Muslim sentiments but also for a new wave of Muslim associationalism. Aghast that terrorism was being carried out in the name of Islam, civic groups issued statements rejecting fundamentalism and political Islam. But the ground was prepared for a new political presence before the events of 9/11. 'Much has changed,' explained one of the leaders of the big national associations to me, 'the connections to the old countries are not what they used to be.'[25]

The groups that are now moving to the forefront were formed in the 1980s and 1990s but then they found unity elusive. Today, the same leader said, the 'functionaries' (by which he meant the leaderships of the old immigrant organizations) are finding it more difficult to defend organizational self-interest in the face of a growing understanding of 'the necessity of the new line.' He defined this as the collaboration by all Muslim groups in a new structure of national umbrella associations capable of representing a pragmatic and de-ethnicized Muslim voice geared to 'the European reality' and national issues. 'The state needs such a collaborator,' he pointed out. 'Muslim unity is a challenge to Western European governments and a help.'

The national associations are either modeled on other pre–existing councils or associations of religious groups, as in the case of the Muslim Council of Britain, for which the Jewish Council of Britain is the ideal, or they are umbrella groups for several associations. However, Europe's Muslim populations are exceptionally diverse and, as was repeatedly pointed out to me in interviews, there is no 'central command' in Islam capable of uniting Muslims who are otherwise divided by politics, national origin, and theological differences.

The emergence of national faith-based umbrella groups or councils is a recent phenomenon. A key difference is the new groups' focus on national political participation and their support for integration as the chief objective. But something about the psychology is different, too. The sentiment that 'we have rights, too' has replaced the modest expectations of the earlier cohorts of immigrants. The first– versus second-generation distinction is misleading, however. People who describe themselves as 'second-generation' representatives are in fact very often foreign-born themselves. The generational label is a metaphor. It describes a perceived change in outlook and strategy rather than a demographic fact.

It is more accurate to speak of a cohort effect to describe the longitudinal shifts in associationalism. The demographic characteristics of a cohort follow from the rules and laws under which migration was allowed.

The German government signed a bilateral treaty with Italy in 1955 allowing a federal labor recruitment office to sign up Italian workers to work in Germany. Similar treaties were later agreed with Italy, Turkey, and Yugoslavia. The Italian workers were largely Catholics and have now been absorbed into the pool of inter-European migrants covered by EU rules. Only Turkish and Yugoslavian workers were primarily Muslims, and they remain in legal limbo.

Other countries followed suit in the following decade, including France, which recruited two million workers from southern Europe. The first wave peaked in 1974–5 when the oil crisis-induced recession caused governments to end labor migration. Immigration nevertheless continued as the first generation of labor migrants were joined by their families in the 1970s.

In Britain, France, and the Netherlands, the colonies were an important source of early migration. Algerian independence in 1962, Idi Amin's expulsion of Asians from Uganda in 1972, and Surinamese independence in 1975 were some of the events that resulted in waves of migration to, respectively, France, the UK, and the Netherlands. Each wave of migration created secondary migrations under family reunification rules. In the UK, the restrictions on immigration imposed by the 1962 Commonwealth Immigrants Act had the perverse effect of pushing immigration to new peaks as men already living in the UK decided to bring their families to join them while they could still do so. A new wave of political refugees and asylum–seekers followed in 1989–92. This drew on a more diverse and more global population of migrants, including large numbers from the former Soviet Union, Arab countries, Africa, and Asia.

Half of Denmark's Muslims today came as political refugees. The other half are labor migrants, mostly of Turkish origin, who immigrated thirty or forty years ago, and their children. However, the distinction between labor migrants and refugees is not hard and fast. I met a number of people who had left Turkey and Morocco for political reasons in the early 1970s, but as it was still possible to acquire a residence permit as a labor migrant, they had not sought asylum status.

British Muslims are primarily first-wave immigrants of Bangladeshi and Pakistani origin. French Muslims are mostly of Maghrebian origin, some from the first wave and others from the second wave. German Muslims are overwhelmingly of Turkish origin and descendents of first-wave labor migrants. Swedish, Danish, and Dutch Muslims are of mixed descent and include many Africans and Arabs who have come as political refugees in the past decade.

Each cohort carries the imprint of the legal and historical context of its migration with it through the decades. The first cohort of labor migrants lacked the skills and experience to become political leaders. The second cohort was mostly women and older family members who arrived under family reunification rules. The most recent cohort includes many illegal migrants, who cannot participate in political activities without risking deportation. It is therefore not surprising that political leadership has been assumed by the refugees and university students who arrived after legal labor migration had more or less come to an end.

The timing of migration and the legal rules under which specific cohorts of migrants were allowed to settle have subsequent consequences for the collective processes of identity negotiation. In the earlier waves of labor migration, sometimes entire villages migrated together and settled in the same area where those who arrived first established a bridgehead. A Turkish-origin Danish city councilor joked that he had to go to Turkey to escape his family. 'I must have sixty cousins in the suburbs south of Copenhagen,' he told me laughingly.[26]

The 'myth of return'—the expectation that they would return to the country of origin after having collected enough wealth to improve social standing at home—was particularly strong among the early wave of labor migrants. It is only now, I was repeatedly told, forty years after the first wave of Turkish labor migration to Germany, that German Turks have themselves abandoned the 'myth of return.'[27] Since mass migration takes place in waves, triggered by historical events ranging from wars and revolutions to the ups and downs of business cycles, personal and collective adjustment is often set to the same clock. The individual migrant's psychological and political adjustment then translates into a cohort phenomenon, and this creates a platform for collective action and political mobilization.

Nadeem Elyas, the president of the Central Council of Muslims in Germany, described in an interview how a 'new self-understanding on the part of Muslim immigrants' emerged in the 1990s. 'We want to keep our identity as Muslims in Germany, as German Muslims. . . . Society does not have a right to decide for us what parts of Islam are acceptable and which are not. That step has to come from us and we have to be willing to use the flexibility of Muslim rules and regulations to develop something you can call Islam with a German character.'[28] The difficulty is that a new consciousness does not automatically translate into new organizations.

European societies are highly organized, and interactions between the state and specific social or economic groups generally take place through formalized channels. Government officials expect interlocutors to be able to show that they speak for their constituents. However, European Muslims are divided by language, by customary differences with respect to the exercise of religion, and by their understandings of Islam. The new associations aim to build cohesion around a shared narrative based upon secularized Islamic value systems, but they compete with each other and often have irreconcilable views of what should be done.

Sometimes, however, diversity works in favor of cohesion. The more fragmented the Muslim population, the sooner host languages—Danish, Swedish, or Dutch—become the lingua franca of intergenerational and intergroup communication. The language shift provides a template for the articulation of a new hybrid organizational identity, as Danish-Muslim or German–Muslim rather than, for example, German-Turkish-Muslim. Language can also be a disability. German-Turkish Muslims numerically outweigh other language groups among German Muslims, and Turkish dominates in many political contexts. From the offices of the Green Party in Kreuzberg to the Turkish association of imams and mosques, Türkisch-Islamische Union der Anstalt für Religion (DITIB), German is not required. Conversely, English has helped build bridges between Muslims from South Asian and Arabic countries, and Africa in Britain.

GERMANY

Article 4 of the 1949 Basic Law, the German Constitution, obliges the state to maintain neutrality in religious matters, but German law does not preclude close cooperation between church and state. Recognized denominations are eligible for federal government assistance in raising a 9 percent church tax, administrated by public tax authorities. Recognized faiths have public rights and responsibilities. As the government states, 'in exchange for administrative and financial assistance from the state, established religious organizations play an active role in German society. They run many hospitals, nursing homes, day care centers and similar institutions in Germany as well as humanitarian aid and assistance programs in the developing nations.'[29] They are represented on government boards, and are allowed to conduct religious education in public schools. There have been efforts to create a comprehensive umbrella association but most Muslim associations now seek instead to obtain some of the benefits of recognition by other means, such as the right to conduct religious instruction in public schools.

One reason for the failure of German Muslims to establish an umbrella organization is the enduring animosity between the two largest Turkish associations. One is Milli Görüs, an exile organization connected to the Refah Party (the Welfare Party), which is banned in Turkey. It is the parent organization of the Islamrat der BRD. The other is DITIB, a Turkish government-funded association responsible for the delivery of religious services to Turks residing in Germany. This animosity has prevented the creation of a unified council to represent Muslims in Germany. One response to this deadlock was the creation of the unaffiliated Zentralrat der Muslime in Deutschland (ZMD), or the Central Council of Muslims in Germany, in December 1994. The organization is modeled on the Central Council of Jews, and brings together about twenty national or regional associations of diverse purpose and origin.

Following German practice, the ZMD is incorporated as a federal 'Verein', but its claim to represent all German Muslims was rejected by an administrative court in Düsseldorf in 2001. The court noted the existence of a rival organization, the Islamrat, and argued that the ZMD was not a true 'Spitzenverband', a peak association, for German Muslims. In consequence, no association has been granted recognition as a representative of the German faith community and Muslims have been denied the privileges of public status as recognized faiths accorded Jews, Catholics, and Protestants.

Relations between Milli Görüs and DITIB have begun to thaw. The former's militancy derived from the rift between the Turkish military and the government parties and the Welfare Party. The November 2002 election, which put Recep Tayyip Erdogan and the Justice and Welfare (AK) Party, a successor party to the banned Islamist Welfare Party, in government, opened the door for a rapprochement between the main associations appealing to Turkish-origin Muslims. DITIB, however, insists that the other groups recognize it as the largest organization of Muslims in Germany. 'One day,' a spokesperson from the association explained to me, 'it is possible to imagine that the other Muslim groups might have representatives on our "Vorstand" (head council).'[30] The difficulty, of course, is that the DITIB is an association of Turkish-built mosques and Turkish-financed imams and owes its size to the unique role of the Turkish government in providing pastoral care to German residents of Turkish origin. Critics of DITIB point out that anything the organization does requires instructions from Ankara. Language is also a barrier. The current secretary-general of DITIB does not speak German.

DITIB representatives complain occasionally that the ZMD represents only '10 percent of German Muslims' but gets all the attention. In the press, Nadeem Elyas, the secretary-general of the organization, is frequently described as 'having ties' to the Muslim Brotherhood (MB). (Other sources estimate the ZMD's membership at 800,000, the equivalent of 25 percent of all German Muslims, but 10 percent seems the more accurate number.) Elyas was born in Saudi Arabia and came to Germany to study medicine in 1964. He was for many years chair of the Islamische Zentrum Aachen–Bilal Moschee (IZA), which was formed in 1964 and has long been regarded as a Brotherhood 'project.' As for the connection to the MB, Elyas says he was never a member of the Brotherhood. A more important factor weighing against discounting the ZMD is that it is based upon volunteer memberships and is the only multiethic Muslim association. It is home to converts as well as a diverse group of Muslim associations organizing Muslims from Albania, Bosnia, Turkey, and Arab and African countries.

The Süleymancis organized their own association in 1980, VIKZ, Verband Islamischer Kulturzentren. They came as labor migrants and were among the first to create permanent schools and mosques in Germany. Today the VIKZ organizes about three hundred mosque communities. The group is named after Süleyman Efendi (1888–1959), a Turkish religious reformer born in what is today Bulgaria. They regard themselves as Sunni Muslims and while they deny that they are a sect within Islam, the VIKZ does not belong to either of the umbrella organizations.

A new type of community-based religious organization has emerged outside the traditional sectarian and political delineations. These groups distinguish themselves by being grassroots organizations, or 'roundtable' (Runden Tisch) groups. Examples are the Hamburg Schura and the Berlin-based Islamische Föderation Berlin (IFB). These are local or regional groups that have grown up around particular functions, such as interfaith collaboration and representation, as in the case of the Hamburg Schura, or provision of services, religious education in public schools, in the case of the IFB.

Perhaps as many as 20 percent of Turkish-origin Germans are Alevites and are outside the main Muslim associations.[31] Theological differences are the issue. Alevites do not regard the Koran as the Prophet's divine revelation, and neither Sunni nor Shiah Muslims recognize them as Muslims. The Alevites do not have mosques but worship in a *cem*, a community house.

Representatives from all the main organizations met in February 2005 in Hamburg to discuss the creation of an encompassing umbrella organization that would seek official recognition as a representative of Germany's Muslims.[32] A number of local associations, including the Hamburg Schura, which acted as host for the meeting, also attended, as did what was referred to as 'leading personalities.' Before the meeting, DITIB announced that it was ready to represent all German Muslims and requested official recognition as 'dialog partner' (Ansprechtspartner), and sole representative, from the state of Nordrhein-Westphalia.

The initiative to try, once again, to create a national umbrella association was prompted in part by another initiative from Nordrhein-Westphalia. The Social Democrats in the state government proposed earlier this year to create a public register of mosques. The purpose of the register, according to the government's announcement, is to create a congregational structure for the mosque communities, which is 'compatible with German church law.'[33] Both initiatives have been greeted with much optimism that a new willingness to find compromise solutions exists.[34] Caution is indicated. In the past, reform efforts have invariably been shipwrecked on organizational rivalries, or have failed to win the approval of the conservative German administrative courts.

BRITAIN

In response to the public questioning of the loyalty of British Muslims, the Muslim Council of Britain (MCB) issued a statement that 'there is no contradiction between being loyal British citizens and being Muslims.'[35] The MCB was formed in 1996 by representatives of a number of national, regional, and local

Muslim organizations, some religious and others civic in nature. A precursor organization, the UK Action Committee on Islamic Affairs, led the campaign against Salman Rushdie's book, *Satanic Verses*. Today people associated with the MCB consider the campaign a mistake and are quick to stress that the MCB represents British Muslims and not the Muslim world community.

Iqbal Sacranie, the MCB's secretary-general, has successfully professionalized the Council's public relations and lobbying activities to such an extent that the group has become a national representative for British Muslims, something that cannot be said for the French Council or the German Zentralrat. The MCB's public role has grown steadily and the Council is frequently cited in the national and international press on matters related to British Muslims. The MCB also lobbies on legislation and is frequently asked for comments on policies and reports, be it a census report showing high poverty rates among Muslims, or initiatives taken by the Blair government to regain support among Muslim voters.

It is, however, not easy to judge how supportive British Muslims are of the groups that profess to represent them. An ICM/*Guardian* poll of 500 British Muslims from November 24, 2004 found that 37 percent said that the MCB generally reflected their views and 45 percent said it did not. The MCB was slightly more popular among Labour voters than among Conservatives, and the most popular among those who said they would vote for the Liberal Democrats, where opinion split 49 to 37 percent in favor of the MCB. I found that support for the organization increased among people I interviewed after the MCB took steps to improve its public image in 2003–4, even as it risked criticism by working with the government. Together with other Muslim groups, the MCB started meeting regularly with MI5 and the Metropolitan police, and sent out a letter to more than 1,000 mosque councils after the Madrid bombing admonishing British Muslims to work with the government to identify radical imams. The MCB also takes on domestic policy issues where the risk of dissension is high, such as polygamy and adoption rights for gays (both of which it opposes).

The associations affiliated to the MCB pursue their own agendas, sometimes at the risk of some public confusion. Two of the larger affiliates are the Islamic Society of Britain (ISB) and the Muslim Association of Britain (MAB). The ISB focuses primarily on community work. Its social activities range from summer camps for young people, soccer tournaments, and study circles to collecting money for various relief projects. The organization regards social activism in Britain as a way of honoring the obligation to do dawah, or missionary work. One of its membership groups is the Association of Muslim Lawyers, which aims to promote the careers of Muslim lawyers and 'to promote the legal rights of Muslims and the availability of advice in accordance with the shariah.' It is one of many professional associations dedicated to promoting religious principles in the professions. Their object-ives are comparable to, say, an association of Catholic social workers or educators, which might promote alternatives to abortion or otherwise pursue Catholic principles in business and social service.[36]

Other groups include the Muslim Parliament, which was launched in 1992 on the wave of anger unleashed by the *Satanic Verses* controversy. The founder, Kalim Siddiqui, who died in 1996, advocated the creation of a 'nonterritorial' Islamic state in Britain. Today the Muslim Parliament is headed by Ghayasuddin Siddiqui, who does not advocate separatism. The Muslim Parliament appears to have only leaders and no followers.

The MAB is regarded as 'Arab-dominated' and works as a political action group. One informed estimate I was given is that it is '50 percent Arab.'[37] The MAB works as a political action committee for Arab-Muslim interests, and tries to corral the 'ummah' behind the Palestine issue. The group is accused of having connections to Hamas, a Palestinian organization with a military wing. It targeted seventy Labour MPs in the June 2005 election because of their pro-Israel votes, and the association mobilizes voters through voter drives in mosques. The MAB, in contrast to the MCB, works with old 'new left' groups, such as the Socialist Workers Party, and is favored by the mayor of London, Ken Livingstone.

Livingstone's relationship with the MAB came under scrutiny when he invited Youssouf al-Qaradawi, a well-known Qatar-based cleric whose pro-grams on al-Jazeera are watched all over Europe, to London as an official guest in July 2004. Al-Qaradawi is also the head of the Dublin-based Euro-pean Council for Fatwa and Research, better known by its French name, 'Le conseil européen de la recherche et de la Fatwa.' The Fatwa Council presents itself as the authoritative source of interpretation of shariah law and fatwas for all European Muslims. The invitation caused much criticism in Britain, but several Muslim associations defended the mayor's invitation. The MCB de-scribed al-Qaradawi as a 'respected Islamic scholar' and accused 'the Zionist lobby' of engaging in a smear campaign.[38] The Muslim Association of Britain and the Muslim Council of Britain both publicly defended al-Qaradawi as a 'moderate.' It is a doubtful label.

The MCB tries to maintain an ecumenical approach to sectarian differences, but the organization has occasionally slipped up. When the Ahmadi commu-nity opened a new mosque in Morden, a suburb of London, which is capable of seating 10,000 congregants, and so has a larger capacity than St Paul's Cath-edral, the MCB issued a dismissive press release: 'In the light of much press interest, the Muslim Council of Britain wishes to make clear that the Qadiyani/Ahmadi Centre which has been constructed in Morden is not a Mosque.'[39] It is not a mosque, the MCB explained, because the Ahmadis are not Muslim. 'So, whilst we fully accept the right of Ahmadis to their own religion, it is clearly misleading to describe them as Muslims. They are not.' (The Ahmadis are also called Ahmadiyyas.) The MCB was repeating the official position of the government of Pakistan, where the Ahmadis were officially declared not to be Muslims in 1974. Ahmadis accept Ahmad as a Prophet, in addition to Mohammed, and are therefore regarded by some Muslims as apostates. In my interviews, other Muslim leaders commented that they did not think the MCB should be in the business of deciding who is a Muslim and who is not.

The diversity of British Muslims is reflected in the panoply of groups that exists, ranging from FOSIS, a student association, to the An-Nisa Society, a feminist group, and *Q-News*, a glossy magazine published by a collective of young Muslims. Some of Europe's most innovative Muslim theologians and public intellectuals are British. Examples are Kenan Malik, Yasmin Alibhai-Brown, Anshuman Mondal, and Ziauddin Sardar, the author of *Desperately Seeking Paradise*.[40]

FRANCE

Several French Muslim associations and the rectors for the Grand Mosques in Lyon and Paris agreed in May 2002 to form a French Council for the Muslim Faith. The new peak organization, Conseil Français du Culte Musulman (CFCM), is made up of twenty-five regional councils, which elected delegates to the national council. The four principal Muslim associations (described below) also sponsored delegates and participated in the election of representatives to the CFCM, as did some unaffiliated regional groups and a number of independent mosque associations. 'After the first elections to the CFCM, in 2003, the activist association, l'Union des Organisations Islamiques de France (UOIF), which is based in Paris, emerged as the winner. In the next elections, held June 19, 2005, the UOIF lost three seats. The winners were the Paris Grand Mosque (GMP) and the FNMF. Nicolas Sarkozy, who as minister of the interior initiated the creation of the CFCM, praised the election as a victory for "moderates" and French Islam but in reality the result owed a great deal to the efforts of the Algerian and Moroccan governments to mobilize votes for "their" associations.'

It brings together mosque groups and branches of associated women's and youth groups. The organization claims to have about twenty local branch offices, some based in community centers and others in mosques. The association's website lists some sixty regional and local membership associations. The UOIF was created in 1983, reportedly with funding from Saudi

Arabia and the Gulf states. The founders were Zouhir Mahmoud Choukr, who was of Iraqi origin, and Abdellah Benmansour, of Tunisian origin.[41] Several of the founders were associated with the Muslim Brotherhood, and the UOIF continues to be described as a 'Brotherhood' organization even though it is also, at other times, described as the 'Moroccan' alternative to the Algerian-dominated Grand Mosque. The Muslim World League (Saudi Arabia), the Algerian, Moroccan, and Turkish governments, Qatar-based clerics, and the Muslim Brotherhood (both Syrian and Egyptian branches) are all external sources of influence, and are as such increasingly under scrutiny.

Whatever its history, the UOIF today draws a multiethnic crowd. The organization's annual meeting in a vacated hangar in a Parisian suburb, Le Bourget, draws huge crowds of young people.[42] The event mixes political speeches and religious sermons with music, food, and fashion displays. The UOIF has a considerable following also among sub-Saharan Africans, and the president, Lhaj Thami Brèze, prides himself on his willingness to make compromises and build alliances across political and ethnic boundaries.

The UOIF has transnational aspirations, most controversially expressed through its links with the Dublin-based Fatwa Council and another organization, the Federation of Islamic Organizations in Europe (FIOE), which is widely regarded as a Muslim Brotherhood association. The UOIF also runs a theological seminary located in a chateau in Burgundy, the Institut Européen des Sciences Humaines, which includes faculty members drawn from the above-mentioned Fatwa Council. The Institut has about 180 students, men and women, both French and foreign. The UOIF preaches a conservative version of Islam, which emphasizes the learning of Arabic and depends upon authoritative statements by clerics to define the rules of the faith in contemporary society, but the association's political language stresses compromise and coexistence.

The FNMF, La Fédération Nationale des Musulmans de France, was created in 1985 with support from the Moroccan government. It is considered more moderate in orientation. The president is Mohamed Bechari, a thirty-seven-year-old, who is also vice president of the CFCM. In September 2004, Bechari became the center of controversy when he went to Qatar with the purpose of trying to negotiate the release of two French journalists, who had been kidnapped and held hostage in Iraq. While in Qatar, Bechari met with Abassi Madani, the exiled leader of Front Islamique du Salut (FIS), an Algerian Islamist organization held responsible for bomb attacks in Paris in the late 1980s. Bechari was widely criticized again in March 2005, when he announced that he had been appointed to the Fiqh Council of the Organization of Islamic Conferences, created in Rabat, Morocco, in 1969, by the heads of states of various Islamic countries as an expression of Islamic unity against Israel.

The FNMF is also linked to other European groups and institutions through membership in the Islamic Educational, Scientific and Cultural Organizations (ISESCO), an umbrella organization of the education ministries of some fifty Islamic countries. Presented as 'the Muslim UNESCO,' the organization was set up in 1969 as a joint Moroccan–Saudi Arabian initiative. (Egypt, Pakistan, Iran, Bangladesh, and 'the State of Palestine' are also members.) Among the European groups and institutions in the ISESCO network are the German Islamrat, the British MCB, and educational institutions such as Al-Aznar University (Egypt), Al-Quds (Israel), and the Oxford Centre for Islamic Studies (Oxford University).

To some observers these interlocking directorates are evidence that Europe is now in the grip of a vast Islamic conspiracy, but this characterization overestimates the influence of such memberships. Sometimes the organizations are Potemkin villages, huge empty facades. Over time alliances break up and new ones are made, and the motives of the membership organizations are not necessarily identical to those of the transnational organizations or other foreign sponsors. Money and institutional support, rather than political fidelity, are sometimes reasons why the national associations rely on outside assistance. Strange alliances are made. The ISESCO and FIOE sponsored, together with the Council of Europe, a meeting I attended organized by FNMF. The sponsorship of the Moroccan embassy was also obvious, as its kitchen staff fed the participants, who also ate from the embassy's plates. Were domestic sources of financing available for associational activities, as is the case in Sweden and increasingly in Germany, affiliations would be a matter of choice and not need.

Two smaller organizations of Turkish origin are also represented on the CFCM, Milli Görüs and the Comité de Coordination des Musulmans Turcs de France (CCMTF), which is the Turkish Diyanet's French arm.

The fourth association is the Grand Mosque in Paris, which is funded by the Algerian government. Successive French governments have treated the Grand Mosque in Paris and its rector, Dalil Boubakeur, who succeeded his father to the post, as the official representative of French Muslims. In the 2004 elections to the Council, the Paris Mosque obtained only six of the forty-one spots on the CFCM's council allocated for elected representatives, but Boubakeur became the president anyway.

The Paris Mosque was built by the French government and inaugurated in 1926 to recognize the sacrifices in World War I by Muslim soldiers from the colonies. Over time it fell into Algerian custody, and the rector is an employee of the Algerian government. The Grand Mosque oversees a network of Algerian mosque associations and imams across the country, and it runs an imam training institute, the Institut de Formation des Imams.

In 1994, the Agricultural Ministry recognized the Paris Mosque as the official issuer of halal certificates, proof that food products have been prepared following religious prescriptions, for which the mosque is paid one franc per kilogram.[43] The grand mosques of Lyon and Evry are now also authorized to issue certificates and share in the derived income. Other organizations have also set up halal certification agencies, but these do not have the government's stamp of approval. The halal certification process has become a source of contention, with critics charging that the mosques do not effectively supervise slaughtering practices. It has been proposed to use a generalized halal 'tax' to pay for the institutionalization of French Islam, and the funds made available to all associations.

The present French Muslim Council is the third effort to create an interlocutor for the government. The most recent attempt, made in 1999 by a Socialist minister of the interior, failed because of disagreements over who should lead the Council.[44] In 2002, the UOIF willingly gave up the directorship to Boubakeur, because it recognized, as Brèze explained to me, that the CFCM would not hold together unless a compromise was forged, and the creation of unified organization was more important than who held the presidency.

The CFCM's cumbersome structure was the result of negotiations between leading associations and the government. Some 1,500 mosques and an undetermined number of associations elect or appoint delegates to regional councils, which elect 150 ('plus or minus' nine electors) representatives to a general assembly. Seven eligible federations and five grand mosques elect another twenty-four organizational representatives. In addition, ten unaffiliated 'personalities'—who are recognized for their moral and spiritual qualities—are appointed to the assembly. The General Assembly elects two-thirds of the sixty-six seats on the Council. The other one-third is filled through appointments.[45] The Council, in turn, appoints a smaller administrative council and an executive bureau. The latter consists of 'eleven to seventeen' members. And then there is a president, various vice presidents, and a general secretary. Deliberations and proposals are sent to various specialized commissions. The vice president of the CFCM, Fouad Alaoui, from the UOIF, unexpectedly withdrew from the CFCM in early May 2005 declaring it 'dysfunctional.' It is not clear, at the time of this writing, if the action signals a real change in the UOIF's policy towards the CFCM or is a ploy to mobilize voters prior to the upcoming elections, which the UOIF is participating in.

Within the first year of its existence, the government provoked a crisis in its relations with the CFCM by passing legislation banning schoolgirls from wearing the Muslim headscarf. To make matters worse, the government refused to even discuss compromise solutions proposed by the associations in the CFCM. The Council has since failed to meet a deadline set by the government for coming up with plans to educate imams in France. Further friction arose when Dounia Bouzar, an anthropologist and one of the independent members of the Council, resigned in January 2005, complaining that the Council had been reduced to logrolling between the representatives of the various associations over appointments to committees. The Council would not become an effective organ for meaningful discussion, she said in her public letter of resignation, until the men of immigrant origin who dominate the Muslim associations were replaced by a more diverse group of native-born Muslims.[46]

Indicative perhaps of the government's increasing impatience with its own brainchild, Dominique de Villepin, the minister of the interior, announced on March 20, 2005 the creation of a 'foundation for the work of Islam in France' (Fondation pour les Œuvres de l'Islam de France), outside the control of the CFCM. The new foundation will provide institutional support for Islam in France from several streams of income, including foreign contributions, a generalized halal 'tax,' and contributions from French businesses and individual donors. The fund will support the construction and maintenance of mosques, the training of imams, and other such expenses. It is to be administrated by a committee of overseers consisting of fifteen members: seven representing the four big associations, and eight 'notabilities' nominated by the CFCM, including two individuals who are not affiliated with the religious organizations. Two different ministries are also to be involved in managing the funds. De Villepin assured the country that this did not violate the principle of *laïcité*. At the same time, it was announced that French universities would start educating imams in September 2005.

THE SMALL COUNTRIES

Swedish Muslim groups are organized in Sveriges Muslimska Råd (Sweden's Muslim Council), which was set up to channel government subsidies to associated organizations. The council mirrors in its name and format the Swedish Christian Council, and it acts as interlocutor with the Protestant and Catholic churches. Bitter conflict exists between the different groups in the council, each centered around one of Sweden's five big mosques. The Stockholm mosque and its associated groups have emerged as the primary representative for Swedish Muslims, reflecting perhaps the political advantage of location.

In the Netherlands, the main interlocutor for Dutch Muslims is Islam en Burgerschap (Islam and Citizenship). In contrast to the other national associations, Islam en Burgerschap was set up in 1996 after discussions between various prominent Muslim public figures as a combination of think-tank and educational association. The group receives public funding and organizes public dialogues between Muslim groups and city representatives in the largest cities with concentrations of Muslim residents. The main aim is to encourage Muslim residents to participate in Dutch public life and to develop a public ethic of Islamic citizenship. Dutch Muslims are primarily of Turkish origin, and as in Germany, the Turkish government plays a large role in providing mosques and imams. The rift between the Diyanet-funded mosque communities and those associated with Milli Görüs divided Dutch Muslims much the same way it has divided German Muslims.

One difference in Holland is the presence of significant numbers of Moroccan, Bosnian, Moluccan, Pakistani, and Surinamese Muslims, who have created a large number of minor and local associations. The result is an exceptionally diverse underpinning of Muslim civic and religious organizations. Increasingly, local associations of interethnic mosque communities have emerged as significant actors in local politics. One example is SPIOR (Platform Islamitische Organisaties Rijnmond), a Rotterdam-based umbrella group for fifty mosques and youth and women's associations. It is involved in the running of Muslim schools, provides assistance to mosque managements, engages in local politics, and conducts public-information campaigns about Islam.

Denmark stands out as the country with the least official interest in developing a dialogue with its Muslim residents. The consistent unwillingness of the Danish national and local governments to engage in coordinating efforts with Muslims goes a long way to explain the comparative disarray of Danish Muslims. A series of groups have been formed only to collapse under the weight of internal disagreement and negative media coverage. Muslimernes Landsorganisation (the national organization of Muslims) was formed in 2002 by two young Danish imams. It is based upon direct individual membership, and despite its name it is neither an umbrella group nor a national organization. Its statement of purpose reflected 'the new line': 'Islam in Denmark is forming its own face, which is not a shadow of the expressions Islam has around the world but its very own face. You can help shape that face.' The group allows only permanent residents and Danish citizens to join. Few have taken up their invitation, and when in Fall 2004 the government for the first time invited a group of Danish Muslims to a 'consultation' meeting about Islam in Denmark, Muslimernes Landsorganisation was not invited to participate. The government preferred instead to meet with individuals, about half of whom were not Muslim but rather experts on immigration. Public funding is available for ethnic minority groups that are not faith-based, but the efforts to create national representation have had a troubled history. One group, INDSAM (the association of immigrants), collapsed in 2002 after press articles on misuse of funding and internal conflict. A year later, a second group, POEM, collapsed when the board was forced to return its funding because it could not account for how the money was spent.

Among the countries not included in this book, Spain, Austria, and Belgium have national councils of Muslims that are in varying degrees consulted by the governments on matters related to Islam and Muslim welfare issues. The councils predate the 9/11 catastrophe, and played little role until government policy towards the Muslim communities became a matter of intense concern. The councils are not fully operative, and the three governments have failed to fully implement the original agreements under which the councils were created. The increased political salience of Muslim civic associationalism in these countries owes as much, if not more, to changes in public consciousness and government policy as to the efforts of Muslim activists and leaders.

One positive outcome of the tragic events of 9/11 was that more Europeans became interested in learning about Islam. Muslim groups experienced a surge of interest from schools, the media, and the general public after the 9/11 attacks, and struggled to keep up with the requests for information and speakers. Initiatives such the 'open mosque day' on October 3, the Day of German Unity, now attract large crowds, and both the Diyanet and the Milli Görüs mosques have participated in the open day activities. Public education remains an important issue for many associations, but increasingly they concentrate their attention on public policy issues ranging from religious instruction and mosque construction projects to social work and advising public authorities on how to approach the Muslim communities.

A desire for greater self-regulation is another source of the new associationalism. Many of the leaders I spoke to expressed fears of 'rogue imams' and warned, in the words of the association president cited above, 'we need to beware of the uprooted imams or the autodidacts.'[47]

RADICAL ISLAMISTS OR CONSERVATIVE DEMOCRATS?

Exiled Islamic radicals and Islamic nationalists are part of the associational landscape. The most important of the old groups include the Ikhwan, better known as the Muslim Brotherhood (Egypt), the Turkish Milli Görüs, the Muslim World League (Saudi Arabia), and the Indian-Pakistani Jamaat-I–Islami (The Islamic Party). Another group, the Tabligh, a missionary organization associated with the Deobandi movement, has focused on spiritual rather than political change. It resembles Scientology in its organizational culture, with its groups of young missionaries who receive their training in madrassas, religious schools.

The Brotherhood was founded in 1928 by Hassan al-Bana (1906–49), who is also known today for being Tariq Ramadan's grandfather. The Brotherhood became radicalized under the influence of the writings of Sayyid Qutb (1906–66), who was executed by Egyptian President Gamal Abdel Nasser.[48] The Brotherhood's importance for today's Islamist political movements is indisputable, but the actual European membership of the Brotherhood in Europe is unknown and likely negligible.

The transnational groups typically have centers and offices in several European countries, often in connection with mosques or Islamic education centers. Their national origins or financial ties with particular donor governments color the groups. The extent of transnational coordination varies.

The Muslim World League (MWL) has channeled Saudi Arabian money to Islamic centers and organizations across Europe, and it has offices in London, Paris, and Copenhagen. (Its focus today is on Africa.) The World Assembly of Muslim Youth (WAMY), the MWL's youth group, worked in the 1970s and 1980s to set up Muslim youth associations and student associations across Europe. Many have subsequently split, as in Great Britain and Denmark, or they have been overtaken by other student groups, as in France and Germany.

The MWL played a critical role by providing seed money for the construction of mosques in the early years of Muslim migration to Europe. Muslim groups and mosques have in recent years moved towards self-financing through zakat, the obligatory contribution to the community that all observant Muslims must pay, or by combining government-funded education and cultural activities with religious activities, and WML's influence has diminished accordingly.

The Muslim Brotherhood and Milli Görüs are now focused on social work and mosque construction. Milli Görüs remains blacklisted by the German federal agency for the protection of the Constitution, the Bundesamt für Verfassungsschutz. The agency's 2003 annual report describes it as by far the largest Islamist organization in Germany and labels the group's social work among youths as 'disintegrative ... antidemocratic and antiwestern.'[49] The blacklisting of Milli Görüs means that government groups and offices are not allowed to include the group in discussions of local problems or even to maintain routine contacts. One local CDU politician complained, 'we cannot meet with half of the Muslims in town because the Verfassungschutz says they are a danger to our values.'[50]

People fear being associated with the group (or being exposed as a member), in part because anyone who has been a member can be denied public sector employment. A recent case involved a ground worker who was refused a job at the airport in Düsseldorf until he could prove that he was no longer a member of Milli Görüs. The Verfassungschutz's embargo was breached, however, when the Islamic Federation of Berlin (IFB), which is affiliated with Milli Görüs, was awarded, by order of an administrative court, a contract with the Berlin government to provide religious instruction in public schools. (All faiths, except Islam, have had the right to provide students with instruction in their own faith in the schools.) Since 2003, the IFB has provided religious instruction to Muslim students in thirty-seven of Berlin's public schools.

What is an Islamist and who are the Islamic radicals? The labels are used indiscriminately to describe theologically and politically conservative Muslims. But conservative interpretations of the Koran are not necessarily harnessed to a revolutionary political project on the lines of the jihadist warriors.

The dividing lines are both political and theological. Religiously conservative Muslims regard the Islamists, who use violence to promote Islam, as apostates who have corrupted a peaceful religion. The 'fundamentalists,' who take a literal approach to the Koran and the hadith, are a small minority. Many religiously conservative people are more accurately described as neo-orthodox, because although they too stress the importance of rituals and Islamic law, they regard these as historically evolved and subject to interpretation. By this definition most of the individuals who are rightly or wrongly associated with the Muslim Brotherhood and Milli Görüs espouse neo-orthodox theological philosophies. The Tabligh, in contrast, qualifies as fundamentalist.

International networks and affiliations do exist, but it is as misleading to regard the French UOIF or the German ZMD as clones of the Muslim Brotherhood. The two have very different styles, one populist and the other respectably moderate, and their membership and associational structures are different. What they have in common is that some of their founding members are individuals who in the early 1980s were associated with the Brotherhood. The Brotherhood may, on a small scale, be described as a recruitment pool for European Muslim conservatives.

Olivier Roy describes the militants who politicize Islam to mobilize anti-government discontent as 'post-Islamists.' A fringe phenomenon, these groups align themselves with the 'old' European far left, such as the Socialist Workers apos; Party in Britain, and exploit the opportunities for dissent created by the European left's opposition to Israel's policies against the Palestinians and the Iraq war.[51] If we draw a historical parallel to Europe's fractious political landscape in the late 1970s, the radical Islamist groups may be likened to the Bader-Mainhof group (also known as the Rote Armee Fraktion) and the Red Brigade terrorists, and the Muslim Brotherhood, as it operates in Europe, to the Euro-Communists of Italy and France. Like the Euro-Communists, individuals who were formerly associated with the Brotherhood now disavow dependency upon the Islamic countries the same way the Euro-Communists disavowed Moscow.

THE NEW TERRORISTS

Europe has experienced political terrorism for decades. Today new radical groups commit violent crimes in the name of Islam. Sympathizers can be found in most of Europe's large cities, some of whom more particularly support terrorism abroad, in Chechnya or Afghanistan.

One Islamist group openly recruiting in Europe is Omar Bakri Muhammed's movement, al-Muhajiroun, which at one point claimed to have about 800 adherents in Britain. It has been associated with terrorist activities, including Richard Reid, the infamous 'shoe-bomber.' Hizb-ut-Tahrir, an international Islamist party, which aims to restore the Caliphate, is banned in several countries—since January 2003 also in Germany—but is legal in Denmark and Britain. The group can be found at most major urban university campuses. It is estimated to have a couple of thousand followers spread across Europe. It received much attention for running in local Danish government elections on a platform that called for the implementation of shariah law in this overwhelmingly Protestant country. The Dutch murderer of Theo van Gogh reportedly had connections to Hizbollah, through a Syrian living in Germany. The March 11, 2004, Madrid bombers had affiliated themselves for ideological (but apparently not operational) support to Bin Laden's al-Qaeda. Like the European terrorists from the 1970s, the new radical Islamist groups combine a global utopianism with a paranoid conception of power. They too aim to use political violence to arouse the complacent masses for whom they pretend to act. Even when it comes to religion, they are not typical of the devout Muslims in Europe. The radicals read the Koran in much the same literalist, context-free way as the leftist terrorists read Karl Marx. Some of their leaders are disenchanted university graduates, like the Dutch Moroccan Mohammed Bouyeri, who is rumored to have written a poem in Dutch celebrating his murder of van Gogh, or they are converts who found faith as adults. Mohammed Atta, from the 9/11 plot, and Reid, the shoe-bomber, were linked to Islamic preachers in Hamburg and London, but neither had grown up with Islam. Reid had converted in prison. Like Mohammed Bouyeri, Theo van Gogh's murderer, Atta grew up in a secular family and 'found' Islam only a few years before he embraced terrorism.

Other radicals focus on a particular conflict, for example the Kashmir problem, or the Israeli-Palestine conflict, and some are traditional left-wing movements. These groups tend to excuse terrorism as a justifiable response to Western repression but they do not endorse it. The British MAB has made coalitions with old European 'new left groups,' such as the Socialist Workers Party, and their main activities include political rallies, demonstrations, and political fairs. The group's activities are above all designed to rally support for the Palestinians against Israel, and it appeals to the ummah much like the old 'new left' used to appeal to the international proletariat.

The Arab European League (AEL), based in Antwerp, preaches an 'Islam is beautiful' nationalism that takes its cue from Malcolm X and the Nation of Islam. Its leader is Dyab Abou Jahjah, a political refugee from Lebanon who was granted asylum in Belgium as a nineteen-year-old. He describes the aims of his organization as 'identity-building' and claims to be for nondiscrimination, albeit not to the point of recognizing homosexuality as equal to heterosexuality. He thinks that socioeconomic integration is good, but rejects the legitimacy of the 'Judaeo-Christian' [*sic*] civilization. In an interview with Rosemary Belcher, published in the *New Humanist,* a British magazine, he also expressed admiration for ETA and the Madrid bombers, and boasts that his people give as good as they get, when they meet 'skinheads.'[52]

Groups like the AEL and radical student groups are oppositional but not terrorist, although we may expect splinter groups to take up terrorism if the parallel with former generations of European terrorists holds. What these groups have in common is the opportunistic exploitation of Islam and a new utopia, which reimagines the ummah as a revolutionary but unawakened subject. They are fringe groups whose appeal is limited to alienated youths and intellectuals. They are also 'homegrown' in terms of leadership and recruitment, and indeed are nauseatingly familiar on the European political landscape.

In contrast, the leaders of the new national associations eschew radical statements and avoid any hint at identity-politics in dress, demeanor, and rhetoric. They represent an increasingly de-ethnicized Muslim constituency. In France, this impels attempts at rapprochement between Algerians and Moroccans, and in the Netherlands between Moroccans and Turks. In Sweden, it means Arab, African, and Turkish Muslims holding meetings in Swedish, because it is the only shared language. Language shifts signal an important transition from the older transnational or émigré associationalism. Once business is conducted entirely in the national languages and between Muslims of diverse backgrounds, the narrative of politics and organizational aims naturally shifts to focus on domestic issues. We then have a new breed of organizations: the national Muslim association.

RESPECT AND RECOGNITION

Muslims who hold public office in the European political system are not religious fundamentalists. They do not insist on a literal reading of the Koran, nor do they aim to create a European Caliphate. Those are media caricatures. Indeed, most of the members of Europe's new Muslim political elite are not well up on theology. 'Most of us are engineers or businessmen,' said a German Muslim, a Christian Democrat, who was also chairman of an interfaith organization. 'How can I debate with a pastor or a theology professor about interpretations of the Koran?' He explained how his views of the Koran and of Islam had changed as he participated in interfaith workshops, and he wished there were educated scholars who could represent Islam in such debates.

The new Muslim elite is not drawn primarily from the native-born descendents of earlier generations of labor migrants. It is largely made up of recent immigrants or refugees whose political engagement predates their arrival in Europe. Most consider Islam very important to their personal lives, but when they describe their political values they emphasize human rights, and concepts such as respect, recognition, and parity. This is a far cry from the radicalism associated with Islamic revolutionaries.

Many Muslim leaders say that they feel tarred by suspicions about their motives, and are tired of being asked to state their willingness to 'bend' Islam to fit with Western democratic values. They protest that the media and the extremists have conspired to misrepresent Islam. Others complain that the representatives of the national Muslim associations are 'fundamentalists,' and should be more forthright about distancing themselves from conservatives and giving support to liberal versions of Islam.

The new Muslim associationalism derives from two independent but interacting factors: the belated but collective realization on the part of Europe's Muslims that they are 'here to stay' and the equally belated effort on the part of governments to come up with policies for Muslims. Government action is, ironically, stimulating Muslim activism, but mostly governments fail to provide avenues for Muslim self-representation. The exception is the French CFCM, which was a deliberate effort to create a Muslim interlocutor for the government. Another is the British MCB which emerged, with government help, as a voluntarist association. Perhaps because the British government was willing to allow the MCB a public role without imposing the sort of demands that the French government made on the CFCM, it is a moderate and cooperative voice for British Muslims.

When I asked Lhaj Thami Brèze, the general secretary of UOIF, what the biggest problem was for Muslims in France, his answer was, 'We have only one problem; it is that they do not respect us and do not recognize us. We demand only one thing: respect and recognition.' The theme came up again and again. A spokesman for the association of Turkish Muslims in France, which is free of the suspicion of ties with the Muslim Brotherhood that surround the UOIF, said about the work of the CFCM, 'Our purpose is to protect the dignity of Muslims and the dignity of Islam. So the Muslims who do not go to the mosque every day, but go only once a week or only twice a year, on Eid or the Feast of Abraham, can feel good about who they are.'[53]

Muslims recognize the essential equality of Christians, Brèze said, so Christians ought to extend the same recognition to Muslims:

People are surprised when I say to Muslims and to our brother Christians here that we Muslims are in part Christians, because we recognize Jesus. Jesus is our prophet, Mary is the symbol of purity, and an example of saintliness. Many verses of the Koran refer to Mary and to Jesus. There is no reason for the lack of mutual recognition between Christians and Muslims.[54]

The eagerness of the national associations to prove their fidelity to national values and moderation in religious matters notwithstanding, many of the elected politicians and other leaders who put their energies into the political parties regard the new Muslim associations with skepticism. The sentiment is that the national governments are making a big mistake by relying on faith councils to regulate Islamic religious expression, because these groups represent 'at most ten percent of all Muslims,' as a German parliamentarian said. The distrust is mutual. The association leaders often do not speak kindly of Muslim politicians either.

NOTES

1. Interview 72, Amsterdam (December 1, 2003).
2. Interview 3, Copenhagen (September 5, 2003).
3. In a subsequent email exchange, Alev contested my version of the conversation and argued that the women could not, and did not, disagree. My notes say otherwise.

4. A group of US-based Muslim feminists have provoked the ire of Muslim leaders, both conservative and moderate, by organizing publicly-announced prayers led by a woman, Aminah Wadud, a professor of Islamic Studies at Virginia Commonwealth University. 'Muslim Group Is Urging Women to Lead Prayers,' *New York Times* (March 18, 2005).

5. Pnina Werbner, *Imagined Diasporas Among Manchester Muslims*, Oxford: James Currey, 2002. For a similar interpretation of French Muslim negotiation of national and transnational identity expressions, see John R. Bowen, 'Islam in/of France: Dilemmas of Translocality,' paper presented at the 13th International Conference of Europeanists, Chicago (March 14–16, 2002).

6. A friendly but critical review of the many applications of transnationalist theory can be found in Steven Vertovec, 'Conceiving and Researching Transnationalism,' *Ethnic and Racial Studies*, 22 (1999) 2: 447–62.

7. John Rex, Daniele Joly, and Czarina Wilpert, *Immigrant Associations in Europe* (Aldershot: Gower, 1987).

8. Yasemin Nuhoglu Soysal, *Limits of Citizenship: Migrants and Postnational Membership in Europe* (Chicago: University of Chicago Press, 1994).

9. Virginie Guiraudon, 'The Marshallian Triptych Reordered: The Role of Courts and Bureaucracies in Furthering Migrants' Social Rights,' in Michael Bommes and Andrew Geddes (eds.), *Immigration and Welfare. Challenging the Borders of the Welfare State* (London: Routledge, 2000).

10. Fouad Ajami, 'The Moor's Last Laugh: Radical Islam Finds a Haven in Europe,' *Wall Street Journal* (March 22, 2004).

11. Niall Ferguson, 'Eurabia?' *New York Times* (April 4, 2004); and 'The Widening Atlantic,' *Atlantic Monthly* (January/February 2005).

12. Again, reliable figures are difficult to find. The estimates are based on country reports in *Intolerance and Discrimination Against Muslims in the EU: Developments since September 11*. Report by the International Helsinki Federation for Human Rights (March 2005).

13. 'Deutsche Bundestag Antwort der Bundesregierung auf die Grosse Anfrage der Abgeordneten Dr. Jürgen Rüttgers, Erwin Marschewski, Wolfgang Zeitlmann, weiterer Abgeordneter und der Fraktion der CDU/CSU.' Drucksache 14/2301, 08.11.2000, p. 5.

14. National Statistics, Ethnicity and Identity. www.statistics.gov.uk/cci/nugget.asp?id=459.

15. John R. Bowen, 'Does French Islam Have Borders? Dilemmas of Domestication in a Global Religious Field,' *American Anthropologist* 106 (2004) 4: 43–55.

16. Interview 91, Paris (November 18, 2004).

17. *Vrij Nederland* (November 22, 2003), 32–6; personal conversation.

18. Interview 66, The Hague (November 26, 2003).

19. Interview 56, Stockholm (November 6, 2003).

20. Interview 8, Copenhagen (September 8, 2003).

21. 'Muslims abandon Labour over Iraq war,' *Guardian* (March 15, 2004).

22. Interview 113, Berlin (November 26, 2004).

23. Interview 98, Boston (June 15, 2004).
24. Interview 76, Paris (May 17, 2004); Interviews 81 and 82, Lyon (May 24, 2004).
25. Interview 106, Berlin (October 19, 2004).
26. Interview 12, Copenhagen, 2003.
27. For an elaboration of the role of the 'myth of return' among Pakistani and Bangladeshi immigrants to Britain, see Roger Ballard, *Desh Pradesh: The South Asian Presence in Britain* (London: Hurst, 1994).
28. http://www.islamfortoday.com/germany.htm.
29. http://www.germany-info.org/relaunch/info/archives/background/church.html.
30. Interview 108, Berlin (October 28, 2004).
31. Ursula Spuler-Stegeman, *Muslime in Deutschland, Informationen und Klärungen* (Friburg: Herder Spectrum, 2002), 36.
32. http://www.Muslim-Zeitung.de/organisationen/5012119610150bc01.html.
33. http://www.nrwspd.de/presse/meldung.asp?ID = 20739.
34. Interview with Aiman Mazyrek, *Süddeutsche Zeitung* (February 26–7, 2005).
35. Secretary-General's Introduction to the 2002 Annual Report, http://www.mcb.org/annual2002.htm.
36. Some of the professional associations are affiliated with the International Institute of Islamic Thought, which has international offices in the United States, just outside Washington, DC, and in London and Paris. The organization's office in Herndon, VA, was raided by the FBI in March 2002. The target of the raid was another organization with which IIIT shared offices. The IIIT is a conservative and reputable organization; see http://www.iiit.org.
37. Interview 25, London (October 10, 2003).
38. BBC News (July, 7 2004).
39. Muslim Council of Britain, press release (October 2, 2003).
40. Tariq Modood and Fauzia Ahmad, 'British Muslim Perspectives on Multiculturalism,' *Theory, Culture, and Society*, forthcoming.
41. 'L'UOIF, le mastodonte musulman,' Hakim El Ghissassi, www.sezame.info, 15/02/2005.
42. The March 25–8, 2005, event can be viewed at http://www.rencontre-uoif.net/directuoif.php.
43. Since the introduction of the euro, the French franc is a paper currency and is used only to calculate the cost of certain transactions to be paid in euros.
44. 'L'élection des représentants musulmans repoussée après les législatives,' *Le Monde* (May 3, 2002).
45. Statuts du Conseil Français du Culte Musulman Article 6.1.
46. The letter was published in full by www.sezame.info and by the newspaper *Libération* (January 6, 2005).
47. Interview 108, Berlin (October 28, 2004).
48. Olivier Roy, *The Failure of Political Islam* (Cambridge, MA: Harvard University Press, 1994).

49. The Verfassungsschutz 2003 annual report has the following to say about the organization: 'Die bei weitem größte islamistische Organisation ist unverändert die "Islamische Gemeinschaft Milli Görüs" (IGMG). Sie betreibt eine faktisch desintegrative Jugendarbeit. Dies und ihre nur vorgeblich auf Integration zielende Politik fördern islamistische Milieus in unserem Land. Die Milli-Görüs-Bewegung ist einem als "Gerechte Ordnung" propagierten umfassenden Regelungssystem verpflichtet, das die westliche Zivilisation, ihren Wertekanon und ihr Demokratieverständnis negiert.' Available at http://www.berlin.de/seninn/verfassungsschutz/publikationen/jb_akt.html.
50. Interview 102, Stuttgart (October 8, 2004).
51. Olivier Roy, *Globalized Islam: The Search for a New Umma* (New York: Columbia University Press, 2005), 323.
52. Rosemary Belcher, 'Europe's Malcolm X,' *New Humanist* (July/August 2004), 8–12. Jahjah's political commitment and belief system also predated his arrival in Europe. He says on this matter: 'I was politically active in Lebanon before I left: I studied politics. The same was true of the others in the founder group.'
53. Interview 78, Paris (May 18, 2004).
54. Interview 85, Paris (May 25, 2004).

2

How Do Muslim Leaders See the Problems?

'It is difficult today to argue that Muslims have special needs,' one Muslim member of the Dutch parliament explained to me. 'All Dutch voters can think about is how they are disadvantaged by the foreigners.'[1] Even if it is acknowledged that Muslims do have special problems, there may be uncertainty about how to define the problems and which to prioritize. It is important also to distinguish between problems shared by Muslims with all immigrants, and those associated with their religion, although these may be shared, in part, with other minority religions in European countries. Moreover, the crucial issues vary from one European country to another, and even in a single country Muslims are not a unified constituency. Ethnicity, gender, political outlook, and class are sources of disagreement and dissent. Calls for a pan-Muslim identity do not appeal to all Muslims. Nevertheless, when I questioned Muslim leaders I found a broad consensus about the problems that face Muslims in Europe. Disagreement grew once discussion turned to solutions, but more about that later.

DO MUSLIMS HAVE 'SPECIAL PROBLEMS'?

Two-thirds of the participants in the study agreed that Muslims did indeed share many special problems. In Denmark, the leaders were more inclined to see the problems affecting Muslims as problems common to all immigrant groups. In Britain and Germany, in contrast, the overwhelming perception was that Muslims suffered particular forms of discrimination. Half of French Muslims (again, caution is in place as this is a small sample) agreed with the sentiment that Muslims have 'many problems,' but contrary to what one might expect after the headscarf controversy, the French participants were, like the Danes, less inclined to alarm than their counterparts. Four out of five of the German leaders agreed that Muslims have 'many special problems,' double the number of the Danish leaders who thought so. The difference in this case was that Danish Muslims tended to see Muslims' problems as part of the problems experienced by all immigrants, whereas German and British

Muslims thought Muslims' problems were specific to their people. Table 2.1 shows the breakdown of answers by country and severity of perceived problems.

I used three different questions to gauge the extent of dissatisfaction. The wording reflected different types of unhappiness, ranging from concrete unhappiness with current policies to feelings about personal prospects. The first question aimed to detect short-term policy discontent and the two others to identify perceptions of more medium and long-term difficulties for Muslims in the different countries in the study. This strategy grew out of early personal interviews, which had led me to believe that different issues might motivate the high level of discontent that people expressed to me.

When I asked a different question about unhappiness, 'Are you generally satisfied with the way Muslims are treated in [country]?,' the picture changed radically. Two-thirds of the participants converged on a 'the glass is half-full and half-empty' position, with three-fifths of the leaders saying they were 'somewhat satisfied' and the rest divided evenly between the extreme views. One-third of the Danish leaders said they were 'generally satisfied.' The reasons for this difference became apparent when I asked the leaders to pick the sources of Muslims' difficulties. Danish Muslims, like British Muslims but for different reasons, see their problems as caused by the current government. British Muslims are unhappy about the Iraq war and the perceived impact of antiterrorism laws on young Muslim men. Their Danish counterparts are unhappy about what they see as a xenophobic government. Interestingly, the views of Danish Muslim leaders were quite polarized between unhappy and happy minorities. I similarly found a small number (one or two out of every ten) of 'generally satisfied' leaders in the other countries, with the exception of the French leaders who admit neither to extreme dissatisfaction nor to general satisfaction.

My last question in the series designed to measure unhappiness with Muslims' position aimed to elicit personal feelings rather than policy-contingent sentiments about living in country X. The answers contained some surprises. British and Swedish Muslims overwhelmingly planned to remain where they were, an answer that I interpreted to suggest a happier long-term assessment than I would have been given had I only asked about current issues. On the other hand, one or two of ten Dutch, Danish, and German leaders are contemplating a move to another country. On balance, when I added up the different measures of short-term and long-term discontent, the British and German leaders were the least satisfied and the French and Swedish leaders the least dissatisfied. Muslim leaders in the UK apparently harbor two contradictory sentiments: anger at the government, and yet a feeling of general satisfaction with life in Britain.

Table 2.1. Perceptions of special problems for Muslims by country

	Denmark (%)	Sweden (%)	France (%)	Germany (%)	Netherlands (%)	UK (%)	Total (%)
Perception of special problems for Muslims							
No special problems	15.6	4.8	0.0	2.2	4.3	0.0	5.1
Some problems	40.6	33.3	60.0	13.0	26.1	24.1	26.9
Many problems	43.8	61.9	40.0	84.8	69.6	75.9	67.9
Total (*n* = 156)	100.0	100.0	100.0	100.0	100.0	100.0	100.0
General satisfaction with treatment of Muslims							
Generally satisfied	33.3	19.0	0.0	10.6	17.4	13.3	17.6
Somewhat satisfied	39.4	66.7	80.0	57.4	60.9	70.0	58.5
Not satisfied	27.3	14.3	20.0	31.9	21.7	16.7	23.9
Total (*n* = 159)	100.0	100.0	100.0	100.0	100.0	100.0	100.0
Expectation to stay in country for rest of life							
Will stay in country	81.8	100.0	80.0	89.4	78.3	93.5	88.2
Will not stay	18.2	0.0	20.0	10.6	21.7	6.5	11.8
Total (*n* = 161)	100.0	100.0	100.0	100.0	100.0	100.0	100.0

Aside from noting that discontent is high in every country, albeit for somewhat different reasons, the evidence could be seen to suggest that content grows with time. British immigration began in the 1950s, and the apparent differentiation between acute discontent with policy and generalized satisfaction with life in Britain is a function of Britons having had more time to adjust to the Muslim presence. However, the large waves of migration to the Netherlands and Germany preceded those of Danish and Swedish Muslims, and there is little difference between Dutch and British Muslims with respect to their historical ties to the country. Swedish Muslim leaders are relatively contented, although Swedish immigration only began comparatively recently, and peaked in the 1990s. This suggests, first, that Sweden has done better by its Muslim immigrants than have most other European countries, and second that there is no necessary relationship between the adjustment of Muslim minorities and the length of Christian–Muslim cohabitation in any particular country. The Swedish case, and other variations between countries, also suggests that Muslim leaders' attitudes to the host country are sensitive to policy and politics. The national variations also weigh against the common argument that Muslims 'have a chip on their shoulder,' or more specifically that Islam has conditioned Muslims to blame others for their social misfortunes.

I was taken aback when several Danish and Dutch Muslim parliamentarians confessed to me that they had thought about giving everything up and migrating to the UK, or alternatively to the USA. Young professionals, about to establish their careers, may be expected to contemplate seeking out opportunities by means of migration. Two German Muslim civic leaders indicated that they considered moving 'back' to the parental country of origin. The country in question was Turkey, and the decision to move back was made contingent on Turkey's prospective membership of the EU, and was tied to business prospects as well as quality of life issues. It is a very different matter, however, when a parliamentarian says that he or she is thinking about emigration as the only solution to discrimination and the lack of opportunities. Still, the opposite sentiment was more common. Often, when I asked about personal experiences, people would answer, 'as bad as it is, this is much better than where I came from.' This was one of the few consistent generational patterns I encountered. The native-born leaders occasionally express an anger growing out of disappointed expectations that the first generation does not feel because they have had the direct experience of political persecution. It suggests that, among some Muslims at least, European states can still draw on a reservoir of goodwill that is about to be depleted by generational change.

Nevertheless, the typical view taken of their situation by European Muslim leaders is a dismal one. There is a high degree of elite consensus that Western

Europe's Muslims have special problems, and that they are serious. This consensus is independent of variations with respect to the personal import-ance of faith and partisan affiliations.

Figure 2.1 can be interpreted as a 'feelings thermometer,' in the sense that it depicts the aggregate distribution of feelings about the seriousness of special problems affecting Muslims. The participants in the study were asked to choose from a list of frequently mentioned problems and rate their import-ance. If a problem was rated 'not important,' the answer was assigned a value of 6. If a problem was rated 'very important,' it was given a value of –6. 'Somewhat important' ratings were assigned a value of 0. The rating system assumed that mild complaining is a natural phenomenon in politics, in order not to overrate unhappiness. As it turned out, the findings indicate very high levels of discontent, with a median answer very close to the most negative possible evaluation.

The probability of getting a distribution of views with a mean so far from the statistical mean by pure chance is extremely low. (A double-sided t-test shows that the chance of this happening is less than 1 in 10,000, with $t = -22.80$, $p = 0.0000$.) It is clear that Muslim leaders are, on average, very discontented. It is worth noting, also, that there is a small right-sided tail towards the satisfied side of the spectrum that suggests the presence of a group of people who we do not hear much about: Muslim leaders who are support-ive of what the European governments and public do with respect to Muslims. But generally the variance of opinion was low, meaning that most leaders

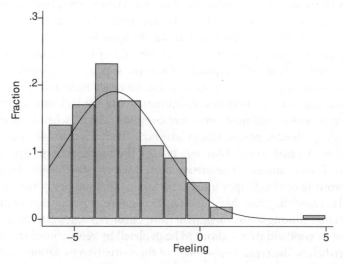

Figure 2.1. Problems for Muslims

Table 2.2. Problems for Muslims by Country

	Mean	Std dev	*n*
Denmark	−3.19	1.72	31
Sweden	−3.00	2.51	21
France	−2.35	1.73	17
Germany	−3.76	1.62	46
Netherlands	−3.57	2.11	23
UK	−3.96	1.82	26

agreed that things are very bad and only a few dissenters thought otherwise. Swedish Muslim leaders were the most contended and British the most discontented. Unhappiness was also high in Germany and the Netherlands, but while agreement about the difficulties was high among German Muslim leaders, it was less so among the Dutch.

Unexpectedly, I also found little difference in perceptions of the severity of problems between leaders, who said that Islam was personally 'very important' and those for whom it mattered less.[2] This suggests that Muslims feel the exposure to bias irrespective of the intensity of their commitments to religion.

'ISLAMOPHOBIA'

In personal interviews, some of the leaders I interviewed made references to 'Islamophobia.' The Runnymede Trust, a British think tank, originally launched the term as an explanation for Muslims' difficulties in a report issued in 1997. The report, *Islamophobia: A Challenge for Us All*, was written by a commission established by the Trust to investigate the causes and consequences of religious prejudices. It concluded that anti-Islamic bias prevailed in public discussions of Islam and the problems of Muslims, and argued that this bias fostered discrimination in employment and schooling, hate crimes, mischaracterization in the media and in everyday life, and a range of other problems experienced by Muslims that derive from these four sources.

The report provided a check list for how to distinguish between an Islamophobic view and an open and open-minded discussion of Muslims and Islam. The list consisted of eight binary assumptions about the nature of Islam that constitute either a fair or a biased presumption. Is Islam regarded as diverse or monolithic, as inferior or different, or as manipulative or sincere, etc.? The list of wrongful assumptions is potentially endless, and not surprisingly the report's recommendations were rather loosely related to the conceptual approach. The Runnymede report received a great deal of publicity and stimulated soul-searching on the part of some media outlets. When I asked British Muslim leaders whether press coverage had improved after the publication of the report, and Islamophobia abated, most felt that this was the case, while continuing to deplore the alarmist reporting of some tabloid newspapers.

One of the report's achievements was to introduce the term 'Islamophobia' into public vocabulary. It is now also widely used outside Britain and has become a popular summary explanation for the difficulties that Muslims face, suggesting, as it does, that anti-Muslim sentiment is a generalized and ir- rational psychological malady. The Islamophobia thesis inverts the thesis offered by culture war theorists to explain conflicts between Christians and Muslims. The culture war theory justifies fears aroused by the Muslim presence in Western Europe, and, at the same time, relieves the West of any responsibility by placing the blame on Islam's antiliberal tenets and Muslims' presumed obedience to those doctrines. The Islamophobia thesis, conversely, explains the hostility that Muslims experience, and blames Muslims' prob- lems on ignorance and irrational fear.

While it is true that Muslims have become a lightning rod for xenophobia and that inappropriate generalizations are often made about the views and inten- tions of a general population on the basis of the actions of extremists, it is simplistic to blame their problems on a sort of collective European psychosis. This is to ignore the fact that many of the problems affecting Muslims are experienced by other immigrant groups, and even by adherents of established minority religions.[3] It also fails to acknowledge the antiliberal strains within some versions of Islam, the anti-Western rhetoric of an uncomfortably large number of Muslim groups and radical clerics, and the real support offered to terrorism by a tiny but highly-publicized and perhaps truly dangerous minority.

WHO IS RESPONSIBLE?

The most commonly cited sources of problems experienced by Muslims are the media and xenophobic political parties. Eighty percent of my respondents said that the press is a very important problem. Negative press treatment of Muslims was ranked as the single biggest problem across the countries in the study, although the condemnation of press coverage was slightly milder in Sweden and Germany. The responses are displayed in Table 2.3.

Discrimination on the part of 'ordinary people' was considered the second most important source of problems in Sweden and France, but it was the least important factor cited in Denmark and the Netherlands. Lack of economic opportunities was considered the second most important source in Denmark,

Table 2.3. Who is responsible for Muslims' problems?

	Denmark (%)	Sweden (%)	Germany (%)	France (%)	Netherlands (%)	UK (%)	Total (%)
Right-wing antiforeigner rhetoric							
Not important	0.0	13.6	4.3	16.7	4.3	0.0	5.2
Somewhat important	28.1	36.4	26.1	44.4	26.1	26.7	33.1
Very important	71.9	50.0	69.6	38.9	69.6	73.3	61.6
Total ($n = 172$)	100.0	100.0	100.0	100.0	100.0	100.0	100.0
Lack of economic opportunities							
Not important	0.0	4.5	4.3	10.5	4.3	3.4	4.1
Somewhat important	21.9	45.5	42.6	36.8	26.1	17.2	32.0
Very important	78.1	50.0	53.2	52.6	69.6	79.3	64.0
Total ($n = 172$)	100.0	100.0	100.0	100.0	100.0	100.0	100.0
Everyday discrimination by ordinary people							
Not important	9.4	4.5	0.0	5.6	17.4	3.6	5.9
Somewhat important	59.4	31.8	42.6	27.8	43.5	42.9	42.9
Very important	31.3	63.6	57.4	66.7	39.1	53.6	51.2
Total ($n = 170$)	100.0	100.0	100.0	100.0	100.0	100.0	100.0
Negative press treatment							
Not important	0.0	9.1	0.0	0.0	0.0	0.0	1.2
Somewhat important	15.2	27.3	27.7	15.8	17.4	3.6	18.6
Very important	84.8	63.6	72.3	84.2	82.6	96.4	80.2
Total ($n = 172$)	100.0	100.0	100.0	100.0	100.0	100.0	100.0

the Netherlands, and the UK, but took a back seat to other problems in Sweden, France, and Germany. One interpretation of the weak but intriguing pattern that the rankings reflect is that in the more 'statist' and elite-centered countries, with long traditions of social and economic planning, elites (the press, other politicians) are regarded as allies but ordinary people are seen as a threat. Conversely, in Denmark and the Netherlands, and to a lesser degree the UK, the greater involvement of civil society groups and oppositional cultural movements creates more contact points for Muslim and national leaders. Finally, it is also possible that the difference reflects variations in intermarriage rates between Muslims and non-Muslims. However, statistics on inter-marriage are inadequate to test this possibility.

German, Dutch, and Danish Muslims were particularly inclined to blame right-wing politicians for their problems. In France and Sweden, right-wing parties were considered much less of a problem. In the Swedish case, it was explained to me, the fact that there is not currently a xenophobic party repre-sented in the Riksdagen, the national parliament, helps keep public debate free of xenophobia, but many Muslims and non-Muslims also predicted that it was only a matter of time before Sweden got its own xenophobic protest party, and that it would then 'become like Denmark.' Swedes generally look with distaste at Danish politics, where a center-right minority government came to power in November 2000 with support from the xenophobic Danish People's Party.

European multiparty systems are highly sensitive to marginal shifts in voter alignments, and the rise of xenophobic parties, which today attract between 5 and 15 percent of voters in most countries, has narrowed the scope for mainstream parties to respond to the preoccupations of Muslims themselves. The efforts of mainstream parties to regain the voters lost to xenophobic parties often take the form of increased verbal commitments to be 'tough on Muslims,' which in turn reinforces the sense of alienation and mischaracter-ization experienced by Muslim minorities.

Pockets of support for extreme right-wing parties exist also in the UK and in Germany, although neither of the parties—the British Nationalist Party (BNP) and 'Die Republikaner' (REP) and 'Die Deutsche Volksunion' (DVU) in Ger-many—are represented in the national parliaments. The Dutch Lijst Pim For-tuyn is not accurately described as right-wing but the party is undeniably xenophobic. The party had collapsed by the time I conducted the survey, and it is reasonable to assume that the Dutch Muslim leaders also had other parties in mind when they complained about xenophobia.

All immigrant groups in Europe are relatively poor and experience some discrimination in the job market. However, Muslims tend to believe that they are the victims of additional employment discrimination. Many times and in several countries I was told of the experience of a friend, a daughter, or a cousin who submitted identical job applications or a personal curriculum vitae under a Muslim name and also under an assumed de-ethnicized name, and received no positive responses on the former but many on the latter.

Studies using a double-blind method can effectively demonstrate purposeful discrimination. Advocacy groups and enforcement agencies typically use this method to detect systematic discriminatory behaviors on the part of service providers, landlords, and employers. The BBC did one such study, which was published in July 2004. The researchers sent out nearly identical job applications under six different identities to fifty employers, who had posted job vacancies in newspapers and on websites. They found that applicants with white-sounding names received an invitation to a job interview 23 percent of the time, while black African candidates got interviews only 13 percent of the time, and of the applications from people with Muslim-sounding names only 9 percent were successful.[4] A French researcher, Jean-Francois Amadieu, sent out seven identical CVs but under seven different names and with different demographic facts; one was a white male with a French name and the other six had 'problem' identities ranging from being a woman or disabled person to having a 'bad' address. The white male received seventy-five offers of an interview and ten rejections. The applicant with the Maghrebian name was by far the least successful and received fourteen offers and twenty rejections. (The study was conducted for an employment agency, AIDA, and published in May 2004.)[5]

It seems reasonable to assume that newspaper accounts of such experiments have inspired an urban legend. The retelling of the experiment as second-hand experience conveys what is perceived to be a moral truth about how educated Muslims, who do 'the right thing,' are victims of discrimination.

While these studies are nevertheless suggestive, there are few reliable statistics about the 'religious penalty' on Muslim job applicants. Survey data are based on small samples and simply ask respondents if they *perceive* they are subject to discrimination. Discrimination may sometimes be deduced from the general data on labor market activity, but most employment statistics are not broken down by religion, except in Britain where the 2001 census included a question on religious affiliation for the first time. In France, indeed, it is illegal for government agencies or government-funded researchers to ask about the faith of respondents.

But even where religious affiliation can be shown to be a factor in employment, this does not necessarily mean that it is because of discrimination. (Activity rates are based upon the question, 'are you economically active or not?' which does not help us determine the causes of joblessness.[6])

The British census did show significantly lower activity rates among Muslims compared to other ethnic minorities. 64.5 percent of Muslim men and only 31 percent of Muslim women are economically active. This compares to

72.7 percent among Christian men (the next lowest group) and 59.2 percent among Christian women, and 74.4 percent of Hindu men and 59.4 percent of Hindu women.[7] Bangladeshi women had the overall lowest activity rates of any population group, only 14 percent, but among the 16–24 age cohort the difference to other groups had already narrowed. (37.7 percent were active compared to 46.7 percent of Hindu women in the same age group.) However, while aggregate statistics on labor market activity is indicative of socioeconomic variations from one demographic group to another, it does not allow us to make solid inferences about the causes of discrimination because other issues, such as differences in educational attainment or culturally determined expectations with respect to women's employment, may also explain why one group fares worse than another.

Cross-national statistics indicate that some countries find it a great deal more difficult to integrate immigrants into labor markets than others. An OECD study from 1999 ranked Denmark, the Netherlands, and Sweden (in that order) as the OECD countries with the worst immigrant employment records.[8] Immigrants were three times as likely to be unemployed in these countries as native born workers, whereas in Canada, Australia, and the USA the difference between immigrants and native-born workers was minimal. But even these figures, which appear to provide a measure of discrimination, do not necessarily do so. The three countries with the worst employment performance are notoriously lacking in low-wage jobs and have high unemployment rates also among native-born groups with poor education and among other hard-to-employ groups. On the other hand, recent cohorts of immigrants are on the average better educated than the native-born population. Other factors may be relevant, ranging from the prevalence in a particular economy of small employers, who are notoriously reluctant to hire ethnic minorities, to the unwillingness of governments to recognize professional qualifications acquired outside the EU.

Other complaints are that children of immigrants are unfairly denied placement in academic tracks—the gymnasium and the baccalaureate or A-levels—and have higher dropout rates than other youths because teachers unfairly judge them to be 'unacademic.' It is also argued that when they do stay in school and finish their degrees, they cannot obtain employment commensurate with their education. Although spotty evidence exists to support these claims, the truth is probably more complex. The 2001 British census shows that young Muslim women marry significantly earlier and have more children and give birth earlier than other immigrants groups. 16 percent of sixteen- to twenty-four-year-old Muslim women are married, compared with a national average of 3–4 percent. Irrespective of faith and ethnicity, marriage and early childbirth work against educational and professional attainment among young women. Families with a nonworking spouse are comparably poorer than families with two working spouses. While the statistics show significant variations across racial and religious groups and confirm that Muslim's socioeconomic status lags behind other groups, we cannot clearly distinguish between the effects of discriminatory behavior on the part of employers from those of other relevant explanatory variables ranging from educational gaps to behavioral patterns, such as the proclivity for early marriage among Muslims.

A general trend may be discerned. Muslim leaders across Europe believe that the media and xenophobic policies have pushed mainstream parties into policies that are detrimental to Muslims and to the prospects for accommodation, and that the situation is deteriorating. Press treatments that homogenize and mischaracterize Muslims are seen as offensive and demeaning. The shift to increasingly assimilationist rhetoric and policies has alienated mainstream Muslim political leaders, not because Muslim leaders oppose integration or think that Muslims do not need to work harder at integrating, but because they are discomfited by the implication that Muslims cannot be 'Western' and retain their commitments to Islam as a source of faith and culture. 'We always have to explain who we are not,' complained a Dutch social democrat, 'we never get to explain who we are.'[9] It was a frequently voiced complaint.

The high levels of dissatisfaction among Muslim political and civic leaders with how Muslims are treated across countries and across other cleavage lines— from party affiliations to personal backgrounds and variations in religious commitment—suggests that we are in the middle of a rapid transformation of Muslim political self-awareness. Yet within the general trend there were also some notable variations. British Muslims are exceptionally unhappy with current policies but their disgruntlement does not appear to reflect the same degree of discontent with the political class as is evidenced in Denmark and the Netherlands. On the other hand, both Dutch and Danish Muslims take a more kindly view of relations with ordinary people than do both Swedish and German Muslims. French and Swedish Muslims are more trusting of the political class.

To sum up, although dissatisfaction is by no means universal, a large majority of Muslim leaders reports strong unhappiness with the situation of Muslims in Western Europe. The tendency of the press to misrepresent Muslims is perceived to be the chief source of their problems. Xenophobic political agitation and the lack of opportunities come a close second. In some countries, but not in all, ordinary people are seen as being unwelcoming and prejudiced. Discrimination and bias are seen as the critical obstacles not just to the free exercise of Islam, but also to the ability of Muslims to integrate and advance in society. A few dissenters insist that the problem is with Islam itself, and with Muslims. Islam, they argue, is illiberal and reactionary.

CHOOSING PUBLIC POLICY FOR MUSLIMS:
PRIORITIES AND PREFERENCES

When I asked the participants in my study what reforms they would like to see, were they free to choose, most opted for a strengthening of antidiscrimination legislation by the including of a clause prohibiting discrimination on the basis of religion. European law varies significantly from US law on questions of ethno-religious discrimination, in part because of the absence of a bill of rights tradition and in part because of the legal legacy of established religions and special privileges for majority denominations. The distribution of support for various policies is reported in Table 2.4.

Ninety-five percent of British Muslims picked such legislation as their first choice of a reform that would make things better for Muslims. German Muslim leaders are also very supportive of increased and strengthened antidiscrimination legislation. Half of the French and Danish leaders picked it as their first choice of reform, but Swedish and Dutch Muslims were less enthusiastic about strengthened antidiscrimination enforcement. The variations in opinion are attributable to different legal frameworks and the framing of national policy debates. In Britain, the current antidiscrimination framework for ethnic minorities is perceived as both successful and flawed. It is thought to have worked well for blacks and other groups who are clearly defined by ethnic or racial attributes but not for Muslims, who are of diverse ethnic and racial backgrounds yet are all subjected to religious discrimination. In the Dutch case, the perceived failure of past experiments with multicultural policies casts doubt on any effort to seek redress by means of legal entitlement.

The wording of the question alluded to an antidiscrimination clause contained in EU law. The Consolidated EC Treaty (Amsterdam plus Nice) restates a prohibition included in Article 21 of the EU Charter of Fundamental Rights, which in contrast to the Charter language is binding.[10] The various rules in one way or another amend language originally contained in the European Convention of Human Rights.[11] The critical difference is that the new EU Treaty language is directly enforceable in national law and explicitly prohibits discrimination on grounds of religion. Prior to this new rule, religious discrimination has generally not been prohibited in national law in Europe.

In Sweden, the tightening up of antidiscrimination law tied as a first priority with the institution of quotas for ethnic minority employment. In the Netherlands, one-third of the respondents picked quotas and another one-third picked church-state reform as their first choice. Mostly, there was little overlap between first and second choices but in the cumulative ranking of priorities—first

Table 2.4. First choice of public policy for ethnic and religious minorities

	Denmark (%)	Sweden (%)	France (%)	Germany (%)	Netherlands (%)	UK (%)	Total (%)
Unified antidiscrimination law including religion	50.0	28.6	50.0	67.4	21.7	93.5	56.1
Public money for religious organizations delivering social services	9.4	19.0	5.6	4.3	13.0	3.2	8.2
Easing access for asylum-seekers and immigrants,	9.4	9.5	0.0	13.0	0.0	0.0	6.4
Quotas for ethnic minority employment	15.6	28.6	16.7	6.5	34.8	3.2	15.2
Church-state reform	12.5	9.5	27.8	8.7	30.4	0.0	12.9
Other answers	3.1	4.8	0.0	0.0	0.0	0.0	1.2
Total	100.0	100.0	100.0	100.0	100.0	100.0	100.0

n = 171

plus second choices of reform—French and German Muslims' support for strengthening antidiscrimination legislation stood out as an area of important agreement. Likewise, the use of quotas to boost minority employment garnered more support in Denmark, Sweden, and the Netherlands.

I also asked respondents to choose their second priority for reform, and here there was less agreement. In Sweden and the UK, the second most pressing priority was the provision of public money for religious organizations to allow them to deliver social services. In Denmark and Germany, the most frequently chosen option was the easing of access to naturalization, and measures to improve policies towards immigrants and asylum-seekers. In France and the Netherlands, church-state reform was the most popular second choice.

One might argue that the difference between a first and a second preference of reform is, if not arbitrary, then perhaps more a matter of the issues of the day than an expression of stable preferences. There was some overlap between first and second choices. In a cumulative ranking of priorities—first plus second choices of reform—the support for strengthening antidiscrimination legislation seemed stronger in France and Germany, and the use of quotas to boost minority employment garnered more support in Denmark, Sweden, and the Netherlands.

State–Church reform—which would imply awarding Islam equal status with other faiths—was a low priority in Sweden, where a reform was completed in 2000 and minority religions given access to public funding. Nor was it favored in Britain, where the Anglican Church, albeit an established church, receives little direct funding from the government. The Church of England's privileges aroused little anger. Disestablishment was rarely advocated. The Church of England has automatic representation in the Lords with twenty-six bishops and archbishops. A few people brought up equitable representation for all faith communities as a desirable reform, for symbolic reasons, and because of the influence that Muslim faith representatives in the House of Lords might be able to exercise in debates. The alternative equitable solution, the elimination of all religious representation in the Lords, had little support. British Muslims think that religion should be represented in the institutions of government, and that reforms which remove faith from the public sphere are a step backwards, because society is already too secular. There is not full agreement on this, however. Some Muslim members of the Liberal Democrats were fully committed to the party's historical stance in favor of strict separation of church and state and opposed any expansion of privileges for religious groups, including Muslims.[12]

Other reform proposals had much less support. Easing naturalization procedures and access for asylum–seekers generated support only in

Table 2.5. Second choice of public policy for ethnic and religious minorities

	Denmark (%)	Sweden (%)	France (%)	Germany (%)	Netherlands (%)	UK (%)	Total (%)
Unified antidiscrimination law including religion	7.1	17.6	23.5	20.5	17.4	0.0	13.8
Public money for religious organizations delivering social services	7.1	35.3	23.5	9.1	13.0	66.7	24.5
Easing access for asylum seekers, immigrants, and naturalization	28.6	11.8	11.8	36.4	17.4	0.0	20.1
Quotas for ethnic minority employment	32.1	17.6	5.9	13.6	21.7	20.0	18.9
Church-state reform	21.4	17.6	35.3	20.5	30.4	13.3	22.0
Other answers	3.6	0.0	0.0	0.0	0.0	0.0	0.6
Total	100.0	100.0	100.0	100.0	100.0	100.0	100.0

n = 159

Denmark and Germany, where some political parties have voiced strongly critical views of existing policies. In fact, the actual policy in the two countries differs significantly. Germany has been among the most generous OECD countries with respect to accepting asylum-seekers, while Denmark has been among the most stringent in limiting asylum. In the Netherlands and Britain, two countries with older and larger immigrant populations, there was no support at all for liberalizing immigration procedures.

The idea that immigrant associations should be awarded public grants—or a 'voucher-based' payment system—created to support faith-based social services received strong support in the UK and moderate support in Sweden and France, but in all cases only as a less urgent priority. Complaints are common that existing social services are poorly equipped to serve elderly and disabled immigrants, whose spiritual and dietary needs are not well-understood by a system based upon the idea of 'solidarity' and 'one-size fits all.' Immigrant social problems are becoming increasingly visible, and many people would tell me that the problems of taking care of the sick and elderly are almost as important as the more visible problems associated with youth unemployment and delinquency. When asked to make choices, however, devolving responsibility for social services to faith-based associations was not an urgent priority. Support for this idea was greater in Sweden than in the other countries. One possible interpretation is that the otherwise generous Swedish welfare system is experienced as particularly unaccommodating by immigrants.

Given the controversies over restrictive immigration policies and the treatment of political asylum–seekers in several of the countries in the study—Denmark and the Netherlands in particular—it is perhaps surprising that few Muslim leaders pick easing restrictions on immigration as an important area for reform. 'We first have to integrate those who are already here,' was a common sentiment. It is evident that conflicts over faith and the problems Muslims experience because of their faith—even if they are secular and do not practice their faith in any rigorous way—outweigh all other concerns.

INTEGRATION VERSUS ASSIMILATION

The meaning of pluralism is contested. There is a 'he said–she said' quality to the public debate and the Muslim response, as it emerges from these interviews. European government leaders and the Greek chorus of talk shows and opinion pages cry, 'the problem with Muslims is that they won't integrate.' And Muslims cry back, 'the problem is that you won't let us in.'

Political discourse has shifted in recent years away from consideration of multicultural or proactive measures for the integration of Muslims towards an increasingly assimilationist rhetoric. Previous policies focused on granting immigrants certain rights and relied on the welfare state as a vehicle for integration. These are now replaced by overtly assimilationist policies and an increasingly coercive approach. In January 2003, Frits Bolkestein, former Dutch Liberal Party leader and EU Commissioner in charge of the internal market, made a speech in Rotterdam that is widely regarded as an obituary on thirty years of Dutch policy and as marking a shift towards a 'tough on Muslims' approach. He signaled a sea change not only in the approach of the Dutch government but also in the way that European governments in general addressed diversity:

Over the past thirty years or so, our country has experienced a large influx of women who find themselves in a disadvantaged situation.... Those who fail to see the discrimination against Muslim women that is going on are simply refusing to face facts. Instead of criticizing this wanton abuse, they gloss over it with references to multiculturalism. We live in a free country where everyone can come and go as they please, pray to the god of their choice, switch from one god to another and exercise the right of free speech.... That said, however, there have to be common standards respected by all. These are anchored in our constitution and no amount of multiculturalism can be allowed to erode them.... And that is why I also reject the slogan 'Integration with retention of identity'.... Why should we not be entitled to criticize Islam and the Koran? Do we live in a free country or not? Let us not mince our words. We should not always see ethnic minorities as victims. They are to be seen not as groups to be pitied but as fully-fledged citizens. We must talk to them, in Dutch, about their responsibilities.[13]

Bolkenstein's speech made a number of concessions to the nativist reaction against immigrants. One was the blunt rejection of value relativism and the announcement of support for a 'common' standard. This implies that double standards had previously existed. His characterization of existing laws as 'good enough' implied that the Dutch do not have to change, and that adjustments must rather be made by immigrants. Immigrants are in the wrong and the Dutch in the right, if for no other reason than because it is 'their' country. But he also held out the promise that if immigrants become like the Dutch, they will *be* the Dutch.

The question then arises: what does it mean to be 'Dutch'? Does it mean that you have to follow the example of Ayaan Hirsi Ali, the Dutch-Somali star of Bolkestein's party and Holland's favorite immigrant politician, and disavow Islam? Many Muslims have indeed concluded that they are expected to give up their faith if they are to be accepted as Europeans. The boundary between integration and assimilation is unclear. However, there are other possible models, such as that offered by the German Christian Democratic founder of a youth association and high-tech businessman whom I quoted in the previous chapter. 'We want to keep our faith but we are German,' he told me. 'There is no reason to live in ghettos. It is nice to keep the language at home but otherwise we want to be integrated.'[14]

Bolkestein's vision of the obligations of immigrants to adjust to national values and institutions contrasts sharply with American ideas about immigrant integration through the 'melting pot,' or the Canadian multicultural pluralism that aims for the coexistence of 'communities.' His party, the VVD, has been particularly forceful in its denunciations of multiculturalism since the rise and subsequent collapse of the Lijst Pim Fortyun. Fortyun was an outspoken critic of what he called the Islamic dilution of Dutch values. The Dutch liberals' outspoken attacks on Islam are not untypical for centrist European parties. They have adopted a remarkably similar rhetoric regarding Islam's treatment of women and targeted the headscarf as an unacceptable feature of Islam.

The idea of the ethnic melting pot implies the fusion of different cultures and ethnicities in a new and thoroughly American identity.[15] It implies that a sense of common national identification is compatible with ethnic loyalty to subgroups, but also that ethnic origin is irrelevant for a person's standing as a member of the civic community. Historians have cast doubt on the factual truth of the concept, contending both that immigrants did not freely choose to become 'Americans' and that integration was conditional on other social cleavages, such as race, gender, religion, or class.[16] Leaving aside questions about the balance between coercion and voluntary adaptation, the concept of the melting pot suggests a model of integration that allows for negotiation of the character of national identity, obligations, and rights that is flexible and encompassing. It implies a reciprocal process different from assimilation and from simple coexistence.[17]

It does not necessarily follow, however, that all the failures of understanding and lack of political sophistication are to be laid exclusively at the door of Europe's governments. How flexible are Muslim elites with respect to what they expect from Western democracies? And how do they define their problems? Are they, as a few Muslim leaders occasionally said to me, the 'new Jews' of Europe? Like Jews, the comparison implies, Muslims are being pushed into ghettos and subjected to discrimination on account of their faith. According to Krishan Kumar, 'Muslims have become the new "other" of Europe.'[18] He adds that 'today the "Jewish Question" in Europe has been largely "solved," mainly by getting rid of the Jews.' The sinister implication is that forced assimilation or forced removal may also be in store for Muslims. This is a dangerous hyperbole, and many Muslim leaders resist the picture of pervasive victimization. In my interviews, people often noted calmly that, despite the troubles, things are 'much better' in Europe than in the Islamic world. These are birth pains, they say, and social peace will evolve over time. A few people even told me that Muslims have 'few problems' and characterized the issues as a question of addressing 'ignorance.'

The emphasis which Muslims place upon religious discrimination as a primary source of their problems leads them to believe that the recognition of their human rights would be a solution. This also exploits the self-image of Europeans as 'tolerant' and 'nondiscriminatory.' In truth, antidiscrimination enforcement and the elimination of public bias will help educated Muslims to get jobs and even to achieve positions of leadership, but many socioeconomic problems will remain, as will problems related to the position of women. Parity for Islam and Muslims—equal treatment of mosques, religious teachers, and scholars, for example—will promote integration and institution-building, but will not resolve the more general problems experienced by Muslims in their daily lives.

The emphasis upon discrimination as the source of problems, and upon human rights enforcement as the solution, also raises large questions about the relationship between individual Muslims and the community. Are Muslims ready to extend the same toleration and recognition to women, and to Muslims who take a view of the faith that differs from the majority? Human rights language has a deceptively attractive logic but in practice it sets a demanding standard.

ANTIDISCRIMINATION ENFORCEMENT

When I asked Muslim leaders about the drawbacks of emphasizing rights and using rights adjudication, their concerns about the costs of a legalistic approach sometimes outweighed the anticipated benefits. In Sweden and the Netherlands there was a widespread feeling that discrimination cannot be fixed by law. Skeptics thought that more legislation would not help to change attitudes, and that only time or education—or both—would gradually ease the pervasive discrimination that Muslims experience. Dutch Muslim leaders were particular skeptical that more laws would resolve anything. 'We already have so many laws,' several people said, 'and none of them are enforced.'

Another argument was that it did no good to create more 'rights' for Muslims, when the general perception is that they already are making too many claims for themselves. It might even be counterproductive to press for reform through changes in the law until public attitudes improved. There was also concern that courts might use rights adjudication against Muslims. The courts' decisions on headscarf bans encourage a certain wariness. (See Chapter 6 for a detailed discussion.)

The understanding of rights as legal freedoms that can be claimed by individuals through the courts against governments is something new in European law and in the public mind, and it is not a well developed idea.[19] Inspired and frustrated by the 1948 UN Universal Declaration of Human Rights, European states created the European Convention on Human Rights in 1950. (The Convention has been amended repeatedly, and is constantly evolving.) Article 14 states that, '[t]he enjoyment of the rights and freedoms set forth in this Convention shall be secured without discrimination on any ground such as sex, race, color, language, religion, political or other opinion, national or social origin, association with a national minority, property, birth or other status.' However, it is only in recent years that courts have begun to enforce this article, in response to efforts by the European Union to create a European 'bill of rights.' The EC Treaty Article 13(5) forbids discrimination based on sex, racial or ethnic origin, religion or belief, disability, age, or sexual orientation, and the article empowers the EU Commission to 'take action.' That means that the Commission can take the initiative and issue directives, which the member states must implement and enforce. Two different international courts watch over the jurisprudence deriving from the European Convention and the EU: the European Court of Human Rights located in Strasbourg and the ECJ located in Luxembourg.

In December 2003, as this study was in progress, two EU directives issued in 2000 took effect in all the countries. The first required member states to implement rules for equal treatment irrespective of racial or ethnic origin, and the second contained new rules on equal treatment in employment outlawing discrimination on the grounds of disability, sex, religion or belief, age, and sexual orientation.[20]

As a consequence of the directives, sexuality, age, ethnicity, religion, and race were added to existing complaint procedures and antidiscrimination enforcement mechanisms. The effects of the directives are limited as they relate only to employment and do not address discriminatory national institutional frameworks for the organization of religion or religious exercise, or even discrimination in housing markets, for example. Enforcement is also an issue. The member states are free to decide on the format of enforcement procedures (all EU legislation is enforced through national implementation) and few countries have introduced significant penalties for discrimination. Typically, wrongfully dismissed persons can rarely be reinstated in their jobs, and oversight agencies can scold offenders but not issue fines. France has defined discrimination as a criminal matter, but with the effect that the burden of proof falls on the victim, and the courts adjudicate so few cases that discrimination goes mostly unpunished.

Muslims embrace rights constitutionalism because of the perceived promise that it will provide a tool to strike against religious bias. Unfortunately, many Muslim leaders underestimate the implications of antidiscrimination enforcement for other aspects of Muslim lifestyles, particularly how what Tariq Modood calls 'Muslim identity politics' creates conflicts with other ethnic and racial minorities and imposes unwanted obligations on Muslim religious institutions.[21] Like gay rights advocates in the USA, European Muslims may wake up one morning and discover that the legal approach has unanticipated and unwanted consequences. In particular, homosexuality and female imams are difficult issues for many (but not all) religious leaders. 'Give us 20 years,' a Swedish civic leader told me. 'Isn't that how long it took the Swedish Church to accept women as pastors?' Others thought it was unimaginable that Muslims would have to deal with gay rights. 'Why would gays want to mess with us?' was one reaction. But the difficulties extend beyond the obligation to address intolerance within Muslim institutions to complicated questions about the implications of religious equity for the legal obligations of imams to, for example, observing nondiscrimination policies when ministering to the mosque community.

In Britain, Muslim civic leaders support strengthening antidiscrimination legislation but are also working to obtain a religious exemption from gay rights clauses, and they have been able to work with the Roman Catholics and the Anglican Church on this issue. It is not the first time that gay rights have been a source of conflict. The Muslim Council of Britain last summer worked together with the other faiths to prevent an amendment to adoption legislation that would have allowed gay couples to adopt.[22]

The religious groups have won round one. The 2003 UK Employment Equality (Sexual Orientation) regulations allow a religious organization to 'apply a requirement related to sexual orientation in accordance with its doctrines or the convictions of its followers' (Clause 7 (3)). In other words, religious organizations can refuse to employ someone who is known to be homosexual, if the organization can prove scriptural reasons for its rejection. The definition of what is a church 'organization' and the degree of theological clarity with respect to sexual ethics are matters of litigation. The Church of England was understandably concerned about having courts and employment tribunals rule on theological questions, and it argued that issues relating to religious prohibitions on same-sex relationships should be left to religious organizations. Unions, on the other hand, contended that this would constitute an unacceptable infringement of their members' employment rights.[23] A similar conflict is being fought out in Sweden, which has an independent gay equality ombudsman, who has made it his number one priority to force compliance with gay rights in Muslim schools. These conflicts over religious exemptions matter greatly for the future direction of European antidiscrimination rules.

The EU's efforts in the antidiscrimination area mean that controversies over clashing rights are destined to spread. All member states faced two deadlines in 2003 for the implementation of more stringent rules on equal treatment and the enforcement on rules against gender, race, and disability discrimination. These would have to be merged with rules prohibiting discrimination on the grounds of age, religion or belief, and sexual orientation. There has been considerable resistance. One year after the expiry of the deadline for the implementation of the first of the two Directives, the EU Commission initiated legal action before the ECJ against six member states (Austria, Belgium, Germany, Greece, Finland, and Luxembourg) for failure to pass new rules.[24] Member state noncooperation is not the only risk to EU action on this front. Another, and more common, hazard is that the expanded application of the law is counteracted by a dilution of enforcement. Employers and many political parties already oppose more rule-making in this area.

A British White Paper, 'Fairness for All: A Commission for Equality and Human Rights,' published by the responsible minister, Patricia Hewitt, in May 2004, proposed the creation of a new Commission for Equality and Human Rights to replace the existing Commission for Racial Equality. According to the minister, the new commission will 'be responsible for challenging discrimination across society and for the first time promote human rights.' The White Paper has already elicited controversy. It was immediately opposed by black and ethnic minority lobbying groups, who argued that it would create a 'hierarchy' of antidiscrimination rights, and dilute existing rights. Religious institutions were exempted from the nondiscrimination rules passed in 2003, and Sarah Ludford, a Liberal Democrat who is a member of the European parliament, protested vehemently that the British government had violated European equal rights law 'in allowing churches and other religious organizations to discriminate against gay people.'[25] The perception that Labour chose Islam over gay rights dominated press coverage of the new equalities bill when it was first presented in February 2005. According to *The Times*, 'Gay rights campaigners have been snubbed by the government for fear of upsetting Muslim voters who are regarded as more important to Labour's election campaign.'[26]

Ten years ago, Mary Ann Glendon, a Harvard Law School professor, lamented that in the USA nearly any social conflict is translated into a discourse on rights and that adjudication has become a substitute for public policy on issues regarding social responsibility. She coined the term 'rights talk' to describe the preoccupation with non–negotiable concepts of 'rights' for the balancing of group interests and public priorities.[27] She held up Europe as an example of an alternative and more sensible approach to the discussion of the balance between rights and responsibilities. One does not need to agree fully with Glendon's view that the preoccupation with rights is detrimental to public virtue to see that she was right about the problems with using adjudication to fix to social problems and the political logic of competitive 'rights talk.' It is also fair to expect that European law-making on antidiscrimination rights will invariably follow this acrimonious path in years to come.

MUSLIM FEMINISTS, ACTIVISTS, AND TRADITIONALISTS

A consistent narrative of Muslims' problems emerges from this study of the views of Muslim leaders. Their chief concern is with religious discrimination. This analysis also suggests the solution: more effective nondiscrimination policies. The larger issues are typically framed in the language of human rights. The moral appeal to human rights is combined with a call on European governments to live up to their own principles, which should encourage legal reforms that promote the equal treatment of Muslims as individuals.

Beneath the consensus, a familiar conflict between left and right discourses on human rights is being replayed. On one side advocates stress dignity and respect as the core of human rights. On the other, the emphasis is rather on equal rights, and social policy is the preferred means of achieving advancement and parity. The division is not sharply drawn, at least not yet, and areas of overlapping agreements on problems and policies exist, but the politicization of Muslim 'problems' invites new agreements and disagreements.

The emerging formation of the 'Muslim' issue also implies a new group-based political identity for Muslims as a religious minority in the West. Thus, a new collectivity of Dutch, Danish, or French Muslims is being forged from what were previously identified as ethnic groups of various national origins, notably Pakistanis, Turks, and Moroccans. As Muslim associations strive to represent 'the Muslim voice' in national politics, dissent and disagreement among Muslims becomes more apparent. This is, of course, as it should be. There are Christian associations and political groups, but there is no one 'Christian voice' in the political life of any Western European state. There is, in particular, disagreement among Muslim leaders as to how the Muslim identity should be formulated. Khalida Khan, a long-time Muslim civil rights activist in the UK and a member of a feminist collective, the An-Nisa Society, complained bitterly about the MCB's conservatism after a fight with the association's representatives (which she lost) over an attempt to update the earlier and highly successful Runnymede Islamaphobia report. In the June 2004 issues of *Q-News*, a left-leaning Muslim magazine, she wrote:

No amount of jiggling with it can get away from the fact that racism is about race and colour and not one's faith identity. Moreover, trying to fit anti-Muslim discrimination into anti-racist strategies simply does not work as Muslims have seen to their detriment. 'Race equality' does not translate into equality for Muslims.[28]

The real issue is not whether anti-Muslim bias is a form of racism or not—plainly it is not, for the reasons pointed out by Khan—but how to address the problems that derive from religious discrimination and what to do about the integration of Islam. The fight between the MCB, which has increasingly emerged as the Muslim establishment, and the Muslim left, represented by An-Nisa, the Forum Against Islamophobia and Racism, and the Islamic Human Rights Commission (and the collective that issues the magazine, *Q-News*, in which Khan's complaint was published), is ultimately about means and goals. Kahn, tellingly, also complains that building mosques is not going to help Muslims get jobs.

Three young men and one woman I spoke with illustrated the consensus that Europeans are having trouble accepting that universal values include Muslims and the diverging lessons that Muslims draw from this premise. They all expressed a rage that derived from disappointed expectations. Were young people more inclined to such anger, perhaps because they had higher expectations of the commitment to universal human rights values than older leaders? I cannot say for sure, but the similarity of expression is striking despite the different vantage points—in terms of origin and political commitment—of the four.

A German Christian Democrat of Turkish origin, the only native-born citizen of the four, and also the youngest, had been one of the founders of an interethnic youth organization, Muslimische Jugend, and was elected as a Christian Democrat to a state parliament. He explained that Muslims, who like himself draw their civic values from their faith, see nothing wrong with a party program that mentions 'God.' That is, he made clear, preferable to the secularists, who will allow no public space for religion. But when religion comes to mean exclusively Christianity and 'occidental values,' then Muslims have to object. Why should Muslims now participate in the CDU? He could, he pointed out, in any case make more money by concentrating on his high-tech business.[29]

Yamin Makri is one of the founders of an interethnic French Muslim youth association, the 'Union des Jeunes Musulmans,' but Makri had 'retired' from youth association work when I spoke with him. He belongs to the theological 'left' and the association was loosely associated with Tariq Ramadan's reformist theology, but Makri embraces even more radical ideas. He had no objection, for example, to women becoming imams, or rather imamas. When I asked what he thought of Huntington's 'clash of civilizations' theory, he placed the blame for the conflict on the narrow French understanding of universal values, which excludes Islam and Muslims from the community of equal respect. He sounded very much like a French intellectual when he explained the issue to me:

Within the context of Islam, one might say, each element is a part: brotherhood, equality, etc., all of those principles. Some say that if those principles are respected, that is sufficient grounds for people to live together. Others dissent: no. They do not think so. More is needed. That is the big issue, the big debate, that is to say: are these values specific to the West and, in particular, a French product or are the universal values really universal? May others (the non-French, author's remark) only live under this ideological domination, where it is not possible to recognize their own values as part of the universal values of others?[30]

Hakim El Ghissassi, a journalist who had also arrived in France as a young adult, complained that the French Muslim leadership stressed religion far too much. However, his principal complaint was that French politicians berate Muslims for not integrating but will not open the door in their own associations for Muslims, nor allow Muslims—or 'foreigners'—to speak about anything other than 'integration problems':

The political problem today is that we had political leaders of Arab origin, from the Maghreb, but they were regarded as servants, that is to say their principal role was to put up official notices (a French derogatory term, author's remark). They were never to be municipal councilors, deputies, never to be eligible for power. That is the problem of the political milieu today. At the heart of French politics today there is a discriminatory approach to the populations of foreign origin. The political parties need to work out how to integrate these people and these populations must not concern themselves exclusively with problems of integration but address all aspects of French politics and society.[31]

A Danish-Iranian human rights activist, trained in international law, also invoked human rights and also stressed the need for reciprocity on the part of Muslim communities when she outlined what she thought needed to be done:

I think it is terrifically important to begin with the Convention of Human Rights and religion. It is essential that all faiths acquire parity so that people have equal access and equal opportunity to exercise their faiths—but within the framework of human rights. The bridge between other religions and the Christian faith community must be based upon understanding and respect for each other by introducing human rights as the essential basic values.[32]

Each of these four young leaders identified value bias and the majority society's inability to recognize the essential equality of Muslims—and of Islamic humanist principles—as the key reasons for the stigmatization of Muslims and discrimination against them. Interestingly, the four approached Islam very differently in their personal lives. One was a nonpracticing Muslim, two were more traditionally observant, and one advocated a radical 'Liberation'–style theology of self-sufficient faith communities. They split evenly on whether or not governments should fund the development of Islamic institutions.

NOTES

1. Interview 74, The Hague (December 2, 2003).
2. A t-test fails to reject the null hypothesis that there is no difference between those who say 'Islam is personally very important' and those who say it is 'not important' or 'somewhat important' ($t = 0.9068$, $P \geq |t| = 0.3659$).
3. A somewhat different and stronger criticism of the Islamophobia concept and its usages can be found in Kenan Malik, 'The Islamophobia Myth,' *Prospect* (January 2005). Also available at:
   http://www.kenanmalik.com/essays/islamophobia_prospect.html.
4. The *Guardian* (July 6, 2004). A young Muslim lawyer told the journalist, 'we have to write a lot more applications than other people to simply get the same result.'
5. The *Institut Montaigne* produced a report based upon the study. Available at: http://www.institutmontaigne.org/groupe.php?id=9. The study was also discussed in the French Senate. Available at: http://www.senat.fr/rap/l04-065//104-0651.html.
6. The UK Home Office relied upon self-reported perceptions of discrimination in a study used to support the inclusion of religion in a proposal to strengthen antidiscrimination law: Home Office Research Study 220, *Religious discrimination in England and Wales*, Home Office Research, Development and Statistics Directorate (February 2001).
7. Economic activity rates for selected religious/ethnic groups, by age and sex, *Focus on Religion*, Census 2001, Office for National Statistics. Available at: http://www.statistics.gov.uk/focuson/religion.
8. OECD, *Trends in International Migration* (Paris, 1999).
9. Interview 66, The Hague (November 26, 2003).
10. *Charter of Fundamental Rights of the European Union*, Official Journal of the European Communities, 18.12.2000/En/C364/01.

11. The language repeats Article 14 in the European Convention on Human Rights, which states that 'The enjoyment of the rights and freedoms set forth in this Convention shall be secured without discrimination on any ground such as sex, race, colour, language, religion, political or other opinion, national or social origin, association with a national minority, property, birth or other status.'

12. The Liberal Democrats appear not to be of one mind on these issues. Lord Dholakia, who was the Party leader in the Lords, when I interviewed him, has sponsored proposals that would broaden rather than eliminate religious representation in the House of Lords. Interview 34, London (March 2, 2004).

13. Speech held in Rotterdam (January 5, 2003). Released in official English translation (January 28, 2003). Available in full at: http://europa.eu.int/comm/commissioners/bolkestein//docs/speeches/20030105-integration_en.pdf

14. Interview 98, Boston (June 15, 2004).

15. For a discussion of the concept and its role in American civic mythology, see Philip Gleason, 'The Melting Pot: Symbol of Fusion or Confusion?' *American Quarterly*, 16 (Spring, 1964) 1: 20–46. A recent example of scholarship on American immigration in this tradition is David Hollinger, *Postethnic America: Beyond Multiculturalism* (New York: Basic Books, 1995).

16. Gary Gerstle, 'Liberty, Coercion, and the Making of Americans,' *Journal of American History*, 84 (September 1997) 2: 524–58.

17. Rogers Brubaker, 'The Return of Assimilation? Changing Perspectives on Immigration and Its Sequels in France, Germany, and the United States,' *Ethnic and Racial Studies*, 24 (July 2001) 4: 531–48.

18. Krishan Kumar, 'The Nation-State, the European Union, and Transnational Identities,' Nezar Al-Sayyad and Manuel Castells (eds.), *Muslim Europe or Euro-Islam: Politics, Culture, and Citizenship in the Age of Globalization* (Lanham, MD: Lexington Books, 2002), 54.

19. Rights constitutionalism, in contrast, is a political-legal principle that awards certain types of law primacy over other legislation, e.g. subordinates acts of parliament and administrative decisions to a bill of rights. See Vicky C. Jackson and Mark Tushnet, *Comparative Constitutional Law* (New York Foundation Press, 1999), 190. For a history of human rights, see Mary Ann Glendon, *A World Made New: Eleanor Roosevelt and the Universal Declaration of Human Rights* (New York Random House, 2001).

20. Council Directive 2000/43/EC of 29 June 2000 implementing the principle of equal treatment between persons irrespective of racial or ethnic origin and Council Directive 2000/78/EC of 27 November 2000 on establishing a general framework for equal treatment in employment and occupation.

21. Tariq Modood, *Multicultural Politics. Racism, Ethnicity, and Muslims in Britain* (Minneapolis University of Minnesota Press, 2005), 160–7.

22. The revised act was issued in January 2003 as The Adoption (Amendment) Rules 2003.

23. A lawsuit was filed by seven unions against the secretary of state for trade and industry, Patricia Hewitt, and a coalition of Church of England and evangelical

schools. The unions claimed that the religious exemption contained in the regulation was in contravention of the EU directive, a claim that the judge did not accept. The judge also did not accept the claim by the schools that religious schools are 'religious organizations' and qualify for the exemption, but applied a narrow definition that limited the exemption to the clergy rather than religious organizations. The judgment is of interest also because the judge's reasoning relied heavily on a comparative methodology including cases from the USA, South Africa, and the European Court of Justice. EWHC 860 (Admin), the High Court of Justice, 26 April 2004 (CO/4672/2003, CO/4670/2003, CO/4880/ 2003, CO/4943/2003, CO/4908/2003, CO/4895/2003, CO/4670/2003, CO/4880/ 2003, CO/4943/ 2003, CO/4908/2003, CO/4895/2003)

24. The press release and statement in support of the complaint to the ECJ are available at: http://europa.eu.int/comm/employment_social/fundamental_rights/news/news_en.htm

25. www.sarahludfordmep.org.uk/story.php?id = 78, posted September 2, 2003.

26. 'Discrimination bill snubs gays to save Muslim vote,' David Cracknell, *The Times*, London (February 27, 2005).

27. Mary Ann Glendon, *Rights Talk: The Impoverishment of Political Discourse* (New York: Free Press, 1991).

28. Khalida Khan, 'Islamophobia: What now?' *Q-News* (June 20, 2004).

29. Interview 98, Boston (June 15, 2004).

30. Interview 82, Lyon (May 24, 2004).

31. Interview 76, Paris (May 17, 2004).

32. Interview 13, Copenhagen (September 11, 2003).

3

Faith and Politics

There has been a lack of concrete ideas about how to integrate Islam in Europe, in part because for decades no serious thought was given to the question. Since September 11, 2001, however, security concerns have forced governments to think again about the situation of their Muslim minorities. Proposals to spend public money on Islamic institutions now appear on the desks of lawmakers, often accompanied by recommendations from the police. *N.B* After the March 11, 2004, train bombing in Madrid, the Spanish government announced a plan (endorsed by the police), which would end the special funding privileges of the Catholic Church and provide public funding for all faith communities, Islam included. After a group of young Muslims was caught plotting to plant bombs in London, the British government proposed a plan—unwisely named 'Operation Contest'—to fund the activities of moderate Islamic intellectuals and generally to encourage the development of a moderate Islam.[1] Neither plan has succeeded, because of furious criticism in the press and opposition on the part of other lawmakers.

Policymakers struggle with two contradictory assumptions that make policymaking seem very problematic. One is that Islam runs counter to fundamental Western values, particularly when it comes to the position of women, and is intolerant of dissent and individual choice. On the other hand, Islam is also perceived to lack coherence and unity because it is a congregational religion, a community-based faith centered around collective worship but without a clerical hierarchy and with no common theology. When government officials look for a responsible interlocutor, they find that the Muslim voice is a cacophony rather than a chorus.

Muslims do express very different views of Islam and draw different conclusions about the implications of their faith for both private and public commitments. For some, Islam is a source of identity and family tradition. For others, it is a source of intense spiritual commitment. And yet others think of faith as a practical problem for Muslims and a source of bias, but not of great personal relevance. And so while Europe's Muslim leaders tend to agree that it is necessary to integrate Islam in European life, this means different things to different people.

Three people whose own accounts of how their faith mattered to them illustrate these differences as well as an agreement that Islam in Europe will be different. One apparent paradox is that the views and aspirations of the first speaker, the most secular of the three, pose the highest bar for integration policies, because, as he puts it, 'what goes for Christians goes for Muslims.'

1. *A secular Muslim*: Seyit (his and the following names are fictional) is a city councilor in a Copenhagen suburb representing a far left party. He is a fit man in his fifties. In addition to his work as a teacher and a local politician, he is also a popular public speaker and lectures at high schools and teacher colleges about integration issues. The family's suburban house, where we met, is spotless. He is so assimilated that he sometimes appears to have appropriated the stereotypical Danish outlook on the world. He does not speak English but has been on a trip to the USA. His native-born friend, who also went on the trip and sits in on our conversation, jokes that all Seyit could talk about was how dirty everything was in New York and how all the cars were dented. Seyit bears out his friend's teasing about him being 'too Danish' by starting to talk about how 'all he saw were black people.'

He talks about how he is 'split'—Danish when he goes out and Turkish at home. The truth of this statement is apparent. The kitchen, where dinner is served, is his wife Samilla's domain. She has cooked a large and delicious dinner for us, but it is explained to me that Seyit bakes the bread, as is the prerogative of Turkish men. He accepts that he is a traditional Turkish male but points out that he does not insist that Samilla puts the food out when he comes home late. He jokes that he and Samilla are a 'cousin-marriage.' They are actually cousins, and the family may have arranged the marriage.

Seyit is proudly nonreligious but Samilla celebrates Eid and Ramadan. Their adult son, who is studying to become a teacher, expresses his appreciation with a pat on his mother's shoulder and a grateful glint in the eye. She nods when I talk about the need for secular families to have access to imams and religious institutions on holidays and for their children. They do not currently belong to a mosque. As Kurds, the family is estranged from the Turkish government imams. Seyit says that, yes, he wants an imam for his family, but he is exasperated with current imams who talk 'nonsense outdated a thousand years ago.' He wants 'Ali from Hvidover' (a Copenhagen suburb) to be educated at the University's Theological Faculty and to become their imam.

In Denmark, Lutheran pastors are civil servants, and Seyit thinks imams should be too. He wants the government to pay for mosques and imams. It is dangerous to accept funding from private parties or foreign governments, because it is imperative to control what is said from the pulpit, and who is doing the talking. The government should consider how Muslims actually practice their faith and institute reforms that fit the realities of the situation. Seyit does not like the local mosque council because they 'meddle in politics.' He tells a story about how, once when he was home in Turkey, the local mosque came by his father's house to collect money for the mosque. He gave them some money, because he did not want to embarrass his father, but otherwise he would 'never pay money to a mosque.' Seyit does not like the local mosque council in the suburb where he lives, either, because they 'meddle in politics'. I later learn that the council endorsed another candidate, also from the left, who had paid the levy to the mosque, for the council elections.

2. *A Euro-Muslim*: Maryam lives in Copenhagen. Her mother is Finnish and her father was a political refugee from an Arab country. Her mother converted to Islam, and Maryam grew up as a Muslim but admits that she did not think much about her faith until she became an adult. A beautiful woman in her twenties, she wears a headscarf. She is studying Arabic at the university and is one of the founders of a Muslim Student Group that reads the Koran and holds weekly prayer meetings. She got the idea for the organization during a visit to UC-Berkeley, where she met with 'progressive Muslims' and was impressed by the love and openness that characterized the group. They were not defensive about their faith, she says admiringly, and taught her a new way to look at Islam. She likes the nontraditional structures that characterize faith groups in the USA, and thinks that is how things will be in Europe. The imams have already lost the monopoly on interpretation, she says.

Maryam thinks of herself as 'a living example of the possibility of being secular and yet a practicing Muslim.' Islam has to be individualized, by which she means that each and every Muslim must find his or her own path to spirituality. She does not regard herself as an ulema (a religious scholar) but she aims to become one once she has educated herself sufficiently. There is nothing in the Koran that prohibits a female imam, imama, and she thinks that she may become one. Mixed marriages are OK, she says, at least between Christians and Muslims. She has some trouble with the suggestion that Jews and Muslims could live together in a marriage.

Muslims must do missionary work but there can be no compulsion and no pressures to convert. She finds it objectionable that there are economic incentives or social pressures for Muslims to convert to Christianity. Maryam wants to separate state and religion, and she understands that to mean that religion should not influence politics. She is not overly concerned about the privileges of the Lutheran Church. It does not matter much to her that Muslims do not have the benefit of tax money with which to build their institutions. Spirituality and respect are more important. She wants to create mutual respect between faiths, but sees the accommodation of Islam primarily as a matter of theological toleration and mutuality. In her view, irreligious equality implies that all religions regard each other as equally valid.

3. *A neo-orthodox Muslim*: Demir lives in a suburb outside Stockholm. A political refugee from an Arab country, he was educated as a physician before fleeing his home, and he has retrained to be allowed to work as an emergency room doctor in Sweden. He is very observant. He is in his early forties. He works incessantly and juggles being head of a Muslim charity with shifts at a hospital in a provincial city an hour away from Stockholm. He has come into town to meet me and also to take part in rehearsal for an orchestra performance. Our meeting takes place during Ramadan, and he is fasting and will not even drink water.

Religious expression is a way to reach God. He stresses the importance of ethical commitment, and cites the Koran, 'If you go to sleep full but your neighbor is hungry, you do not belong to us.' Faith, he says, is not a question of rules but is about ethics and existential problems. There are many problems among Muslims, who increasingly are giving in to drug abuse and criminality, and are affected by social problems. Muslims need to be mobilized to find a way to express their religion, to find ways of living as Muslims. He is tired of the talk about rules, about the headscarf, or how long the sleeves should be on a woman's dress. He would prefer to see more emphasis on the spiritual aspects of Islam. Islam is for everybody, he says, and quotes from the Koran, 'Come whoever you are. . . .' It occurred to me that he was possibly trying to convert me.

Demir says that Muslims in the West must focus on the expression of Islam in poetry, and in music, and find Swedish ways to convey the universal message of Islam. Too often the question is which kind of Muslim you are. If you are from the Middle East, he says, political aspects often dominate, but Muslims elsewhere are more interested in the expression and practice of religion. What is happening in the world is intruding on our way of thinking and the result is political Islam, and as a consequence the spiritual aspects of Islam are becoming less important. Demir disapproves of that. People from Bosnia and Somalia think very differently. They do not have many problems living with Christians and Jews. In the Balkans, there is a long tradition of coexistence, going back to the Ottoman era. European Muslims can learn from that experience but, for now, they face a question of survival.

Demir does not think that it is possible to develop a new interpretation of shariah law or to combine different traditions within Islam.[2] Compromise is not possible, he thinks. Muslims must accept that a millet system is not possible in the West. The state sets the laws. If we do not have an Islamic society, we cannot have Islamic law. Therefore European Islam must be different. He envisions a universal 'church' of Islam. Civilization is a question of the expression of your religion, and Muslims in the West must embrace an existentialist interpretation of Islam. Demir detours into a lecture on Islamic universalism and cites Sartre and Kirkegaard to persuade me of the prominence of existentialist tenets in Islam.

The real issues, says Demir, are the lack of faith in the society as a whole and the many social problems. He mentions drugs and alcoholism. Religious Christians are also marginalized. And there are many problems with young people. All religious people have common issues to discuss. But Muslims have big problems among themselves, he says, and he specifies particularly the shortage of educated Muslims, and the fact that those who are educated do not participate in public life. Muslims are always explaining who they are *not* and never have a chance to say who they *are*. Muslims must change that, he says.

These three individuals share a desire to find a new expression of Islam that is both modern and European. Yet their disagreements also illustrate why common ground can be hard to find between Muslims when it comes to shaping public policy. The picture that emerges from my interviews and the surveys suggests that faith alone does not determine the views that individual leaders formulate about the future of Western Europe's Muslims.

It can mean different things to say that Islam is 'personally important.' An affirmative answer may reflect a spiritual commitment, and it may also describe identity and family origin. It may even allude to both faith and identity. The term 'Kultur-Muslim,' or 'culturally Muslim,' is used in Germany and Scandinavia to describe individuals of Muslim origin who do not observe the rituals of faith but are Muslim by family background. Muslims often object to the term because it implies a distinction between an ethnic Muslim and a 'religious' Muslim, and they regard any attempt to distinguish between degrees of faith as pernicious. In any case, they argue, 'Islam' is a religion and not a culture. This is obviously true, in the sense that there is one faith and many cultures: Arabic, North African, Pakistani, Bangladeshi, etc. Arguably, even these categories are much too broad. Further divisions can easily be introduced.[3]

Objections aside, the term 'Muslim' reflects a sociological fact, the fact of being 'Muslim' in a 'Christian' society. European Islam invariably reflects the variety of faith commitments. Some Muslims attend the mosque only rarely, perhaps on the day of the Feast of Abraham or Eid al-Fitr. Others follow the daily prayer schedule. As a Danish imam said to me, complaining about the small-mindedness of many Danish Muslims, the issue is not how long the sleeves should be, but how to organize a Danish Muslim wedding? Which rituals do you include and which do you reject?[4]

CHOICES FOR THE INTEGRATION OF ISLAM

Most leaders agreed that European Islam must be integrated through 'home-grown' institutions and the dependency upon the Islamic countries for funding and imams must end. They also tend to agree that the established laws and arrangements that regulate relations between the state and other religions can be adapted to accommodate Islam, provided that the necessary political will exists. There were, however, dissenting voices. One significant minority is concerned that adaptation implies the assimilation of Christian practices. Others would prefer Muslims to be left alone to develop their faith in their own way.

N.B.

Yamin Makri, who was quoted in Chapter 2, put the anti-institutionalization view to me succinctly. When I asked him what he thought about the government's desire to create programs for educating imams in France, he responded: 'What is the purpose? So that imams can become like the *curé* (Catholic parish priests, author's remark)? We have a chance to be free to develop Islam. We must protect that. Why should we become like the Catholics or like the Jews?'[5] His vision of Islam was a congregationalist ideal of a community-based and non-hierarchical faith without a clergy and with no central authority. When I asked if women could be imams, he pointed out that the question only made sense if you had a clergy and a hierarchy. Without a clerical authority, who would there be to rule out imamas? Of the Paris mosque, the Islamic 'high church' in France, which over the years has been much favored by French governments as a representative of French Islam, he said disdainfully, 'that is not a mosque; that is the Algerian embassy!' The French press often describes Makri as an 'Islamiste,' but his views are not those of a fundamentalist. His unorthodox religious beliefs compel him to support the separation of church and state, and he speaks approvingly of liberty.'[6]

FOUR MODELS FOR INTEGRATING ISLAM

I asked the participants in the study a series of questions about public policies. These were designed to investigate how basic theological propositions about the nature of Islam shaped their preferences with respect to policies for religious accommodation and institutionalization, and in particular policies for imam recruitment, sources of funding for Islam, and the application of the shariah in democratic societies. Aside from a few people, like Makri, whose views could not be classified, the participants in the study matched one of four templates for religious accommodation.

The four positions can be described as the result of the cross-tabulation of two basic epistemological questions (see Table 3.1). Is Islam compatible with Western values? Should Islamic religious institutions be integrated into existing frameworks regulating relations between church and state? Those who answered both questions affirmatively I call secular integrationists. Those

Table 3.1 Typology for approaches to the integration of Islam

		Q: Should Islam be 'mainstreamed'?	
		Yes	No
Q: Is Islam compatible with Western value systems?	Yes	Secular Integrationist 23.5 %	Voluntarist 33.8 %
	No	Anticlerical 14.7 %	Neo-orthodox 27.9 %

who agreed that Islam was compatible with Western values but did not want institutional integration may be described as Euro-Muslims. Those who think that Western norms are incompatible with the exercise of Islam and oppose the integration of Islamic institutions to existing European frameworks for the exercise of religion are neo-orthodox. People who think that Islam is incompatible with Western norms but favor assimilation are anticlericals.

It is apparent that Muslim leaders have very different views on what should be done to integrate Islam in Europe. I shall describe the four different models for religious integration in some detail, before moving on to discuss demographic and partisan differences that account for some of the disagreement. Although the leaders differ with respect to basic propositions about the nature of Islam, areas of overlapping agreement exist on practical questions, such as the need to educate imams in Europe and to develop domestic sources of financing for Islamic institutions. Many differences can be traced to national origin and to ethnic-cultural variations within Islam. Muslims of Turkish origin are much more supportive of 'mainstreaming' than are Muslims of South Asian origin, and British Muslims are notably less supportive of the institutional cooptation of Islam within the frameworks that apply to other religions.

Two out of five of the leaders in the study view Islam and Western values as in some measure incompatible, and they are skeptical about the prospects for the normalization of Islam in Europe. They arrive at these conclusions from different starting points. Within this group are some who oppose the integration of Islam in Europe because they worry that Islam will be compromised. Their priority is to safeguard religious purity, and they prefer to do so by creating a diasporic religious community. Others opposed integration because they are anticlerical and dislike religion in general. Some say that Islam is a faith beyond repair, and irredeemably antiwoman and antidemocratic. One young Swedish Muslim, who had grown up in Sweden and belongs to the Green party, told me firmly, 'we do not need imams here.'[7]

The two groups opposed to integration had different reasons for the stance they took. The anticlericals thought that Islam was irredeemably illiberal. The neo-orthodox believed that European liberalism was anti-Islamic. Nevertheless, they described Islam in similar terms. They regard the religion as 'fixed' and often used essentialist terms to describe the believers. At the same time, most neo-orthodox Muslims concede that some measure of government help is necessary to facilitate observance, and they argue that it is possible for Muslims to live separately, but as loyal citizens in the West. And anticlericals would sometimes acknowledge that Islam was important to a close relative, and reluctantly admit that something should probably be done about integrating Islam.

A majority thought that the integration of Islam within European value systems and legal frameworks was nonproblematic, but disagreements existed on the appropriate policy measures and the role of governments. Some feared assimilation to liberal value systems, yet they all stressed choice, individualism, and saw no role for shariah, except as a private matter. They agreed on the need for theological renewal and rethinking, particularly on questions of the role of women. Interestingly, within this camp, I also encountered individuals who shook their head at notions of 'European Islam' and argued that Islam is a faith with plenty of flexibility and is 'good enough' as it is to fit with Western values. They disliked theological discourse and discussions of faith. For them religion is 'something you do' and the less said the better, it seemed. Many stressed the right of European Muslims to exercise their religion and to settle on their own ways of religious observance.

The integrationists worried about the ability of Muslims to practice their faith in acceptable circumstances. They often expressed concern about what they saw as the inadequate training of the existing imams, and the imams' lack of understanding of national cultures and rules. The inability of foreign-trained imams to speak European languages was a frequently mentioned concern, as were worries about 'self-appointed' imams who spoke [political] 'nonsense.'

There are two camps of integrationists. One would like existing church-state policies to be extended to cover Islam. The other favors more autonomy for Muslims to build their own institutions. Both support extending to imams the legal rights and obligations that pastors or priests enjoy. This seems an innocuous demand, at first glance, but it raises complicated questions about the certification of imams, the autonomy of religious communities, and the relationship between religious and secular family law. Legal parity in such matters will invariably, for example, imply that imams also must recognize civil divorces as binding in religious law.

A few imams expressed their concern about lacking legal protection, when they try to help daughters and wives, but because imams are largely independent, women can usually find a sympathetic imam to support their case.[8] A more important problem is that the courts and the state do not recognize the legal standing of Muslim marriages. Consequently, women married in religious ceremonies cannot make claims against their husbands in secular courts, and access to social benefits is often problematic.

Granting the legal obligations and immunities that currently apply to priests and pastors will radically transform the position of imams. It will also change recruitment patterns. It is unlikely that European governments will start extending legal rights and obligations to imams in the absence of a certification requirement.

This did not worry the leaders who wanted to regularize the employment situation of imams, and imams with whom I discussed these issues saw no conflict between religious and secular law (although some supported legal reforms that would give shariah optional legal standing for Muslims.) It was the advocates of a nontraditional 'new theology' who most disliked the idea of formalizing the status of imams, preferring to have recourse to secular law to deal with judicial problems and to religious law for spiritual problems.

THE SECULARISTS: SEEKING EQUITY

Leaving aside for the moment the views of the neo-orthodox, the main disagreements among those who favored the integration and even assimilation of Islam to European established church-state models centered on how much assimilation Muslims should accept. One group, whom I call 'secular integrationists', favors a uniform approach to all religions. This wish to extend existing church-state relations to state–mosque relations sometimes inclines the secularists to support unexpectedly radical solutions. The sentiment is that what applies to other faiths should also apply to Islam. Many secularists prefer the strict separation of church-state and, if this was already the established rule, their first preference is that the state provides no assistance to religion. But given that state neutrality is generally not an option, the secularists want equity. One Muslim councilor from Berlin expressed this view very clearly:

What goes for the Christian confessions goes also for Muslims. So if the Christian churches [the Protestant and Catholic synods] send in clergy to teach religion in public school, then Muslims should be allowed to do that too. But it would be best if we had a change of the constitution and created a completely secular system, in which case there should be no religion taught in schools.[9]

Another city councilor, also from Berlin, wrote in the same vein:

In a multicultural and multireligious society like Germany, there should be compulsory education in ethics which would give all children knowledge of other worldviews and faiths, so they will know how to interact and have a dialogue. Confessional-based education in religion is a mistake and harmful![10]

Secularists often admitted that they had cared little about religion in the past, but had changed their views and come to the conclusion that Islam must be normalized. A central demand is that the education and recruitment of imams must be established in existing universities and other educational institutions. As most European countries have public universities and clergy, except for some minority faiths, are generally educated at theological faculties, governments should step in to ensure that Islamic scholars are taken on by universities to provide instruction in Muslim theology.

A Danish city councilor thought that if pastors are civil servants and paid from taxes, then clergy of all faiths, including Islam, should be supported in the same way. He pointed out that the Scandinavian social democrats had always favored public subsidies for religion, because allowing the state to have a hand in the education and running of religious institutions kept religious sectarianism in check. A free–market approach in religious matters, he explained, is bound to lead to excess, with competitive proselytizing, and entrepreneurial preachers whipping up their flocks for selfish purposes.[11]

For these reasons, and because he personally was loath to pay for religion but recognized that other people felt differently, he would have the mosque financed through taxation and prohibit private funding. He took a cynical view of the Turkish government's continued practice of sending state-educated imams to minister to Turkish communities abroad. 'They want to keep tabs on us and they want our money to keep flowing back to Turkey.' He was equally cynical about the political role of mosques in local politics. Although 'these people' (by which he meant the Danish Turks) vote for the left, and for the social democrats in particular, they are deeply conservative and support conservative causes and groups in Turkey. The European left is mistaken, he thinks, if it assumes it can count on the immigrant Muslim vote. Once the right drops its xenophobia, religious Muslims, who are naturally value-conservatives, would give their support to conservative parties.

Political scientists have concluded that Turks residing in Western Europe are overwhelmingly supportive of left-wing parties. Some studies have estimated that two-thirds of Turkish origin voters tend to support the large social democratic parties.[12] As a consequence, both the right and the left have taken the left-leaning proclivity of Turkish Muslims for granted. But recent research supports the Danish city councilors' intuition and suggests that it is a mistake to do so. Two Turkish political scientists, Ayhan Kaya and Ferhat Kentel, who conducted a survey of German and French Turkish-origin immigrants, found that among those who took an interest in Turkish politics, which turned out to be only about half of the people interviewed, a plurality of about one-third identified the Justice and Development Party, the party of Recep Tayyip Erdogan, as their party. They also found that German Turks (25 percent) were a great deal more likely to vote in Turkish general elections than French Turks (8 percent).[13] A Dutch survey also found much greater support for the Christian Democrats among Turks in the Netherlands than among other immigrant-origin groups, with Dutch Turks splitting themselves evenly between the social democrats and the Christian democrats (16 percent voted for the Greens).[14] It is probably a mistake to take the loyalty of Turkish-origin voters to the left for granted. On the other hand, it is also the case that many Turkish-origin residents in Europe are *not* value-conservatives and Turkish-origin Muslims often hold strongly anticlerical views, like the city councilor who despaired of Turkish conservatism.

Secularists are reluctantly giving in to the cross-pressures they experience between their secular values and their attachments—personal and cultural, and in some case spiritual—to Islam, on the one hand, and their awareness of religious conflict on the other. They often brought up their worries about teenage children or elderly parents in need of spiritual support and cited their personal experiences of bias and discrimination, or recalled anti-Muslim statements by people in high places, when they came to explain how they had reached the conclusion that something has to be done to create 'safe' mosques and to weed out unqualified preachers. Global politics was seldom mentioned, although the French headscarf ban was occasionally raised as an example of how Muslims cannot forget who they are in Europe. However, secularists did often point to the Iraq war or the conflict in Palestine as reasons why Muslims need to organize and become self-aware.

The secularists are averse to theological discussion, and think above all about practical problems and obstacles to the free exercise of religion. They often and freely complain about this or that imam, who talks 'nonsense,' and they worry about politicization by 'the mullahs' or mosque councils. They do not like proselytizing and prefer that people be 'left alone to make up their own minds.' They do not like the headscarf and think Muslims should integrate, if not assimilate; yet they consider the headscarf legislation discriminatory and an infringement of Muslims' rights. 'It is a crime to force a woman to wear a headscarf,' said a Dutch Islamic scholar and religious instructor, who had strongly integrationist preferences, 'and it is a crime to prevent her from wearing it.'[15]

THE VOLUNTARISTS: INTEGRATION
BUT WITH RESERVATIONS

The 'voluntarists' are skeptical of the intentions of Western governments, and worry about the assimilationist pressures associated with accepting public financing. Nevertheless, they agree that public assistance is needed to create educational institutions, and that there should be certification procedures for imams. They disagree with the secularists, however, on the role that governments should play in the general scheme of institution-building and financing for religious institutions, from imam salaries to mosque construction. Their preferred remedies emphasize reliance on private initiative and tax exemptions for mosque communities. A conservative Danish Muslim businessman had no problem with the Lutheran Church's public funding—'it is absolutely OK that the Evangelical-Lutheran Church has privileged status in Denmark, but other faiths should qualify for tax-exempt status.'[16]

The voluntarist approach to the development of Islam is perhaps the most well-developed agenda of the four different approaches described here. It favors the integration of Islam within European society through religious self-government and voluntarism. States are expected to give recognition and respect to European Muslims, and to refrain from putting legal obstacles in the way of religious exercise but, aside from neutrality and equal treatment, the rest is up to European Muslims themselves. In contrast to the secularist integrationists, the voluntarists do not hanker after equality or parity between faiths. They want state neutrality. With time, they say, Muslims will be able to support their own faith. They do not think Islam's value compatibility with European liberalism presents a problem. They assert, as a matter of course, that religious law must be subordinate to secular laws—with the notable exception of gay rights, which they do not think secular states have the right to impose on religious people. Women's rights are uncontroversial.

The voluntarists are pragmatists. They support policies fitted to the national modes of integration and state accommodation for religious exercise. They want to end reliance on foreign funding but they do not want to replace it with state funding from domestic governments, except as a stimulus to self-help. They want to create imam-training institutes in various European countries, and stress the importance of 'modern' imams who speak the language of the country. Imams must be educated people, who are knowledgeable about the legal frameworks and sociological realities that European Muslims live with. Three-fourths of the women in the study held views that put them in this camp.

The voluntarists disagree with the secularists primarily on questions about the legitimate reach of states and in their views on the intentions of governments. They see national integration not as a necessary evil but as a good thing, as a new opportunity for Islam, but they also believe that government should not interfere with the theological development of European Islam. They worry that if governments provide too much financial and institutional support, Muslims will be asked to make concessions that will imperil the faith. The worries are sometimes quite concrete, for example that 'official Islam' will have to condemn women who wear the headscarf. Sometimes the concern is diffuse and centers on the dilution of faith—or religious 'laziness'—that afflicts state-sponsored religion. If public recognition of Islam and religious parity require Muslims to assimilate to national norms and expectations, many leaders prefer a little bit of inequality and less acceptance.

The secularists and the voluntarists agree on many issues. They see eye to eye on the need to subordinate religious law to secular law, about the need to create national seminaries for Islamic education. They want national theological institutions to educate a 'homegrown' Islamic intelligentsia. Both groups consider dependency upon the Islamic countries to be a corrupting influence. They yearn for respectability and want to see Islam represented in Europe by educated and learned men and women.

THE ANTICLERICALS

The anticlericals are suspicious of all established religions. A Danish social democrat declared that all religion is 'old-time superstition.'[17] They acknowledge that Islam is inequitably treated in European countries, but they prefer to eliminate public help and privileges for all religions, Christian or Muslim. Some individuals in this group had formerly been Marxists and they belonged mostly to the left or far left. Ali Lazrak, a Dutch parliamentarian who was expelled from the small Socialist Workers' Party in February 2004 after I spoke with him, is a prominent exponent of the anticlerical view. In Sweden, anticlericalism has become associated with a group known as 'the Iranian Marxists,' a group of political refugees who are now active within the Social Democratic Party. Nevertheless, I also met a few right-wing politicians who expressed anticlerical views.

Other Muslim leaders and colleagues occasionally described the anticlericals disdainfully as the 'Muslim anti-Muslims.' One example is an Iranian political refugee, who came with his parents to Sweden after the Iranian revolution. When I asked him what was the biggest problem for Muslims in Sweden, he did not hesitate to say that they 'find it difficult to accept

Swedish norms and laws,' and excoriated 'the sexism that permeates Islam.'[18] He was also not persuaded that there was any need to built mosques or buildings for religious worship for any other faiths.

A young Dutch woman explained that she does not feel or act as a Muslim, and therefore she is not treated any differently from other Dutch people. And as for the need to make special accommodations for Islamic religious law, she said, 'If you would like a law that is based on Islam, you should find a country to live in that allows that.'[19] She pointed out that the Dutch detest laws against 'hate speech' because they give religious people more rights than nonreligious people. Religious people can say something derogatory about other people, for example that gays are sinners, as long as it is said in the name of faith, but non-religious people cannot respond in kind, she objected.

NATIONAL MODELS AND CHOICES FOR THE INTEGRATION OF ISLAM

Worries about pressures to assimilate to a 'French' or 'Danish' Islam played a large role in shaping policy preferences. Leaders who were unconcerned about the pressures to assimilate were often Social Democrats, and were in general supportive of state provision of social and cultural services in other contexts. Conversely, leaders who mistrusted the intentions of governments wanted to preserve some measure of Muslim autonomy. They invoked minority protections and spoke about religious rights, and worried less about 'religious equality' than 'religious freedom.' Freedom matters more than equal resources, in their view, and they oppose direct government financing for Muslim institutions, although they concede that indirect help and temporary subsidies are required in order to free European Muslims from the need to rely on foreign sources of financing and assistance.

The higher up the Muslim leaders were in the national political system, the more likely they were to be secularists. Nearly all the parliamentarians I spoke to are resolutely secularist and some hold anticlerical views. The neo-orthodox were found either in Muslim associations or as participants in interfaith groups, except in Britain where many city councilors are neo-orthodox.

One explanation of the difference between various elites may be that recruitment to higher office screens out the more religiously conservative leaders. The pressures to assimilate to party conventions are strong on any politician who makes it to the top of the political parties.

Table 3.2 Policy choice for integration of Islam by country of residence

	Denmark (%)	Sweden (%)	France (%)	Germany (%)	Netherlands (%)	UK (%)	Total (%)
Secular integrationist	20.8	37.5	60.0	25.0	13.6	10.7	23.5
Voluntarist	33.3	37.5	30.0	30.6	59.1	17.9	33.8
Anticlericals	33.3	12.5	0.0	22.2	9.1	0.0	14.7
Neo-orthodox	12.5	12.5	10.0	22.2	18.2	71.4	27.9
Total	100.0	100.0	100.0	100.0	100.0	100.0	100.0

$n = 136$

Scandinavian and French Muslims were more likely to support state-centered institutionalization than British, Dutch, and German Muslims, who in contrast tended to favor noninterference by the state in religious affairs. Table 3.2 above displays the distribution of support for the various options for how to integrate Islam across the countries included in the study.

These differences reflect to some extent the different preexisting national frameworks, with public funding for religion already the norm in some countries and banned in others. The study is too small to allow a systematic comparison of the relative importance of ethnic origin and national institutional frameworks in explaining preference patterns. Clearly, the high level of support for voluntarism or traditionalism, both of which go with calls for the state to keep away from the regulation of Islam, corresponds with British and, since 1983, also Dutch norms for the separation of church and state. In contrast, the Scandinavian countries and Germany already provide public funding for the recognized churches (Islam excepted). However, differences of opinion were both less principled and more ambiguous when the discussion turned to specific policies.

ETHNIC ORIGIN AND POLICY PREFERENCES

Muslims of Bangladeshi, Pakistani, or Indian background were disproportionately inclined to subscribe to traditionalist views. British Muslims, or their parents, tend to come from these countries. Muslims of Turkish origin are more inclined to be secular or even anticlerical in their outlook, although those who belong to Milli Görüs tend to be value-conservatives and resist assimilationist pressures. Table 3.3 shows the distribution of Muslim leaders across the four models for religious accommodation by country of origin.

Table 3.3 Policy choice for integration of Islam by country of origin ($n = 132$; 44 missing)

Country of Origin	Secular integrationist	Voluntarist	Anticlerical	Neo-orthodox
Denmark	0	0	0	2
UK	1	1	0	3
Netherlands	0	2	1	3
Germany	2	2	1	4
France	3	2	0	1
Turkey	11	21	14	5
Bosnia-Herzegovina	0	2	0	0
Morocco	4	5	0	0
Arab*	4	2	4	2
Africa**	2	1	0	2
India	1	3	0	2
Pakistan	4	0	0	9
Bangladesh	0	2	0	4
Total	32	43	20	37

* Tunisia, Iraq, Syria, Lebanon, Egypt.
** Ethiopia, Somalia, Ghana, Zanzibar, Malawi.

The relationship between ethnic origin and religious orientation is ambiguous. I identified twelve different ethnic groups among the leaders, each of which had more than three members. (This involved collapsing some African and Arab countries into a generic category of 'Africans' and 'Arabs.') Leaders of Turkish origin may be found in all four categories, but were markedly more inclined towards secularist views than were leaders of South Asian origin. Fourteen of the twenty leaders who were classified as anticlericals came from Turkey. Half of the voluntarists were also of Turkish origin. (Leaders of Turkish origin were the single largest ethnic group in the study, representing 51 out of the 132 leaders who provided information about their origin.)

Fifteen of the thirty-seven neo-orthodox leaders came from South Asia, and no leaders from this background were anticlericals. This supports the anecdotal observation that many Muslims from Pakistan and Bangladesh, and less so from India, often take fairly conservative views of Islam. Nevertheless, there are also many who take a more integrationist position. Surprisingly, the native-born leaders were also predisposed to neo-orthodox views. Many spurious generalizations are made about the second generation, which was described to me as both more and less observant than the first generation. The numbers are small, and it is best not to draw any general conclusion from them.

'EURO-ISLAM': THE SOCIOLOGICAL BASES
FOR THEOLOGICAL REFORM

The secular integrationists and the voluntarists are the driving forces behind what might be described as 'Euro-Islam.' The label is ambiguous because it is used variously to describe a theological project of Islamic renewal and simply to indicate Muslim assimilation to European lifestyles. The *Guardian*, a British newspaper, for instance, used the term in a Pollyannaish essay on Britain's ethnic future to deduce new consumer demands, and proclaimed, 'Euro-Muslims will achieve wealth.' The Internet will encourage more net-working and solidarity between different Muslim communities across bor-ders. Euro-Muslims will increasingly use their numbers to exercise political pressure on governments in matters of concern, for example, Middle East policy. Islam will become a cultural heritage rather than a religious practice for many second-, third-, and fourth-generation Muslims—much as Chris-tianity is for many Europeans today. Elements of Muslim culture will be adopted as counterculture platforms by rebellious and spiritually thirsty Europeans.'[20]

The *Guardian*'s rosy scenario takes a happy ending for granted. True, both Eid ul-Fitr, the end of Ramadan, and Eid ul-Adha, the feast of celebration that follows two months later, have become occasions for Muslims to spend money and occasions for special merchandizing in department stores and supermarkets in large European cities, but the blithe prediction of Muslim assimilation ignores too many questions. Exactly what 'Euro-Islam' will look like is very much under negotiation, and it is by no means certain that the outcome, ten years from now, for example, will be that Muslims think of their faith only as 'cultural heritage.' Nor is it at all clear that the majority society will think of 'Muslim' as an ethnic or a cultural category, similar to, for example, 'Jewish' or 'Italian.'

Another usage is suggested by the addition of a national label. In Sweden, references are made to 'blue-yellow' Islam to suggest the blending of Islam with essential Swedish qualities. The linking of Islam with the national colors creates a sports metaphor, which suggests that the Muslim 'team' could play in Swedish colors.

Social scientists sometimes use the term Euro-Islam to describe the socio-logical processes of community formation, or assimilation to European reli-gious-cultural patterns of behavior.[21] Some European Muslims use the term to describe a strategic goal, or a program that demands both theological innov-ation and sociological adaptation. A Danish Muslim student organization,

Kritiske Muslimer, describes Euro-Islam as an objective and an open-ended process of self-realization. 'In Europe, one can observe a moderate form of Islam that is described as "Euro-Islam." There is no definitive definition of the concept just as there are no fixed definitions of what Islam is or it means to be a Muslim. We can describe Euro-Islam as a tendency, a movement, and a dynamic process.'[22]

This group espouses the ideas of Tariq Ramadan, a controversial Swiss-born professor, who has become a proponent of Islamic renewal. Ramadan has urged European Muslims to 'be at the same time fully Muslim and fully Western.'[23] His 1998 book, *To Be a European Muslim*, has been translated into fourteen languages and his taped lectures are distributed at meetings and conventions of young Muslims everywhere in Europe. I encountered study groups using his books in Sweden, Denmark, and the Netherlands, and many people made references to Ramadan's 'five basic principles' in interviews. The principles are, says Ramadan, 'a virtual consensus among both Islamic experts and the Muslim communities of Europe.'

The first principle is that Muslims need not worry about conflict between being a good Muslim and living in the West, and can participate fully in public life and should embrace without reservation the idea that they can live full lives and be Muslims in the West. 'The old concept of the dar-al-harb ("the land of war," i.e. territory controlled by unbelievers) is outdated,' said Ramadan, and other concepts that put 'the Muslim presence in Europe in more positive terms' should be used.[24] In his newest book, Ramadan goes further and argues that European Muslims have a historic opportunity to develop a purer version of Islam freed of the ethnic practices and diversions that characterize religious exercise in the Muslim world. His ideas excite many young people, native-born Muslims in particular. Ramadan has many critics, also among Muslims. The skeptics do not disagree on the fact; they accept that European Islam will be different. They disagree about the need for a new theology or, alternatively, they have no need for theology. 'Islam is just fine as it is,' one person said, 'the problem is with public policy.'[25] Interestingly, many neo-orthodox who are otherwise cautious about accepting the practical and legal constraints of institutional integration, are also supportive of the notion that Islamic theology should and will change to reflect the social and political realities of living in Europe.

NB The Euro-Muslim agenda combines a new and pragmatic epistemology of Islamic flexibility with a practical approach to public policy that accepts the dual imperatives of integration and institutionalization. It respects the community's prerogative to decide the pace and extent of integration, but integration is the goal. It has to be accomplished without seemingly giving in to pressures to assimilate and sterilize Islam to suit the tastes of biased European publics and governments. However, attempts to constrain Islamic observance by legislation, through measures such as the headscarf bans or prohibitions on ritual slaughter, force many Muslims to worry about how to promote integration while retaining autonomy.

THE NEO-ORTHODOX

It is a mistake to think that religious traditionalism (or neo-orthodoxy, which is the more accurate label) conflicts with liberal commitments. The complexity of the relationship between religious orientation and political values is illustrated by the fact that many of the most pious leaders in the study identified their political orientation as either centrist or on the left. The neo-orthodox did not argue for turning Europe into a Caliphate but for the right to exist as a religious minority and to live, by choice, according to religious law. I did not encounter anyone who argued for the forcible imposition of Islamic law on Western states—not even the radical imam who declared that human rights were good because they allowed radicals like him to carry on the quest for an Islamic revival.

The neo-orthodox reject both what they see as attempts to 'Westernize' Islam and the Islamist politicization of Islam. Devout Muslim leaders regard the Islamist fringe groups as parasitic and abusers of Islam. Mosque community leaders who oversee pastoral activities speak freely about their fear of infiltration by radicals and of the dangers of extremism among young men in the local communities. This is, of course, denied by radicals. The radical Danish imam cited earlier in this chapter insisted that the dangers of radicalism are entirely invented by governments and by those who hate Islam.

The fringe groups are sociologically and theologically different from the neo-orthodox. The followers of these groups are young radicals, sometimes converts, and often university students or urban dropouts. The neo-orthodox, in contrast, are men and women based in mosque organizations, engaged in local politics, or affiliated with the new national Muslim associations. Some are imams and religious scholars. They often mentioned one or another of the radical groups as examples of the dangerous politicization of Islam and 'bad' theology. 'They are not really Muslims,' people would occasionally say to me to put as much distance as possible between themselves, their faith, and the extremist Islamists. 'In my opinion,' Imam Abduljalil Sajid, a shariah law expert, says, 'the word "Islam" should be used exclusively for the Divine way of Life based upon its divine sources: The Holy Book known as Quran, the word of God, and Sunnah, the proven practices of the Holy Prophet.' He argued, with the literalist perspective of a religious scholar, that the political fundamentalists should be described simply as 'criminals' and disbarred from using the term 'Islam' to describe their project.[26]

N.B- The neo-orthodox care a great deal about religious doctrine. One exponent of neo-orthodoxy, who was associated with a British Muslim association, responded to my question about the need to use the flexibility of Islam to develop something you can call an Islam with British character, that 'the basic tenets of Islam are not for "modification," and are such that they can be applied in any culture which allows the freedom to practice cultural values, which until very recently was the case in Europe.'[27] In this view, Islam is not up for interpretation. 'Islam is what it is,' was a typical statement made by the neo-orthodox in response to my questions about the need to adjust to European norms and behaviors.

Because they regard the hadith and the Koran as the authoritative sources of faith, they argue that it is meaningless to speak of Islamic theology because religious scholarship is about reading the book and knowing tradition. They believe in authority and in the derogation of interpretation to the experts. A minority of the neo-orthodox thinks it is best to continue to bring imams and scholars from the Islamic world, because they are better schooled in Islam and tradition than anybody educated in Europe can be expected to be.

They stress that the Koran tells Muslims to obey the law of the land they live in, but their emphasis upon the binding nature of Islamic religious law for Muslim individuals nevertheless creates tensions with secular personal law, particularly in family law cases and especially in matters related to marriage and the dissolution of marriage. The neo-orthodox support amending secular law to allow for the codification and application of religious law in secular courts. There are precedents for these kinds of arrangements, which are often described as 'legal pluralism,' in British court cases that involve adjudication in matters of personal law between noncitizen British residents, when courts are obliged to take foreign law into consideration, and in Canada and the state of New York, where orthodox Jews have acquired the right to have religious law applied in secular courts.

HOW TO BE MUSLIM AND SECULAR

The culture war thesis invokes a view of Muslims as remote-controlled agents for a hostile culture that is antagonistic to liberal individualism. As the findings discussed here show, the commitment to faith and cultural identity remains important among Muslim leaders but views vary widely about how daily life and political institutions should reflect those commitments. European Muslim leaders are overwhelmingly secular in outlook and supportive of core liberal values about individual choice and the separation of religion and politics.

The need for domestically educated imams is widely accepted and this implies support for policy change and for the adaptation of scriptural interpretation and a new hermeneutics of theological debate and knowledge accumulation. Large majorities agreed that imams and Islamic scholars should be educated locally, particularly in Denmark and Great Britain, where four out of five agreed with this proposition.[28] The importance of the issue was confirmed in my conversations with parliamentarians and city councilors, where my interlocutors brought it up in different contexts but invariably as a matter of urgency.

'What good is a Saudi Arabian imam to me?' asked Yasin Ahmed, of the Stockholm mosque. 'I am a Swedish Muslim. The Saudi Arabian imam does not understand my life and who I have become.'[29] Parents talked about how difficult it is to find educated imams who speak the language of their children, be it Dutch, Danish, Swedish, or even English.

Imams and Islamic scholars and instructors also worried aloud and at length about the difficulties of recruiting imams and the lack of recognized national theological institutions.[30] Concerns about imam recruitment touch upon multiple issues ranging from pastoral care and the ability to build stable religious communities to the public presence of Islam in interfaith dialogue, the media, and negotiations with local and national governments.

Revelations about rogue imams recruiting among disaffected youth cause Muslim leaders much concern for reasons of both national security and legitimacy. 'Every time one of those idiots get caught,' said a Danish imam, 'things get much worse for the rest of us.' The lack of university-level institutions capable of representing Islam and educating Islamic scholars and clerics is a welfare problem as well as a problem for the institutionalization and integration of Islam. The anticlericals excepted, the general consensus is that European Muslims will not be comfortable until it becomes possible to educate a European Islamic intelligentsia and a cadre of religious scholars, a new ulema, but ideas about how to achieve this objective within a reasonable timeframe are in short supply.

It is important to acknowledge that religious revival does not necessarily take the path of fundamentalism. Fundamentalism implies a rejection of pluralism of faith, a return to literal readings of the scripture, and the assertion of a timeless religious community. The religious revival that the leaders described to me takes the opposite form. It regards Islam as a historically and contextually defined faith, and sees adjustment and adaptation to European lifestyles as a source of innovation and revitalization. Language and culture matter as sources of pluralism and difference. Respect for national law and the subordination of religious law to secular law are high priorities. Faith is a matter of the individual's spiritual choice, and as I was repeatedly told, 'no one can decide who is a good Muslim and who isn't.'

Neo-orthodoxy is part of the revival but it is only one stream. It is their free commitment to neo-traditionalist religious observance that sets the neo-orthodox European (or American) Muslim apart from the Islamist or the Salafist from the Islamic world. In Europe, religious commitment often becomes a source of countercultural identity, but it is invariably also a highly individualist choice.

As has been the case among orthodox Jews, the neo-orthodox blend a modern lifestyle with self-chosen commitments to traditionalist interpretations of religious obligations, albeit with modifications. Educated and professional women embrace and simultaneously defy tradition by turning to the Torah or the Koran, and by insisting that they and not the imam or the rabbi read the book and draw their own conclusions.[31] The family is a unit of power and authority, and feminists will disagree about how equitable gender relations can be in a family where the differences between men and women are taken as religiously given. Nevertheless, one should never jump to conclusions about how neo-orthodox women behave and interpret their faith.

Aminah Mohammad-Arif describes how young South Asian Muslims in the USA, who are overwhelmingly highly educated professionals, react to what is perceived as discrimination and integration by dedicating themselves to religious immersion. They do not turn to the local mosque or imam for instructions on spiritual matters, but pursue self-discovery through independent religious studies and set up their own Koran reading groups. She cites as a typical expression of this sentiment the following statement:

What I love in the US is that we can practice the Islamic religion in the purest way, without all the cultural stuff of the first generation.[32]

In practice, neo-orthodoxy is a demanding lifestyle and involves protracted engagement with reinventions and reinterpretations of religious texts and doctrines. The fallacy of regarding neo-orthodox religiosity as 'fundamentalist' is particularly evident when women choose to 'have it all': conservative theology, professional careers, and feminism.

ISLAM AND HUMAN RIGHTS

One frequently made argument for mutuality between Christianity and Islam
is that dignity and respect are essential and shared values in the two religions.
One version of the argument is that Islam recognizes Jesus as a Prophet, and
that Christians should therefore extend recognition to the Prophet, Mohammed. The young woman cited at the beginning of the chapter who had started
a student group that focused on reinterpreting the Koran, thought that
conflict could be prevented if Christians and Muslims extended mutual
recognition to each other and regarded each others' faith as equally valid.[33]
The Swedish doctor, who explained the universalistic principles of Islam, also
stressed that it is incumbent upon any Muslim to extend charity to another
person irrespective of his or her faith. Many people stressed that Islam
recognizes all prophets as deserving of respect, and has no problem coexisting
with other faiths. In Britain, several people argued that it is unthinkable that a
Muslim would say derogatory things about Jesus, and therefore blasphemy
laws should be extended so Muslims can have the same right to respect against
blasphemy that Christians have. These might be described as faith-based
arguments for human rights and the obligation to treat all human beings
with dignity and respect. Religious Muslims are comfortable with concepts of
'equal worth' and 'dignity,' concepts which in Europe have often been advanced by Catholic social activists. They are less inclined to use the socialist
tradition's equivalent terms, 'rights' and 'equality.'

N.B.

Not all appeals to human rights were as sincere. A Danish imam invoked
human rights as an opportunity for the exile community to use Europe as a
base for bringing religious renewal and 'the failed Islamic project' to the Arab
world. He praised human rights as a god-given opportunity to praise Allah
and to seek conversions. Although he was careful to say also that political
violence is unacceptable, he was an Islamist in the sense that his goal was the
creation of an Islamic constitution. He repeatedly denounced Europeans
for not living up to their own ideals when they criticized radicals like him.[34]
He also made it clear that his objective was to use liberalism to restore Islam to
its rightful place and so to diminish the scope of the secular state. Other
religions, he implied, would have the same protection that Islam had been
given. It was a chilling message that caused me to consider where my own
boundaries for toleration might be. The appropriation of human rights for a
fundamentalist cause gave me pause, as did the barely concealed threat
implied by the invocation of reciprocity to imply moral equivalence.

?

an ultra-montane Catholic bishop
in 19th century U.S.A.

More often, however, I encountered generous and principled defenses of human rights, such as that made by a British Liberal Democrat, who was faithful to his party's historical opposition to the privileged position of the Church of England and fully committed to the separation of church and state. He favored the extension of antidiscrimination legislation to cover religion, but this (then) city councilor was entirely consistent in his Kantianism. He opposed public funding for Islam and any remedies for the current difficulties that would involve special protection for Islam and Muslims. In his view, human rights involve a radical commitment to the reciprocal respect of all faiths, lifestyles, sexual orientations, etc. He strongly supports antidiscrimination enforcement, even if that means that Muslims would have to accept gay or female imams because that is what the commitment to human rights is about: nondiscrimination.[35] And he was lukewarm about proposals to extend blasphemy laws to Islam and favored instead the abolition of current laws, which restrict free speech to protect Christians against blasphemy.

More commonly, no particular right or principle was invoked, and the demands for equal treatment of Muslims were framed as a generalized evocation of the right to dignity or some unspecified norms of equality. Occasionally someone would refer to the 1948 United Nations Declaration's Article 1, which states simply: 'All human beings are born free and equal in dignity and rights.' The more common reference was to the right to practice one's faith, which is listed in the UN Declaration's Article 2: 'Everyone is entitled to all the rights and freedoms set forth in this Declaration, without distinction of any kind, such as race, color, sex, language, religion, political or other opinion, national or social origin, property, birth or other status.' A common remark, however, was, 'you know, they signed the Declaration but it means nothing at home.' A few people complained, 'they will always say, why don't you fix the problems in the Islamic world first' or 'once you tolerate Christians, we will tolerate Muslims.' And then add, 'but, you know, I am refugee from there.'[36]

NOTES

1. *The Sunday Times* (London) (May 30, 2004).
2. The shariah is the code of law derived from the Koran and from the teachings of the Prophet. It is the task of religious scholars to interpret the meaning of the shariah and how religious law applies to the circumstances of present-day issues.

3. Gerd Baumann, *Contesting Culture. Discourses of Identity in Multi-Ethnic London* (Cambridge: Cambridge University Press, 1996).

4. Interview 20, Copenhagen (September 15, 2003).

5. Interview 82, Lyon (May 24, 2004).

6. I worried after speaking with him that I might end up misclassifying him as 'neo-orthodox,' because of his opposition to national institution-building. I subsequently checked my coding, and discovered that he—correctly—had been labeled 'unclassifiabel.'

7. Questionnaire 02.81.

8. There are parallels among orthodox Jews, where women whose husbands deny them a religious divorce after the collapse of the marriage are unable to remarry in an orthodox synagogue. If the woman remarries in civil ceremony, the children are considered illegitimate.

9. Questionnaire 05.44.

10. Questionnaire 05.10.

11. Interview 22, Copenhagen (September 16, 2003).

12. Andreas Goldberg and Martina Sauer, *Konstanz und Wandel der Lebensituation türkishstämmiger Migranten in Nordrhein-Westfalen* (Essen: Zentrum für Turkeistudien, 2003), Table 34; Lise Togeby, 'Migrants at the polls: an analysis of immigrant and refugee participation in Danish local elections,' *Journal of Ethnic and Migration Studies*, 25 (1999), 4: 665–684.

13. Ayhan Kaya and Ferhat Kentel, 'Euro-Turks: A Bridge or a Breach between Turkey and the European Union?' A Research Report, Center for Migration Research, Istanbul Bilgi University (September 2004).

14. Eddie Nieuwenhuizen, 'Political participation of migrants in the Netherlands,' Research Report, Landelijk Bureau ter bestriding van Rassendscriminatie (no date).

15. Interview 61, Rotterdam (November 24, 2003).

16. Questionnaire 01.19.

17. Questionnaire 01.42.

18. Questionnaire 02.13.

19. Questionnaire 04.53.

20. *Guardian*, Special Report (January 9, 1999).

21. Press Release (February 8, 2002);
    http://www.uni-essen.de/zft/news/mitteilung/en/2002.

22. http://www.kritiskemuslimer.dk/euroislam.htm.

23. *Christian Science Monitor* (May 19, 2003). Available at:
    http://www.csmonitor.com/2003/0519/p07s02-woeu.htm.

24. Tariq Ramadan, 'Europe's Muslims find a place for themselves,' *Le Monde Diplomatique*. April 1998.

25. Interview 25, London (October 10, 2003).

26. Interview, Oxford (July 24, 2004).

27. Questionnaire 03.71.

28. The statement to which respondents were asked to agree or disagree was: 'We should educate imams and Islamic scholars here because they can translate Islamic principles to the life of Muslims living outside the Islamic world.'
29. Interview 49, Stockholm (November 4, 2003).
30. Yvonne Yazbeck Haddad, 'The Globalization of Islam. The Return of Muslims to the West,' in John L. Esposito (ed.), *The Oxford History of Islam* (Oxford: Oxford University Press, 1999), 625.
31. Debra R. Kaufman, *Rachel's Daughters: Newly Orthodox Jewish Women* (New Brunswick, NJ Rutgers University Press, 1991); Lynn Davidman, *Tradition in a Rootless World: Women Turn to Orthodox Judaism* (Berkeley: University of California Press, 1991).
32. Aminah Mohammad-Arif, 'Young South Asian Muslim Identity in the US,' unpublished paper (no date), 9.
33. Interview 2, Copenhagen (September 4, 2003).
34. Interview 17, Copenhagen (September 12, 2003).
35. Interview 23, Oxford (October 9, 2003).
36. Interview 10, Copenhagen (September 9, 2003); Interview 57, Rinkeby (November 6, 2003).

4

From Integration to Culture War

Islam has quickly become a part of the accommodating religious landscape in the USA, and Muslims were added to the already existing 'rainbow-coalition' of religions.[1] In Europe, religious pluralism is a new social fact that has yet to be fitted into legal frameworks and public practices. Indeed, institutions established long before the arrival of significant Islamic minorities have found it difficult to respond to the needs of Muslims who have decided that they need to build their own religious institutions and are no longer content to rely on pastoral services from the 'old country.'

A painful reconsideration of the role of religion in public policy has begun in Europe, but so far with contradictory results. On the right, politicians assert the importance of Christian values to European identity in ways that marginalize and even denigrate Muslims. On the left, lawmakers tend to think that states should not fund religion at all and stress principles of state neutrality and secularism. They would eliminate all funds for religion, if they could, and are unwilling to support public funding for conservative religious Muslims. On the right, politicians are often tied to the Christian establishment and favor protecting current privileges given to the national churches. Yet, as immigrants and their children settle and become citizens, their aspirations must be taken into account by political parties and the state. And since security issues have risen to the top of the agenda since September 2001, it is obvious that governments must find ways to promote the institutional assimilation of Islam, or else they will leave the door open for Islamic countries and movements to assume sponsorship of immigrant communities.

In practice, many current conflicts have little to do with any global 'clash of civilizations' and everything to do with often tedious details of policymaking and the application of norms and rules. These range from zoning rules that inhibit the construction of mosques to workplace regulations that do not accommodate prayer schedules or religious holidays and animal welfare laws that prohibit or restrict access to ritual slaughter.

To be sure, Islam is not the only minority religion to suffer discrimination. Hindus as well as Muslims cannot follow traditional burial practices in municipal cemeteries. Baptists may also have trouble financing the education of their clergy in the same way as Muslims do. Scientology is a prohibited sect in Germany and France. Many of the problems experienced by Muslims—sometimes more severely than other groups—are the product of European frameworks for the exercise of religion. Nevertheless, Muslims do have particular problems.

The conflicts are repeated across Europe, with slight variations in themes and emphasis and despite different national legal and religious contexts. The same questions crop up again and again. Who should do the adjusting? What legal changes are required? All six of the countries in my study provide public funding for independent schools, including religious schools, but Muslims have found it difficult to establish schools in practice, and their schools are often subjected to extreme scrutiny. Controversy over Muslim dress, from the headscarf to the more severe jilbab (a floor-length coat-like dress that is worn with a headscarf that covers the forehead and neck), has produced court cases everywhere, although only in France and Germany has the headscarf been banned in particular contexts. Muslims have found it difficult to bury their relatives in municipal cemeteries. Ritual slaughter, coeducational physical education, the teaching of Islam in school curricula, arranged marriages, the provision of prayer rooms at work and in educational institutions; these are some of the issues, large and small, that have captured the public mind and occupied local and national policymakers. The list lends credence to the perception that Islam and Europe are on the brink of a 'culture war' due to the unwillingness of Muslims to accept secular norms. However, Europeans tend to ignore the fact that their established norms and policies are not necessarily secular, but may reflect long-standing practices that were instituted in order to appease national churches.

Consider three case studies of controversies that have evolved over the past decade. Each centers on one country but has parallels in other countries. The first is about a decade-long struggle to open an Islamic cemetery in Denmark. The second case study details the efforts to educate imams in Britain. Two degree programs have been established with ties to universities, but structural problems persist. The third case is the story of how kosher slaughter was allowed under a religious exemption from German animal protection law but halal slaughter disallowed. In 2002, the German Constitutional Court in theory permitted Muslims the same exemption to carry out ritual slaughter that Jews enjoyed, but the court based its decision on a regulatory model for oversight of businesses that left many obstacles in place.

AN ISLAMIC CEMETERY FOR DANISH MUSLIMS

The national Lutheran Church—Folkekirken, or the People's Church—has near-total control over the burial process. Danish law provides the Lutheran Church with the responsibility of registering all births and deaths, as well as the exclusive administration of cemeteries. All deaths must be reported within forty-eight hours to the municipal church office, the office of the local pastor in the national church, irrespective of the deceased's religious affiliation. Everybody has a right to a funeral and burial in the local church and cemetery. It is more or less also the only option available. People may also petition the Minister for permission to scatter the ashes of the dead over the ocean, provided that environmental rules are observed.

Denmark's old religious minorities include about 6,000 Jews, about 34,000 Catholics, and small communities of Baptists, Methodists, and Jehovah's Witnesses. The Jewish community is unaffected by the Lutheran Church's legal monopoly, as it was given special royal permission to buy land for burial grounds, first in 1675 in a provincial town, Fredericia, with a history of accommodating dissidents, and then in 1794 in Copenhagen. Catholics have made special arrangements with some twenty cemeteries belonging to the national church.

There are 250,000 Muslims in Denmark but the country has no Islamic cemetery. Families can at present send the bodies of relatives (in special zinc caskets) back to the countries of origin to be buried there. Alternatively, they can negotiate with local Lutheran pastors and church councils for permission to bury the deceased in a spot in a local cemetery reserved for what used to be called the 'nonbelievers.' (The church authorities have recently adjusted the terminology and now speak of 'nonmembers' to connote the 15 percent of the population who belong to minority religions, of which Islam is the largest.)

At present, five cemeteries belonging to the national Lutheran Church have created special sections, where Muslims may be buried. By law, all burials, take place in a casket or by cremation. Given the difficulty this requirement imposes on Muslims, the Ministry of Ecclesiastical Affairs—'the Church Ministry'—announced in 2002 that, if the local parish council gives permission, Muslims may petition the Minister, who is also the head of the national Lutheran Church, for permission to follow Islamic burial requirements and hold a burial without using a casket. The opportunity to seek ministerial permission to follow ritual burial requirements is the result of a long and difficult conflict, in which some pastors and parish councils have taken the side of Muslims and others have objected to any concession.

Muslims who wish to use the nonsacred part of the cemetery must pay, like other nonmembers of the Lutheran Church. The fee is about $250. The Church Ministry publishes a price list for the acquisition of burial plots and maintenance, to be applied by local church authorities. Plots are free for the 85 percent of the population who are members of the national church, and they are also given discounted prices for other services.

The fee is not the difficulty. Local church councils have refused to let Muslims use nonsacred ground in the cemeteries for reasons of space constraint. Danes often prefer cremation. Urns do not take up much space. Muslims do not use cremation. Other complaints are that Muslims want to be buried at odd angles because the dead must face Mecca. Lutheran graves face in the direction of sunrise. Muslims do not allow burial plots to be disturbed and think of a grave as an eternal resting spot. Used to efficient land use, Danish custom is to reuse burial plots after twenty-five years. Some municipal cemetery councils have allowed Muslims to be buried in nonsacred areas of the cemeteries but without following Islamic ritual requirements.

A coalition of civic groups has tried to establish Muslim cemeteries. They have several times located suitable land, but a thicket of zoning and land use rules as well as environmental regulations have presented insurmountable obstacles. Lack of funds is another impediment. Danish Muslims came as labor migrants in the 1960s and 1970s, or have arrived in recent decades as political refugees. They are generally poor, and land in Denmark is expensive.

Pastors and local church authorities from the tax-supported national Lutheran Church have argued that it is unconstitutional for the government to use tax money to help the Muslim minority. In support, they cite Article 68 of the Danish constitution, which prohibits making anyone pay for faiths other than their own. Representatives of minority religions argue that current arrangements violate this paragraph and it supports their case. Religious minorities note that the paragraph allows taxpayers who prove that they are not members of the national church to be exempted from paying direct church taxes. Church taxes are collected together with general taxes by the national treasury and administrated by the Ministry of Ecclesiastical Affairs. But the Lutheran Church is partly financed also by general taxes and consequently non-Lutherans, including Muslims, are made to contribute to the Church. Changing this arrangement would mean either ending the Lutheran Church's special privileges, which most Danes strongly oppose, or allowing minority religions an arrangement similar to that used to support it. The prospects for reform are poor, and in the meantime, the cemetery initiative turned to government for help.

In Fall 2001, a mayor of a suburb of Copenhagen announced that he had a suitable piece of land that he would sell to the Muslim community to create a cemetery. The government—at the time, Social Democratic—proclaimed that a solution had been found. When it turned out that the land the mayor was selling did not belong to him but was the property of the municipality of Copenhagen, responsibility for the transaction fell to the mayor of Copenhagen. The latter had expressed enthusiasm for the idea before he knew who the real owner of the land was. However, he found himself obligated to act. Copenhagen decided to proceed with the sale, but the project stalled for lack of money. The Social Democratic government decided to appropriate 18 million Danish crowns, approximately $2.5 million, for the project, but the appropriation was stopped on a floor vote in parliament by a filibuster from the Danish People's Party, a xenophobic and anti-Muslim party. Shortly afterwards an election was called, which the Social Democratic government lost. The election brought a new center-right minority government to power, which depended upon the People's Party for its governing majority.

Tove Fergo, the new Minister of Ecclesiastical Affairs (she has since moved on), who was herself a parish pastor in the Lutheran Church, explained the new government's position by pointing out that it was not proper for the state to subsidize a Muslim cemetery. 'The way it is in Denmark,' Ms Fergo said, 'is that the members of the People's Church pay for their burial plots, citizens who aren't members of any faith pay for their burial plots, and the Mosaic Community pay for theirs, and religions outside the official church pay for theirs.' She concluded that since everybody in Denmark pays for their own burial plots, there is no need for Muslims to be treated differently and to have their cemetery financed by the state.[2] She neglected to mention, however, that there is no Islamic cemetery and that the People's Church holds a monopoly on cemetery land. Although it is possible for Muslims to be buried in a Lutheran churchyard—or in a municipal cemetery designed according to Protestant norms—a Muslim cannot be interred in sacred soil. The minister also did not mention that the Lutheran cemeteries are public property and that the caretakers are public employees. In sum, Muslims help pay for Christians to be buried but Christians are disallowing Muslims to have a religious interment.

On February 9, 2005, the right-wing government was reelected. The Danish People's Party gained votes, and as the third largest parliamentary faction it provides the minority government with the votes it needs to stay in power. For the Social Democrats, it was the worst election since 1920. At the time of writing, no progress has been made on establishing a cemetery. Nor does Denmark have a single purpose-built mosque.

A twisted causal chain runs from a handful of Muslim immigrants looking to bury their dead following religious rules to the collapse of a sympathetic government, which illustrates how mundane matters of public policy can become the symbolic focus of a 'culture war.' The first obstacle is the clash of practices between Christian and Islamic burial customs. It is a matter of public policy because current rules cannot easily be adjusted to accommodate Muslims in the absence of a forthright assessment of the public privileges enjoyed by the Lutheran Church. Political reluctance on the part of local politicians to help Muslims were overcome, perhaps because there are enough Muslim voters in Copenhagen that the city's mayor saw good reasons to be responsive to their needs. Had the Muslim community's poverty not been an issue, there might have been no need for government assistance beyond the need for a permit from the Minister of Ecclesiastical Affairs. But the effort to create a Muslim cemetery in the suburbs of Copenhagen became an issue in national electoral politics, inviting large statements about the centrality of certain practices and norms—Lutheran versus Muslim—to Danish law and identity.

Conflicts over Muslim burials and unaccommodating cemeteries are common all over Europe. France is committed to a public philosophy of strict secularism—*laïcité*—and Denmark to a national Lutheran Church, but the difficulties are strikingly similar. Sometimes local authorities are accommodating, but mostly they are not. Aside from Sweden, which recently issued directives to all cemetery councils to work with local imams to facilitate proper Muslim burial practices, no laws stipulate equitable access to religious burial. In both France and Denmark, as is the case across Europe, cemeteries are generally owned by municipalities and fall under the control of mayors, city councils, or independent boards with clerical representation. And most cemeteries, despite their public nature, are run following Christian burial practices.[3]

A team of French journalists and sociologists who tried to chart the availability of cemeteries for Muslims published a report in December 2004. They found a severe lack of burial space. The authors identified seventy locations across France that accommodated Muslims.[4] In these cemeteries, Muslims are allowed a special area so that burial may take place facing Mecca rather than east, as is the Christian custom. The largest is Thiais, which is managed by the mayor of Paris. A tourist destination because of its many memorials, including one for the Second World War Resistance, Thiais became a municipal cemetery under the 1905 law which separated church and state in France. The law transferred ownership of many church properties to the municipalities, and although the rules of operation reflect Roman Catholic norms, Thiais has special sections for other faiths.[5] The report noted that, aside from permitting the different orientation, there was no difference between the Muslim section and other sections. Non-Muslim spouses may be buried next to a Muslim. Some graves are decorated with pictures of the deceased, in breach of the proscription in Islam against human and animal pictures in sacred spaces. While this may be unproblematic and even a gain for secular Muslims, the consequence is that believers have no alternative compatible with a stricter interpretation of the requirements of Islam.

WHERE DO IMAMS COME FROM?

There are about 250 mosques in Sweden, 150 in Denmark, 400 in the Netherlands, and probably 1,500 each in Britain and in France.[6] A recent survey put the number of mosques in Germany at 2,600.[7] There is at least one imam attached to each mosque, and in many cases two or three. The single largest source of imams in northern Europe—with the exception of Britain—is the Turkish government. When 'guest workers' began to appear in large numbers in Scandinavia, Germany, and the Netherlands, the governments of those countries entered into contracts with Turkey to supply pastoral care for what was at the time considered to be a temporary population of Muslims. Although church and state are formally separated in Turkey, the Turkish government oversees Muslim religious facilities and education through its directorate of religious affairs, the Diyanet. The Diyanet regulates the operation of Turkey's 75,000 mosques, and employs local and provincial imams, who are civil servants. It also supplies imams—or *hoyas*—to Turkish communities resident abroad. The imams are paid by the Turkish government while abroad, and are granted temporary visas, usually for up to four years, by the national governments. Turkey sends imams to Scandinavia, the Netherlands, Germany, and France. France also has country-to-country contracts with Algeria. Diyanet imams account at the most for 10–15 percent of all imams in these countries. No one knows where the rest come from or what education they have, if any.

The local supply of imams in Europe is severely restricted by the lack of institutions for training them. As a result, most come from abroad. Of those who are European citizens, some are autodidacts and part-timers who have been recruited from within the immigrant community. Some are religious entrepreneurs, who make a living out of the mosque. A few are converts or second generation Muslims who, at their own expense, travel to Islamic universities in Egypt or Saudi Arabia to become Islamic scholars.[8] Many mosque communities do not have an imam but are served only by a *khatib*, someone who leads prayers on Friday, and many mosque councils cannot afford regular pay for imams.

Beginning in September 2004, new Home Office rules for 'overseas ministers of religion' came into effect in Britain. The rules require 'imams and priests [...] to show knowledge of, and engagement with, British civic life, including an understanding of other faiths' within a year of having been in the country. David Blunkett, then the Home Secretary, said, 'We hope that faith groups will continue to work closely with us during the second half of the year to ensure that overseas ministers of religion, like all migrants, engage with the communities in which they live.' The new rules further require 'imams and priests to have professional qualifications,' but it is not clear how 'professional qualifications' can be determined. The Muslim Council of Britain supported the new rules.[9]

The British rules are not exceptional. Several other European governments have implemented more restrictive rules with the aim of regulating the recruitment of imams from abroad. The Dutch authorities have imposed similar requirements, but in addition require that imams attend a compulsory 'introduction course' and take a language test. Turkish government-funded imams are taught German before they are allowed to transfer to Germany. New Danish rules prohibit the issue of visas to imams who do not already speak Danish, and only Danish-speaking imams have permission to conduct marriages. The effectiveness of such rules is questionable. Few new mosques are being built, and those in existence already have imams. Another issue is whether it makes sense to close the door to imported imams in the absence of educational opportunities at home, in the form of recognized Islamic seminaries or training programs within existing theological faculties. Where the recruitment of imams is difficult, religious leadership often falls to autodidacts.

Most British imams are trained abroad and recruited by local mosque councils. There are thought to be about 2,000 imams in Britain, under ten percent of whom have been trained in the UK. So long as a mosque council guarantees that it will provide an income for the imam, work permits have not usually been a problem. But Muslim community elders tend to recruit from the villages that they come from. Imams recruited in this way have often been educated in madrassas—Islamic seminaries that are dedicated to particular versions of Islamic law dating from the ninth or tenth century. When they come to Britain, there is no additional training or oversight. 'They are honest men and I do not blame them,' said Moulana Shahid Raza, from the Muslim College in Ealing, west London, 'but they are like people driving a car without having learnt how to do it.'

The Muslim College in Ealing is trying to address the issue of local training for British imams. It offers a diploma in Islamic studies in collaboration with Birkbeck College of London University. Women are admitted and wearing the hijab is optional. The college is nonsectarian and focuses on textual interpretation of the Koran. But the course also stresses the importance of critical skills and of relating beliefs and practices to the British context. Interfaith dialogue, mosque administration, and social studies are part of the curriculum. The college also offers a separate master's degree in imamship. The head and founder of the college, Zaki Badawi, hopes that mosque councils will eventually require a certificate from imams, like the one his college offers, before they are employed.

The Markfield Institute of Higher Education in Leicestershire offers Britain's second program in Islamic chaplaincy. It is associated with the Islamic Foundation, a decades-old center of Islamic education, and is affiliated with Loughborough University. The Markfield Institute and the Muslim College annually produce only about fifty graduates from their imam courses. Another twenty-five more traditional seminaries are operating in Britain, where imams are educated following course plans that are transposed unchanged from Islamic countries, and in which the language of instruction is Arabic or Urdu.

As in other European countries, British politicians and civil servants are proposing to educate imams at home and considering ways to restrict or manage the inflow of foreign imams. A new requirement is that they demonstrate a command of the English language and an understanding of British society as a condition to receive a visa. A Muslim Labour peer, Nazir Ahmed, argued for doing something about the imam problem: 'Young British Muslims go to the mosque and hear an imam delivering a sermon in a foreign language about the past. It has no relevance to … the problems affecting Muslims in Britain. At the same time, it fills them with absurd notions about the British. They leave the mosque feeling angry and confused and walk straight into the arms of extremist groups such as al-Muhajiroun which talk to them in a language they understand.' Ahmed, along with the *Guardian*, called for state funding of imam training. The Home Office appeared supportive of the idea but nevertheless rejected a first request for a £250,000 ($450,000) grant for imam education from the Muslim College in Ealing.

There are many reasons why governments call for control of imams and yet step back from direct involvement in imam education. In the UK, one problem is how to reflect the diversity within Britain's Islamic community. There is the danger of seeming to favor one strand of Islam against others. On the other hand, perhaps it is right for the state to favor seminaries that teach liberal doctrines or that encourage interfaith dialogue.

Another problem is the employment conditions for imams. There is general agreement that Western education of imams is a collective good, but the demand for educated imams like the ones produced by the Markfield Institute and the Muslim College in Ealing is too small to make the programs viable. Some graduates are foreign students who have opted to be educated in Britain because it is more prestigious, and plan to return to Indonesia or elsewhere in South Asia after graduation. Among those who stay, most become teachers in Islamic schools or seek employment in prisons or social services. Employment conditions for imams are generally unsatisfactory. They typically have no job contract, no pension, and no benefits. In many cases, they have no regular salary. The income provided by mosque councils may be sufficient for someone who is recruited from a Bangladeshi village, but it will not satisfy a young British Muslim who compares herself or himself to friends with business degrees or working in information technology.

A French security agency conducted a census of French imams, which remains unpublished but the findings were described by the author of the study, Barnard Godard, on *sezame.info*, a French blog edited by Hakim El Ghissassi.[10] The study identified over a thousand imams, about half working full-time. Only 45 percent are paid regularly and the rest are paid in kind or unpaid. Of those who are paid, Turkey supports sixty, Algeria eighty, and Morocco only two. Saudi Arabia pays the salaries of about a dozen, who have graduated from Saudi Islamic universities, but none of them are Saudis. Less than twenty percent of the imams are of French nationality, mostly naturalized. Very few are French-born. Half of the imams are either of Moroccan or Algerian origin. Over half are over fifty years old. One-third speaks French with ease, another third speaks it with some difficulty, and the rest does not speak it at all. The countries from which the imams are recruited would be different, but we may otherwise surmise that a similar census would yield comparable results in any Western European country with respect to employment conditions, educational background, and the general lack of language competency and non-national legal status.

Counterterrorism policies targeting mosques and growing concerns about radical preachers have directed attention to the desperate need for European-educated imams and Islamic religious scholars. The French and Spanish governments announced plans to establish government-approved imam institutions in 2004, but little progress has been made. In France, the task of producing an educational plan was entrusted to the newly formed umbrella organization for French Muslim associations, the CFCM, which missed the deadline for producing a proposal. The Dutch government has funded a degree program at the Free University in Amsterdam, which according to the press release will begin in September 2005 to 'train Islamic spiritual leaders and clergy.' The program is located in the Faculty of Theology, and aside from offering bachelor's and master's degrees, it will also provide naturalization courses for imams.

An important issue is what to do about the imams already in the country. In the absence of new mosque building and radical changes in the structure of mosque governance, the demand for educated (and expensive) imams will not be sufficient to absorb imams with diplomas from newly created European theological institutes. Newly minted imams with diplomas from 'mainstream' seminaries will most probably find employment at a limited number of elite mosques and public institutions, including prisons and hospitals and other institutions that can pay regular salaries. Ultimately, policymakers will have to consider how employment laws and other laws affecting clergy should be applied to imams. All of this must raise questions about where the money for imam education and salaries will come from.

ANIMAL RIGHTS AND RITUAL SLAUGHTER

Animal rights laws require that animals be stunned or otherwise anaesthetized before butchering, so they feel no pain. Sometimes a pragmatic argument is advanced that it is better for consumers because the meat changes in undesirable ways in reaction to pain. However, the argument is generally put in moral terms. As formulated in a recent amendment that was proposed to the Swedish animal protection law (Djurskyddslagen) by the Christian Democrats, a small Protestant party: 'the idea that humans have responsibility for the protection and shielding of all living beings is one of the basic pillars of the Christian democratic worldview.'[11] Interestingly, Sweden exempts chickens from the prohibition on butchering without prior stunning. It is not clear if it is because scientific opinion is that chickens feel no pain (which animal rights advocates dispute) or because Sweden has a substantial chicken industry that was capable of fighting off regulation.

In principle, these and similar laws and regulations affect Jews and Muslims equally. In fact, kosher butchering is disallowed in Sweden, while a compromise has been made regarding halal butchering, which involves desensitizing the animals before butchering. The meat is packaged with a halal certificate, but critics challenge the accuracy of the labeling. There is some internal disagreement among Muslims as to the acceptability of stunning, if it does not stop the animal's heart. Efforts to find a compromise solution that satisfied both animal rights groups and religious representatives failed.[12] Imported halal and kosher meats are available in both Norway and Sweden, often from Denmark or the USA. Since Swedish and Norwegian consumers already mostly depend upon imported meats, consumers of ritually slaughtered meats are not paying excessive penalties for being unable to buy local meats.

The German animal protection act (Tierschutzgesetz) from 1972 prohibits the slaughtering of animals without prior stunning, except in the case of hunting or on religious grounds. Article 4 of the act stipulates that exemptions may be allowed on grounds of 'compulsory' religious prescription against stunning. The prohibition was strengthened in 1988 after a public outcry about immigrants butchering animals in bathtubs, but halal butchering was permitted. Complaints about animals in apartments were common at the time. Turkish labor migrants were often from peasant backgrounds, and some continued to keep chickens or rabbits as they had done before migrating. This caused friction with neighbors.

A number of cases were brought before Länder courts, in Hessen and Berlin, and in 1995, the federal administrative court in Hessen ruled that while Jews had a right to an exemption under Article 4, Muslims did not. Islamic law experts at the Al-Azhar University in Cairo were consulted by the court and asked for a statement about Islamic law on the requirement of ritual slaughter. Hoping perhaps not to make life too difficult for Muslims in the West, the experts said that Muslims could eat meat that had been conventionally slaughtered if ritually slaughtered meat was not available. The Jewish experts stated, however, that Jews absolutely must eat kosher meat. As a result, halal butchering was legal from 1988 to 1995, and made illegal thereafter.

The decision was appealed to the federal constitutional court by a Muslim butcher, who complained about the impact upon his business. The Zentralrat (ZMD) took a strong interest in the case, and helped move it along. The constitutional court granted the application on the grounds that the law allows for religious exemptions and the butcher had a right to the free exercise of his profession. The fact that Jews had an exemption entered into the argument only as evidence that a religious exemption from the animal protection act's general prohibition was possible.[13] There was no discussion of the requirements for equitable treatment of the two religions, and the decision was based entirely on the butcher's right to conduct business.

The issue is far from settled yet. A few months after the constitutional court's decision, on May 17, 2002, the Bundestag passed an amendment to Article 20 of the constitution to make the federal government responsible for the protection of animals. The new Article 20a of the German Basic Law affirms that the state 'takes responsibility for protecting the natural foundations of life and animals in the interest of future generations.' The amendment was seen as a concession to animal rights advocates, who had opposed the court's decision. At present, kosher and halal slaughter is permitted, but new legal challenges on animal rights grounds are likely to occur. Muslim leaders also complain that the regulatory agencies granting permits to halal butchers are excessively strict in their interpretation of health rules and requirements with respect to equipment, training, and certification. German commercial organizations rely heavily on a model of formal apprenticeship and certification through trade associations, which is not an easy fit for immigrant small businesses, where skills may have been informally acquired.

Another difficulty for European regulators is that interpretations vary as to the exact requirements of halal slaughter. These tend to be more flexible than those applied by orthodox Jews in the case of kosher meat, but halal is not just a matter of butchering techniques. The halal requirement affects many aspects of life. At a talk at the UK Meat and Livestock Commission, an expert from the Halal Food Authority stated that in Arabic 'halal' means, simply, 'permissible' food and 'haram' means the opposite, disallowed foods.[14] But what, precisely, is forbidden?

Because of the development of industrial food processing this is no simple matter. The basic requirement is that animals must be alive and healthy at the time of slaughter, and they must be alive when butchered by severing the jugular vein, carotid artery, and windpipe with a single swipe of a sharp knife. Eating blood is forbidden, so all the blood must be drained from the carcass (which is why the heart must be kept beating as long as possible). In addition, a recitation must be made dedicating the meat for consumption. Further, like Jews, Muslims are not allowed to eat pork and food products with derivatives from pigs or other nonhalal meats.

The technical differences between halal and kosher slaughter are minimal, except that the recitations are different and in the case of halal meat the blessing must be done by a Muslim (any Muslim) and kosher meat must be certified by an approved rabbi. Occasionally additional requirements are added, as in the case of the expert from the Halal Food Authority who added that 'in the interest of animal welfare, the animal has to be fed as normal and given water prior to slaughter, one animal must not see the other being slaughtered, [the] knife should be four times the size of the neck and razor sharp, and as far as possible the slaughterer and the animal should face Qibla or Mecca and the animal must not be suffering with any ailments or any lacerations.'[15] Particular rules of this sort notwithstanding, halal slaughter is sometimes seen as more easily reconciled with animal welfare rules because many Muslim authorities accept stunning with the argument that it does not stop the animal's heart from beating and the animal therefore remains alive at the time of butchering.

Predictably, an industry has grown up around the provision of halal products. One institute, the UK-based Halal Control, tests products to see if they are in fact free of traces of prohibited—nonhalal, or haram—products.[16] Sugary candy often contains gelatin, which is made from animal carcasses. Haribo candy, a widely available and popular sweet in Europe, was found to have traces of pig DNA making it unacceptable for strictly observant Muslims (and Jews). Companies exist that specialize in locating and providing approved halal foods to airlines, prisons, educational institutions, and restaurants. Websites list which products are halal (aspartame and BHA or BHT, which are generally bad for you and contained in processed foods) and haram (collagen, not ingested but used in cosmetics).

When faced with a request from a coalition of Muslim interest groups and halal food purveyors, the New Jersey Attorney General's Division of Consumer Affairs held a hearing and resolved not to regulate religious labeling. The request was that consumer protection law be used to establish standards for who may use labels such as 'halal farms' or 'halal products.' The Division declined to issue such guidelines, citing both US law on the separation of church and state and technical incompetence. An inaudible sigh of relief can be detected in the agency's statement that 'the Division believes that any attempt to license halal certifying agencies would violate State and Federal constitutional provisions relating to separation of Church and State.'[17] Buyers beware, it advised, 'consumers are encouraged to evaluate various certifying agencies to determine whether those agencies' standards meet or exceed their own.'

The Attorney General did, however, issue guidelines for record-keeping and disclosure forms to be used by businesses claiming to sell halal meats. In sum, the agency did not want to get into who could say something was halal or not, but it did amend the Halal Food Consumer Protection Act to require businesses, nursing homes, and summer camps to disclose where their meat comes from and to guarantee that it has been properly cared for and butchered.

The difficulties associated with the regulation of halal slaughtering are in some respects not different from any other example of business regulation. Is the product what the seller says it is? Is it safe? And does the law treat business owners in an equitable manner, or are some business owners discriminated against by the nature of the laws or by the application of the law?

A natural initial reaction to the German constitutional court's complicated reasoning about the possibly discriminatory impact of the animal welfare law upon the occupational freedom of the Muslim butcher is that the court missed the point. The court should have broached questions of religious freedom and the equitable treatment of faiths, some critics say. It is obviously the case that German Muslims will perceive the fact that kosher slaughtering is allowed and halal slaughtering disallowed as discriminatory. But the Muslim butcher who filed the complaint was not a German citizen and the constitution's article about equal treatment therefore did not protect him. Moreover, his problem was not that he was prohibited from exercising his faith but that his business was put at risk.

It is perhaps fitting that the court's decision was based upon the butcher's right to conduct his business. Most Muslims—like most Jews—do not exclusively consume ritually slaughtered meat. Most people buy their meats in supermarkets and not at specialized butchers. And as a German Muslim social democrat of Turkish origin said about her constituency, 'they care mostly about how much it costs!' This is probably true, but one should not conclude that Muslims who do not routinely buy halal meat do not think it is important that it is available. They may know someone who cares deeply, perhaps even have parents who do. And then there is the symbolic aspect. As it was sometimes put to me by secular Muslim leaders, 'If Jews have the right, Muslims should too.' The more religious leaders were inclined to present it as a matter of religious rights. Even if only a minority of Muslims practice their faith in this way, the government does not have the right to make it impossible for them to do so. No Muslim leader defended to me the viewpoint of animal rights activists. A few religious leaders pointed out that the Koran disallows mistreatment of animals, but no one conceded that ritual slaughter violated the animals' rights.

It is also clear, as appears in the New Jersey amendment to consumer protection law, that human rights law need not enter into the solution to many issues of religious accommodation. The integration of Islam and the equitable treatment of faiths are often a matter of reforming the mundane application of routine laws and regulations. It is in this context that the sensitivity of courts, government officials, and lawmakers to the disparate impact of seemingly neutral rules on different groups becomes important. European courts are at a particular disadvantage as they are unaccustomed to second-guessing governments on the implementation of policy. The concept of 'disparate impact' is exceedingly difficult for jurists, who are used to making decisions based upon precedents and the strict reading of legal texts, and are unaccustomed to estimating the social consequences of their decisions, or of using sociological evidence.

The common theme running through the three stories recounted here is the tendency of government policymakers to react to the problems of religious pluralism in a restrictive and piecemeal fashion. As long as reform proposals related to the integration of Islam in Europe elicit the reassertion of Christian or other 'national' values, the perception that they are discriminated against will grow among Muslims. Existing laws could instead be adjusted, through new implementation rules and flexible legal interpretation, to accommodate religious pluralism. This would promote integration. Unfortunately, in most cases, little foresight is displayed about how public policy has to change to reflect the social change that follows from other liberal values, such as the freedom to choose your own religion, human rights, and economic policies that have stimulated international migration and mobility.

IDEATIONAL, ECONOMIC, AND INSTITUTIONAL SOURCES OF RESISTANCE TO PLURALISM

Nearly all European countries now have a xenophobic party. In some cases, older nationalist parties have assimilated anti-immigrant rhetoric and gained new support; in other cases, new parties have emerged. The program of Pia Kjaersgaard's Danish People's Party states: 'Foreigners should be absorbed in Danish society, but only under the condition that they do not pose a threat to social security and democracy.'[18] The party supports revoking citizenship and expulsion for naturalized citizens convicted of crimes that result in jail sentences, and it has pushed through parliament new restrictions in access to naturalization. The party strongly defends the Lutheran Church's special privileges as the national church. It is at present the third largest political party in Denmark.

Nativist parties have also done well elsewhere in Europe. In September 2001, Carl Hagen's Progress Party became the third largest party in Norway with fifteen percent of the vote. In June 1999, the Belgian Vlaams Blok received ten percent of the vote and in the next five years it won up to one-quarter of the votes in Flanders, its core catchment area, but it was forced to disband after the Belgian Supreme Court declared the party illegal in November 2004, due to its racist nature. In the October 1999 Austrian Nationalrat election, Jörg Haider's Freedom Party got 27 percent of the vote, and became the second largest party in the national parliament. As is often typical for populist protest parties, the Freedom Party subsequently split, and its influence has diminished. The Dutch Lijst Pim Fortuyn, a new party, shook up the party system in 2002 by claiming that Muslims were bigots and had diluted Dutch liberal values. The Lijst became the second largest party almost overnight, with 17 percent of the vote, after the assassination of Fortuyn by an animal rights activist. But without Fortuyn, the Lijst collapsed as a national party. It lives on in Rotterdam where the party is part of the city government under the name of Levbar Rotterdam. However, the influence of the xenophobic voter bloc remains after the party that first crystallizes this sentiment collapses. Typically, mainstream parties begin to use similar rhetoric in an effort to coopt the support of more radical voters. In the Netherlands, the Liberal Party (VVD) took over as the chief defender of Dutch values after Fortuyn's death. The rhetoric of both parties has suggested that only Muslims who have renounced Islam can be Dutch.

In the UK and Germany, the electoral system creates high barriers to new parties, and the British National Front and the German Republikaner Party and Deutsche Volksunion (DVU) have remained largely regional or local parties. The British National Front was, at its peak, able to win only seventeen seats in local council elections. The Republikaner Party achieved representation in the Baden-Württemberg state legislature in 1992 with 10.9 percent of the vote and in 1996 with 9.1 percent, but they failed to cross the 5 percent barrier necessary for representation in the 2001 election. The Sverigesdemokratarna (Sweden-democrats) are strong in southern Sweden but have failed to garner national support comparable to that of its predecessor party, Ny Demokrati (New Democracy).

The influence of xenophobic parties is not to be measured by their votes alone. Conservative, centrist, and social democratic parties have sought to coopt the nativist reaction by offering policies that are tough on immigrants and protect national values. References to the menace of foreign cultures and the threat posed by immigrants in general, and Muslims in particular, to social solidarity and cultural homogeneity have become part of mainstream public dialogue. If Conservatives focus on 'national identity politics,' the Social Democrats focus on social solidarity.

Both sets of values can be turned against Muslims. In the 2002 German election campaign, the CSU/CDU party leader, Edmund Stoiber, proclaimed that 'the homeland builds identity and civility'—and added warnings against 'uncontrolled immigration.'[19]

Two years later, Stoiber ridiculed a proposal from the Greens to make the end of Ramadan a German holiday. The government, of which the Greens are part, had just proposed to eliminate a few of Germany's many holidays, including one from the week-long Easter holiday. 'Eliminating national or Christian holidays and introducing Islamic holidays; that is how far it has come in our country! That is not toleration, not integration, but the surrender of our cultural heritage. It must be stopped. Our country has been colored ('geprägt') by Christianity and not Islam for 1500 years.'[20] The idea that public holidays should be neutral with respect to the religion they favor or, at minimum, provide some measure of parity for all faiths, was lost in the outrage.

In France, the center-right government has similarly asserted responsibility for defending essential French values against Islam. In February 2004, in a speech accompanying the introduction of the new legislation prohibiting students from wearing the Islamic headscarf, the prime minister, Jean-Pierre Raffarin, stated unequivocally that assimilation to the French language and values was a requirement. He announced a new package of legislation that would present 'a contract' between new immigrants and the state, with stricter language requirements and rules for 'attachment' to France as pre-conditions for obtaining residence permits.[21] Other European governments are increasingly stipulating that it is not sufficient that immigrants are law-abiding and learn to speak the language. They must also assimilate to the values and norms of the French, the Germans, and the Danes with respect to religious observance, conduct, and other moral codes.

Anti-immigrant sentiments reach well beyond the minority that is willing to support far-right parties. Forty-eight percent of Danes believe that the Muslims currently living in the country are 'a threat to Danish culture and religion,' and only nine percent think that they are a source of cultural and religious renewal.[22] In January 2004, the British polling organization, MORI, reported that according to respondents, race and immigration was the third most important issue facing Britain—ahead of the economy, and law and order.[23] Support for immigration control is not by itself indicative of xeno-phobic attitude. Many Muslims and other immigrants agree that Europe is not in a position to welcome more immigrants until current problems have been worked out. It is indicative, however, of substantial discomfort with increased societal diversity. By the end of 2004, a poll conducted by the *Wall Street Journal Europe* found very high levels of anti-Muslim perception across most European countries, but the highest levels were found in Sweden, where 78 percent reported that they thought Muslims were disapproved of, the Netherlands (72 percent), and Denmark (67 percent), three countries that historically have prided themselves on social inclusion. In comparison, only 39 percent of Britons thought that Muslims were disapproved of.[24]

N.B.

SOCIAL SOLIDARITY AND PLURALISM: THE NEW ANTIMONIES?

One of the anomalies of European anti-immigrant rhetoric is that it serves up diluted versions of the high rhetoric used in earlier decades to compel the rich to pay for the poor. It reflects in part the success of the post-1945 welfare state consensus that it shapes the current generations' view of the obligations of states and rights of citizens. The slogans of reform—'One Nation Britain' and 'The People's Home' in Sweden—appealed to national restoration.[25] Prewar reformers anticipated wartime rhetoric and the postwar communitarianism. Sociologists contributed to the pursuit of solidarity. In 1931, R. H. Tawney wrote that, 'what a community requires...is a common culture, because, without it, it is not a community at all.' The nationalist idiom that was once used to build support for national solidarity today lends itself to distinctly antipluralist sentiments. The normative visions of egalitarianism as the basis for community were articulated in the concept of 'social citizenship,' which was a slogan masquerading as an analytic concept.[26] William Beveridge, in his 1942 report, recognized that a system of social insurance would require 'a sense of national unity overriding the interests of any class or section.' In a 1942 lecture, he said: 'One of the weaknesses of many reformers in the past is that they have not taken account of the immense feeling of patriotism in the British people, or that loving pride which we have in our country.'

European reform movements have emphasized collective action rather than individual rights. The consolidation of mass democracy took place in many Western European countries in a context of economic stagnation, war, and mass emigration. As a consequence of war, displaced populations were foremost on the minds of lawmakers. Emigration and stagnation made the accommodation of immigrants a hypothetical question, with no practical consequences. With the exception of the UK, where the term 'ethnic minority' has taken hold, 'minority' refers to this day to territorially displaced persons, exemplified by ethnic-German Russians, Swedish Finns, Danish Germans, or German Danes.

The democratic transformation of European societies took place in the shadows of the events of 1848 and 1917. Socialists focused on class and not religion, and social democratic and socialist parties often remain uncomfortable with religious groups. Conservatives aligned themselves with Church hierarchies. Religious dissenters usually turned to the small liberal parties and more often than not failed to find allies supportive of state–church reform. Some emigrated to countries that were more accommodating, often to the USA or Canada, which today are also favored destinations for emigrating Muslims.

In his book, *Hellfire Nation*, James Morone describes the central role of religion in US political history as a force for change, sometimes propelling abolitionists and social reformers like Jane Addams, and at other times inspiring conservative reactions.[27] With the notable exception of Great Britain, where social reformers often came from religious backgrounds, a similar book could not be written about European social movements. In this regard, as in so many others, Europeans find no preexisting template for understanding the many ways in which religion can motivate political and social action.

The continental European constitutional traditions focused on resolving the conflicts between state and government and the powerful established churches. They have not historically emphasized the rights of nonconformists or worried about state neutrality in matters of faith. Constitutions typically contain equality commitments and promises of freedom of thought, but no language or requirement concerning the equal treatment of religions. Law

N.B.

and rights were in any case regarded as antitheses, as national liberals and social democratic reformers mistrusted courts and judges and regarded law as an instrument of reaction and conservatism. Suffrage and parliaments were regarded as the more dependable avenues for reform. Minority guarantees were concessions made to recalcitrant elites, and popular sovereignty was expressed through electoral majorities.

N,P

Social scientists have conventionally regarded xenophobia and nativist electoral mobilization as a protectionist response on the part of the weak to the consequences of economic competition from immigrants in localized housing and labor markets.[28] Nativism is a political movement that discriminates on the bases of origin. It seeks policies that will deny immigrant-origin persons the rights and privileges given to native-origin persons.[29] Xenophobia is the perception that foreigners, as a group and as individuals, pose a threat to national values. The two 'isms' go hand in hand, but one is a political movement and the other a disposition. Nativism is a political movement seeking particular policies. Xenophobia is an attitude that can be exploited for multiple political and social purposes. The crystallization of the latter into political action requires political leadership and policymaking. Voters may be xenophobic but that is not a sufficient condition to make nativism a policy.

Economic historians have argued that heightened exposure of native-born populations to competition from foreign-born groups motivated the surge of anti-immigrant legislation in the USA in the 1920s.[30] Political scientists agree that contemporary anti-immigrant legislation fits the pattern of earlier nativism and is also primarily economic in origin. Support for Proposition 187 in 1994 correlates with the cyclical downturn in the California economy and, further confirming the assumption that nativism is a protective instinct of the weak, anti-immigrant sentiment was concentrated among voters of lower socioeconomic status.[31] Interestingly, European attempts to replicate economic explanations for anti-immigrant sentiments in the wake of recent decades of mass immigration to Western Europe have failed. Studies have found that rising unemployment rates have had no or negative effect on support for European far-right parties.[32]

One reason for why rising xenophobic sentiments cannot be explained by socioeconomic variables is that the European welfare states cushion people against the ill effects of the business cycle. Recession is today associated with a marginal shift in votes towards the left. In Europe, the welfare state has eliminated the historical link between recessions and right-wing mobilization. Moreover, scholars have failed to establish a robust link between nativist attitudes and socioeconomic status among European voters.

The research supports the obvious observation that contemporary European nativist rhetoric differs from past populism by purporting to defend national culture—including the welfare state—against exploitation by immigrants.[33]

It is evident that ideas about the roots of social problems play a large role in shaping policy preferences. A policymaker who thinks that Europeans are anti-Muslim because they are used to governments subsidizing their faith over other faiths, will clearly advocate different policies from someone who thinks that immigration presents a threat to social security and that Muslims are too welfare-dependent. One thinks that religion and public policy with respect to the exercise of religion is at the crux of the matter. The other thinks that religion is incidental to the problem and that the real issue is social policy. Yet, culture and economics need not be competing explanations of anti-immigrant sentiment. Alberto Alesina and Edward L. Glaser, two Harvard economists, have argued that cultural conflict arises because economic institutions—the welfare state in particular—engender certain norms and behaviors.[34]

In a controversial article entitled, 'Too Diverse?' in the February 2004 issue of the British magazine *Prospect*, David Goodhart, the magazine's editor, suggested that a tradeoff exists between diversity and solidarity and that possibly, 'Britain [is] becoming too diverse to sustain the mutual obligations behind a good society and the welfare state.' The argument suggests that perceptions of economic and cultural threat may be mutually reinforcing and that therefore cultural and economic theories of nativism should not be regarded as mutually exclusive.

Arguably, it is economically rational for small countries with relatively few low-skilled native workers to oppose labor migration and to prefer free trade. If you can have protectionist labor market measures that shield high wages and taxpayers against the welfare loss associated with an inflow of large numbers of low-skilled migrant workers, and still reap the benefits of abundant labor by trading with countries with few or no welfare restrictions, you can have the best of both worlds: high social protection for your own community and cheap goods from communities with no such protection.[35] It is unclear how this calculus works in practice, but electorates and politicians seem to pursue a short-term calculus of costs and benefits of this sort. The free trade model that sees low wage immigrant labor as a boon to growth is arguably less attractive in small countries with generous welfare states than in large countries with low-wage and highly mobile workforces already characterized by a high share of immigrant labor, like the USA.

INSTITUTIONAL RIGIDITY
AND PSYCHOLOGICAL REACTIONS

The normative appeal of a culture of solidarity looms large in the anti-immigrant rhetoric. Michele Lamont recounts how French blue-collar workers took umbrage at the immigrants' large families and presumed boundless reliance on public monies for income.[36]

A Dutch study used a controlled-experiment methodology to test respondents' generalized collective and personal-individual perceptions of threats to economic and cultural well-being that are posed by specific immigrant groups. Its findings confirm the primacy of cultural over economic concerns in fueling xenophobia. Paul M. Sniderman, Louk Hagendoorn, and Markus Prior concluded, 'a perception that Dutch culture is threatened is the dominant factor in generating a negative reaction to immigrant minorities.'[37] The authors conceded that because low self-esteem was positively correlated with feelings of vulnerability to both economic and cultural threat, cultural and economic sources of bias are closely related, and perceptions of either are ultimately a matter of self-assessment and not actual exposure. Nevertheless, they conclude, 'our results, both experimental and nonexperimental, show that concerns over national identity are more of a driving force than concerns over economic interest.'[38] As they also point out, if the root source of xenophobia was economic, economic growth would offer a solution. It is much more difficult to address perceived conflicts of identities and values.

Europeans are wedded to a commonsensical understanding of culture as 'how we do things here,' which asserts the existence of an ahistorical national identity. With few legal and historical reasons to distrust national homogenization and the primacy of electoral majoritarianism, publics and governments alike find it difficult to think about conflict issues in terms of the requirements of pluralism and the toleration of nonconformist religious behavior.

Public reactions to the perceived 'Islamization' of European societies have the marks of a moral panic. Stanley Cohen, a British sociologist, coined the term to describe media coverage of youth fashion, 'mods,' and 'rockers' in England in the late 1960s.[39] Panics arise when it becomes widely believed that a particular group is dangerously deviant and a menace to social stability. According to Cohen, moral panics are contemporary witch-hunts characterized by a disproportionate response to threats to public values and mores. The threat may be a real one (drug abuse or terrorism) but is exaggerated, or it may be an imagined one (witchcraft or UFOs). Moral panics have a predictable course. They develop when the general public becomes aroused by the perpetuation of stories that are retold many times, encouraged by public personalities and amplified by TV and the tabloids. The stories typically take the form of anecdotes told as facts. Moral panics are a cause for concern because they pose obstacles to sensible and pragmatic solutions to societal problems. The distinction between the real danger to the public and the imagined danger is lost.

Many aspects of the current debate over Islam in Europe seem to suggest that it is a 'panic,' which in due course will quieten down as the public moves on to other issues. But then there are also aspects that suggest the conflict has deeper institutional and structural roots. The Muslim leaders often seemed to debate with themselves what is going on.

A Danish convert described the hardening of Danish self-perceptions as he had experienced it. 'When I think back to the Denmark I knew in my childhood, some changes are positive, and others negative. Today people have a very restricted perception of what it means to be Danish. Everything that is outside the framework of a Morten Koch movie [a Danish film series from the 1960s that idealized agrarian life] is regarded as un-Danish. It is incomprehensible that a well-informed and well-off people can become so unbending and prejudiced. Danish law has started to resemble Apartheid now, with special rules that target particular population groups who are regarded as un-Danish, Turks or Pakistanis, for example.'[40]

Europeans are used to the public facilitation of faith and unused to the social demands and public ethics associated with state neutrality and self-chosen cultural and religious identities.[41] To the extent that belief in Islam is a source of stigma and social differentiation in contemporary Europe, Muslims are driven to formulate a collective defense. The importance of faith or cultural affinities in shaping Muslim leaders' belief systems is an early warning of the growing political salience of religious issues. Islam is becoming, in effect, the functional equivalent in the present social and political context to ethnicity as a source of differentiation and identity-formation among the otherwise ethnically and linguistically very diverse European Muslim populations. Religious bias pays as little attention to theological differences as racism pays attention to hues of skin color.

There can be no doubt that many European Muslims experience the process described by identity theory as truth. Muslim leaders often argue that the discriminatory homogenization of Muslims to a hostile mold victimizes individual Muslims and deprives them of their rights. Muslim distinctiveness is not 'born whole' but is the result of a complex process of stigmatization and self-assertion of collective identity. A controversy over British antiterrorism enforcement policies that rely on what in the USA became known as 'racial profiling' is an interesting example of the processes of identity-formation. It is, of course, absurd to use the term 'race' to describe Muslims. The term 'racial profiling' derives from the state police's policy of stopping black drivers on the New Jersey Turnpike to boost the success rate of drug-related stop and searches. Applied in a British context to describe policies affecting Muslims, the term reinforces the idea of Muslim 'groupness.'

KULTURKAMPF ONCE MORE

'Kulturkampf'—or culture war—was the term used to describe the struggle between the Catholic Church and the Prussian government and the secular (predominantly Protestant) Liberals in the Bismarckian period from 1871 to 1891. The chief issue was the balance between faith and public control of German intellectual life and science, in the universities and in the institutions of government. The term was subsequently used by the National Socialists against the Socialists and the Communists, once more to describe the battle between contradictory world views and views of the role of government for control of German minds in the 1930s.

Huntington initially argued that an era has dawned comparable to the cold war. 'In the post-cold war world flags count and so do other symbols of cultural identity, including crosses, crescents, and even head coverings, because culture counts, and cultural identity is what is most meaningful to most people. People are discovering new but often old identities and marching under new but often old flags which lead to wars with new but often old enemies.'[42] In his 2004 book, Huntington changed his focus to domestic politics and argued that Western civilization, specifically the USA, will fall into decline if Americans fail to assert their core values—which Huntington defines as Anglo-Protestant—and wage a *Kulturkampf* against the cultural influence of immigrants at home and stand tall abroad. Committed to fundamentally hostile principles for reasons of their faith, Muslims are, he says, an 'indigestible minority.'[43]

The 'clash of civilizations' theory is widely accepted in Europe. It endows every conflict between Muslims and the West with moral purpose, and it implies that the defense of secularity and rationality against fundamentalism and faith is at stake at all times. It is not a theory that is conducive to a 'small steps' approach to dialogue and compromise.

Not all historians see Christian–Muslim relations through the centuries as a coherent history of epic and relentless conflict. In a review in the *New York Review of Books*, William Dalrymple traces an alternative mother lode of history writing to Sir Steven Runciman's history of the Crusades, a three-volume work published in 1955. Runciman takes the view (here cited from Dalrymple) that Western civilization has grown out of 'the long sequence of interaction and fusion between the Orient and the Occident.'[44] In this view, it was the Byzantines and the Damascus caliphate that were the civilized inheritors of the Greek and Roman civilizations, with their emphasis on art and toleration, and the Christian crusaders who were the Barbarians.

Conversely, a few of the more theologically minded European Muslims that I interviewed brought up the collapse of multicultural Grenada in 1492 as an example of how Islamic toleration was suppressed by Christian mono-religious domination. In 2002, Muslim activists entered the Cathedral of Cordoba to conduct prayers and were arrested. The present cathedral is superimposed upon a mosque dating back to the eighth century. For centuries, Christians and Muslims shared the space but the mosque was subsequently converted to a Christian Cathedral and remains so today. One Spanish Muslim group has initiated a petition to the Vatican to reinstate Muslims' rights to religious exercise in the space, which is today a historic site registered by UNESCO. The main Spanish association of Muslims, ICCM, nevertheless said that it was nonsense that any such claims were being made.[45] The Cordoba mosque incident illustrates that the political usage of symbols pits not only Muslims against Christians, but also Muslims against Muslims.

Symbols are the raw material of all political mobilization. Dale F. Eckelman and James Piscatori put contention over symbols at the core of Muslim political activism in the West. Muslim politics is, by their definition, the 'cooperation and contest over the form, practice, and interpretation' of Islam.[46] The process owes more to the skill of politicians than to real conflicts over fundamental norms or, as Huntington postulates, 'civilization values.' The headscarf issue is a case in point: French and German lawmakers decided to make a symbol of the headscarf; British lawmakers decided not to.

Notwithstanding Huntington, it is evident that there are many areas of overlapping agreement between Muslims and Christians. The problems faced by Muslims in Western Europe are widely shared by other faith groups. Rabbis and imams regularly work together to change zoning rules and laws that penalize religious minorities. Christian and Islamic religious scholars and clergy agree that secularism has gone too far, and that much of what is wrong in Europe today is due to public hostility to spirituality and faith. A starting point for addressing the 'clash of practices' that results from current policies is to use the discretionary powers of existing laws to solve practical problems and to diminish the obstacles to the integration of Islam that exist. Post-Christian religious pluralism is a social reality that has to be faced.

NOTES

1. Yvonne Yazbeck Haddad and John L. Esposito (eds.), *Muslims on the American-ization Path?* (New York: Oxford University Press, 2002); Mohamed Nimer, *The North American Muslim Resource Guide: Muslim Community Life in the USA and Canada* (New York: Routledge, 2002).

2. www.folketing.dk/Samling/20012/sporgetime_sc/US20.htm.

3. http://www.mcb.org.uk/mcbdirect/features.php?ann_id=133; http://www.open-democracy.net/articles/ViewPopUpArticle.jsp?id=5&articleId=865.

4. 'La toussaint musulmane, une enquête sur les cimetières musulmans de France,' by Hakim el Ghissassi, Yacine Chaib, and Olivier Géhin. Available at: http://www.sezame.info/index.php?action=article&id_article=87528&print=1.

5. http://www.paris.fr/fr/Vos_demarches/obseques/cimetiere_thiais.ASP#.

6. This section builds on my essay, 'Is there an imam problem?' *Prospect* (May 2004).

7. *Dokumentation. Frühjahrsumfrage: Neue Daten und Fakten über den Islam in Deutschland.* Nr. 1/2004 15. Mai, 2002. Zentralinstitut Islam-Achiv-Deutschald. Soest-Diringsen.

8. An article in the French newspaper *L'Express* described in unusual detail the difficulties of funding and institutionalizing religious institutions; see 'Enquête: L'argent de l'islam,' *L'Express* (November 21, 2002); http://www.lexpress.fr/forma timp/default.asp?idarticle=364510&url=http://www.lexpress.fr/info/societe/dos-sier/mosquees/dossier.asp?ida=364510.

9. Immigration and Nationality Directorate. New Immigration Rules on Switching and Ministers of Religion (July 22, 2004); http://www.ind.homeoffice.gov.uk/ind/en/home/news/press_releases/0.textonly.html; BBC news: http://news.bbc.co.uk/go/pr/fr/-/1/hi/uk/3917057.stm.

10. 'Formation des imams: état des lieux,' by Bernard Godard (February 16 2005); http://www.sezame.info (article = 120635).

11. Motion till riksdagen, 2004/05:MJ506

12. Report available at: http://www.sjv.se/startsida/amnesomraden/djurveterinar/ djuridiken/djuridiken12004/rapportomreligiosslakt.4.7502f61001ea08a0c7fff 41510.html.

13. Bundesverfassungsgericht, BverfG, 1BvR 1783/99 (January 15, 2002).

14. The UK Meat and Livestock Commission was established under the 1967 Agri-culture Act and is funded by a tax on slaughtered animals. The commissioner is a government appointee but it is a paragovernmental organization working for the industry.

15. http://www.halalfoodauthority.co.uk/compliance.html.

16. http://www.halal.de.

17. Halal Food, Division of Consumer Affairs, New Jersey Register (September 7, 2004), 36 (17).

18. http://www.danskfolkeparti.dk.

19. 'Heimat schafft Identität und Geborgenheit.'
20. Speech by the party leader and Bavarian premier minister, Edmund Stoiber, at the CSU annual party meeting (November 20, 2004).
21. Projet de loi relatif à l'application écoles collèges du principe de laïcité dans les et lycées publics. Allocution du premier minister, M. Jean-Pierre Raffarin, à l'Assemblée Nationale. Paris (février 3, 2004); http://www.diplomatie.gouv.fr/actu/print_bul.asp?liste=20040204.html.
22. Poll conducted of 1,348 respondents by Mogenavisen Jyllands-Posten (May 20, 1997); http://www.dupi.dk/webtxt/dupidok/1997/del4_97.htm.
23. MORI Social Research Survey, *Prospect* (January 22, 2004).
24. The question asked respondents to report what they thought 'Europeans' thought of Muslims. The polling organization had originally sought to ask respondents directly what they personally thought of Muslims, but many national polling organizations refused to ask the question that way. The cross-national variations nevertheless suggest that the respondents answered based on their perceptions of collective feelings about Muslims. In that sense, the poll responses measure the level of hostility to Muslims; 'A Test to Multiculturalism,' *Wall Street Journal Europe* (December 10, 2004).
25. Michael Mann, *States, War, and Capitalism: Studies in Political Sociology* (New York and Oxford: Basil Blackwell, 1988).
26. For an example of the deliberate use of appeals to communitarian self-interest in welfare state expansion, see the works of Alva R. Myrdal, *Nation and Family: The Swedish Experiment in Democratic Family and Population Policy* (New York: Harper, 1941); and Gunnar Myrdal, *Beyond the Welfare State: Economic Planning and Its International Implications* (New Haven, CT: Yale University Press, 1960).
27. James A. Morone, *Hellfire Nation: The Politics of Sin in American History* (New Haven, CT: Yale University Press, 2003).
28. Timothy J. Hatton and Jeffrey G. Williamson, *The Age of Mass Migration: An Economic Analysis* (New York: Oxford University Press, 1998).
29. Nativism is named after the Native American Association formed in 1837 by American Protestants alarmed by the influx of Catholic immigrants. US nativists supported legalized discrimination against immigrants, mandatory Americanization, and national origin quotas intended to keep out the least desirable immigrants. The Chinese Exclusion Act (1882), the Bureau of Americanization (created in 1917), and the national origins quota system (1921 and 1924) are examples of nativist legislation.
30. Claudia Goldin, 'The Political Economy of Immigration Restriction in the USA, 1890–21,' in Claudia Goldin and Gary D. Libecap (eds.), *The Regulated Economy: A Historical Approach to Political Economy* (Chicago: University of Chicago Press, 1994); Asheley S. Timmer and Jeffrey G. Williamson, 'Racism, Xenophobia, or Markets? The Political Economy of Immigration Policy Prior to the Thirties,' National Bureau of Economic Research, Working Paper 5867 (December 1996), Cambridge, MA.

31. See Michael R. Alvarez, and Tara Butterfield, 'The Resurgence of Nativism in California? The Case of Proposition 187 and Illegal Immigration,' *Social Science Quarterly*, 81 (2000) 1: 167–79. Proposition 187 is an initiative measure that was submitted to the voters of the State of California in the November 8, 1994 general election. It passed with 59 percent of the vote and became law the next day. It required California law enforcement, social services, health care, and public personnel to verify the immigration status of persons with whom they come in contact and to deny services to out-of-status individuals and report those persons to state and federal officials. The act limited attendance at public schools to US citizens and lawful aliens. The courts voided parts of the act and it never became effective. In 1999, Governor Grey Davis withdrew the state's challenge to the court's decision and Proposition 187 was effectively annulled.

32. Using a pooled time-series research design on a cross-section of six Western European countries between 1984 and 1993, Pia Knigge found that unemployment and inflation had no effect on support for extreme right-wing parties; 'The ecological correlates of right-wing extremism in Western Europe,' *European Journal of Political Research*, 34 (1998), 2: 249–79. Using more sophisticated econometric data from Germany in 1989–98, Marcel Lubbers and Peer Scheepers also found no evidence that higher levels of unemployment increase the support for extreme right-wing parties; 'Explaining the trend in extreme right-wing voting: Germany 1989–98,' *European Sociological Review*, 17 (2001), 4: 431–49. A third study found a correlation between high levels of unemployment and high immigration, but failed to find an independent effect of unemployment on electoral success of extreme right wing parties; see Matt Golder, 'Explaining variation in the success of extreme right parties in western Europe,' *Comparative Political Studies*, 36 (2003), 4: 432–66.

33. The 2002 party program of the Danish People's Party states, for example, 'Foreigners should be absorbed in Danish society, but only under the condition that they do not pose a threat to social security and democracy.' Available at: http://www.danskfolkeparti.dk.

34. Alberto Alesina and Edward L. Glaeser, *Fighting Poverty in the US and Europe: A World of Difference* (Oxford: Oxford University Press, 2004).

35. The model presumes that immigrants' entitlement to benefits cannot legally be set at a different (lower) level than that of national origin residents. In fact, governments have in recent years tried to introduce increasing differentiation of benefit structures based upon legal status. Dietmar Wellisch and Uwe Walz, 'Why Do Rich Countries Prefer Free Trade Over Free Migration? The Role of the Modern Welfare State,' *European Economic Review*, 42 (1998), 2: 1595–612.

36. Michele Lamont, *The Dignity of Working Men: Morality and the Boundaries of Race, Class, and Immigration* (Princeton, NJ: Princeton University Press, 2000).

37. The authors translated the Dutch term 'allochtonen' as 'ethnic minorities.' Strictly speaking, it means means 'foreigners' and is used in statistics, policy documents,

and daily speech to contrast the foreign-origin population—even when legally Dutch—to the 'autochtonen,' the Dutch-origin population. Paul M. Sniderman, Louk Hagendoorn, and Markus Prior, 'Predisposing Factors and Situational Triggers Exclusionary Reactions to Immigrant Minorities,' *American Political Science Review*, 98 (2004), 1: 35–49.

38. Ibid, 46.
39. Aristide R. Zolberg and Long Litt Woon, 'Why Islam Is Like Spanish: Cultural Incorporation in Europe and the USA,' *Politics and Society*, 27 (1999), 1: 5–38.
40. Interview 20, Copenhagen (Sept. 15, 2003).
41. Jytte Klausen, 'The Re-Politicization of Religion in Europe: The Next Ten Years,' *Perspectives on Politics*, September 2005, 554–7.
42. Huntington, *The Clash of Civilizations*, 20.
43. Huntington, *Who Are We?*, 188.
44. William Dalrymple, 'The truth About Muslims,' *New York Review of Books* (November 4, 2004): 31–34.
45. http://www.islam-online.net/English/News/2004-04/20/article07.shtml.
46. Dale F. Eickelman and James Piscatori, *Muslim Politics* (Princeton, NJ: Princeton University Press, 1996), 4.

5

Christian and Muslim Europe

'European culture cannot be defined in opposition to a particular religion (such as Islam),' concludes a high-level report issued by Romano Prodi, the departing president of the European Commission in October 2004. Nevertheless, the report admits that, in effect, Europe sees itself as Christian, and the authors acknowledge that religion is a political matter. 'Even in Europe, where modernization and secularization appear to go hand in hand, public life without religion is inconceivable.' Yet while recognizing that there are institutional barriers to the integration of Islam, they take refuge in vague generalizations. 'The only feasible path...consists in understanding the consequences of transplanting Islam into a European context.'[1]

In Europe, church and state are still intertwined in ways that secular Christians hardly notice but which nonetheless penalize religious minorities. National policies are often bewilderingly inconsistent. The continued importance of legal privileges for Christians is most evident in those European countries that have established churches, i.e., a church recognized by law as the official church of a state or nation, and given civil authority. In practice, however, the differences between countries with constitutionally privileged national churches—Lutheranism in Denmark and Norway, Anglicanism in Great Britain, Greek Orthodox in Greece, and Roman Catholicism in Portugal—and those that do not formally have a national church is often small.

Europeans have followed two different models for organizing church-state relations: religious monopolies or state-sponsorship of particular recognized national religions. The US model of strict separation of church and state has not found favor anywhere. Typically, European governments fund religious schools, maintain church property and cemeteries, and educate the clergy at public universities. Religious pluralism is a new social fact with which European states have yet to come to terms and, country by country, they are plunging into national debates about religion and public policy and how to accommodate growing numbers of nonconformist believers. Muslims are, for many reasons, at the center of the controversy.

HOW CHRISTIAN ARE EUROPEANS?

European electoral politics is no longer a 'religion-free' zone. Public debates refer with increasing frequency to the importance of religious values, and even secular politicians on the left may invoke the Christian heritage as a source of national identity.[2] As voters have increasingly supported extremist parties, the large parties on the left and right have been driven to adopt a nativist rhetoric.[3] To take one near comical case, a Danish social democrat and former prime minister, Poul Nyrup Rasmussen, spoke during an election campaign of 'the irreconcilable differences between Danish and Muslim cultures' [*sic*]. He also said it is unacceptable that Muslims interrupt the working day with prayers, 'because in Denmark, we work when we are at our jobs.'[4] He forgot about the union-negotiated coffee-breaks.

When even in officially Anglican England the media gave huge publicity to the outpouring of emotion that accompanied the death of John Paul II, some elements of the press declared that a 'Catholic renewal' was under way in the country.[5] Catholics were surprised too. 'It was like a miracle,' said Father Michael Seed, an advisor to Cardinal Cormac Murphy-O'Connor. 'Tony Blair, Prince Charles, Lady Thatcher, John Major, Michael Howard, Charles Kennedy, the Lord Chancellor, half the Cabinet and the entire diplomatic corps, plus the Union flag at half mast and prayers in mosques.... This is a time of God's blessing on the earth.'[6] But the Father spoke tongue in cheek. Britain has not turned Catholic and old religious conflicts are still causing political friction.

In October 2004, the proposed new commission for the EU was rejected by the European Parliament (EP) largely because of one commissioner's views on homosexuality. Rocco Buttiglione, nominated for the post of commissioner responsible for justice and security, was opposed by the left parties in the EP because in his confirmation hearing he had said that homosexuality was a sin, and that the purpose of marriage is to protect women and children. The EP accused Buttiglione of repudiating the EU law prohibiting discrimination against homosexuals, which he would be required to implement as justice commissioner. Buttiglione eventually withdrew but a senior Vatican official, Cardinal Angelo Sodano, commented to the press: 'This is not the first time that Catholics, Christians, men of the Church find themselves confronted by problems of this type and in danger of becoming victims of isolation and discrimination.'[7]

When the new constitution of the EU was drafted, German, Italian, Polish, and Slovakian delegates argued that a reference to 'God' and to 'Christian values' should be incorporated in the text, and they were supported by the former French president, Valéry Giscard d'Estaing, a Roman Catholic.[8] Greece, Denmark, and Ireland fought to include a preemptive paragraph (Article I-51(3)) that protected existing church privileges against the convention's antidiscrimination clauses, arousing the ire of the British Humanist Society and the International League of Nonreligions and Atheists (IBKA), a German-based association of atheists.[9] Nonetheless, academics have also voiced the view that the moral identity of Europe rests on secularized Christian values, which other faiths (by implication, Islam) are perceived not to share.[10]

Prominent political leaders have also acknowledged the importance of Christianity to their political engagement. Lionel Jospin, the French socialist prime minister from 1997 to 2002, grew up as a Quaker, and says his faith inspired his early antiwar position in connection with the Suez crisis and the Soviet invasion of Budapest in 1956. Helmut Kohl, the German Christian democratic chancellor from 1982 to 1998, was a Roman Catholic. Tony Blair has described himself as a Christian socialist, and Jacques Chirac has allowed the public to know he attends church regularly. Chirac's wife interceded on behalf of her favorite Mother Superior, so that she would be exempted from a new rule requiring women to remove head coverings in ID photos.[11] (The nun wanted to be photographed in her wimple.) Most European parliaments make prayer rooms available for representatives. In the German Bundestag, about twenty members pray daily. The room accommodates both Protestants and Catholics, but there is no prayer room for Muslims.

What about ordinary people? Empty pews in churches suggest that Europeans care less and less about religion. But if Europeans are not in general actively Christians, they are, by their own assessment, passively Christian in large numbers. Surveys show a recent increase in the number of Europeans who express religious commitment.[12] When the Eurobarometer Survey asked respondents to identify their faith, 70–90 percent of the sample in Austria, Belgium, Italy, Ireland, Spain, and Portugal described themselves as Catholic, as did 64 percent of the French and 40 percent of (West) Germans. In Denmark, Finland, and Sweden, 60–80 percent described themselves as Protestant. So also did 40–45 percent of Britons and (West) Germans. In a few countries, notably France, Britain, and Sweden, between a third and a fifth of the population describe themselves as nonbelievers. 'Non-believers' constitute a majority in the Netherlands (57 percent) and the former East Germany (68 percent).[13] Europeans are obviously less inclined to belief compared to Americans, 90 percent of whom say that they believe in God. However, even in Western Europe, the majority of people tell pollsters that they do believe in God. Even in ungodly Scandinavia, 56.6 percent of Danes say they believe in God, although only 36 percent of Swedes say they believe.

The Gallup International Millennium Survey provided an international comparison of patterns of belief and observance, and Europeans are certainly unusual in global terms. Gallup found that 88 percent of Western Europeans declare that they belong to a denomination, yet only 20 percent report that they attend services regularly apart from weddings and special occasions.[14] This average disguises large-scale national differences, from less than 5 percent of the population in Scandinavia to nearly one-third in Great Britain who regularly attend church services.

The 'empty pews' comparison presumes that if you do not go to church on Sunday, you do not care about religion. But religion matters more to Europeans than their Sunday behavior lets on. Europeans pay their governments to support their churches, and assume that the church will be there when they need it. The consumption of essential religious services—baptisms, confirmations, weddings, and funerals—has been remarkably resistant to change. Denmark and Sweden are often described as the epitome of European secularism, but 85 percent of the population in the two countries belong to the national Protestant churches. Swedes are more prone to church weddings (61 percent) than are Danes (43 percent). Danes, however, are more partial to confirmations (80 percent). About three-quarters of the newborns in both countries are christened, and they get christened even if the parents are not married.[15] The Danish and Swedish national churches provide 90 percent of the population with a religious burial. One has to conclude that many Swedes and Danes who profess not to believe in God nevertheless turn to the church for assistance throughout their lives.

Religious leaders often despair over these numbers. They complain that Europeans approach faith the same way they think of savings: the government will take care of it.[16] Nonetheless, the established religions are also beneficiaries of practices and institutions that guarantee their continued existence in spite of the apathy of their flock. Muslim leaders sometimes worry that accepting state subsidies will have a similar pacifying effect on Islam, and oppose extending existing templates for religious accommodation to state–mosque relations for this reason.[17] Others, however, see it rather as desirable that the government should sustain Islamic institutions that discourage religious zealotry.

ARE MUSLIMS MORE RELIGIOUS?

It is difficult to make a direct comparison between European Muslims and Christians with respect to habits of religious observance. It may also be misguided to do so. Communal prayer is one of the pillars of Islam. Attending church regularly is also important for some Christian denominations, but for many it is a minor duty of faith. That is not the only difficulty. Surveys of religious observance have produced wildly different estimates of the balance between the highly observant and the nonobservant. Methodological difficulties account for some of the inconsistency, but a more important complication is that researchers disagree about basic definitions of 'observance' and 'fundamentalism.' MORI, a British polling organization, has also pointed out problems associated with the polling of small subgroups, such as British Muslims. Randomized surveys include too few members of subgroups—of Hindus or Muslims, for example—to enable generalization. The Euro barometer surveys, which are otherwise a convenient source of European polling data, include so few Muslims from each country that meaningful analysis is impossible. An alternative sampling procedure is to poll a particular area with a high concentration of the subgroup, or to select respondents based upon last names. (However, among some ethnic groups, many names are not immediately recognizable as 'Muslim,' and converts do not necessarily change their names.[18])

There are a few specialized studies of Muslims' religious habits, but they use different methodologies and define religious observance in different ways, which make them problematic sources of comparison. One US study of about 1,300 Muslims in twelve of the thirty-three mosques in Detroit and the surrounding metropolitan area found that only eight percent of those polled—who were drawn from the mosque audiences—said they abided by strict, traditionalist interpretations of Islam. The researcher, Ihsan Bagby, concluded that this finding buttressed the argument that American Muslims are overwhelmingly 'moderate.' Considering that Americans are usually more observant than Europeans, we might expect European Muslims to have become acculturated to 'lazy' patterns of observance, but European studies have tended to find higher rates of strict observance. A German study conducted among Turkish-origin Muslims in 2001 in Nordrhein-Westphalia suggested that a large minority was irreligious while a majority was fairly religious: 40 percent described themselves as either not at all or just a little religious, 49 percent as religious, and only eight percent as very religious. Women were slightly more observant than men and younger people less religious than older.[19]

A French study from 2001 found that only ten percent of 4–5 million Muslims are 'pratiquant,' religiously observant.[20] Michèle Tribalat, a French demographer, reported that 60 percent of Muslim men and 70 percent of Muslim women are not observant, although they respect what she calls 'cultural attachments' to Islam by not eating pork, not drinking alcohol, not smoking, and fasting during Ramadan. Tribalat supports the idea that assimilation is necessary. It is, she says, 'the process of learning the principles and the ways of French society,' and argues that the secularization of religious practices is as important as learning to speak the language.[21] In her view, 'the French sociopolitical system cannot survive without the erasure of some [immigrant] cultural peculiarities.'

But what you find seems to be a function of what you ask. A telephone survey of 500 French Muslims conducted in December 1997 and January 1998 by SOFRES and *Le Nouvel Observateur*, a French news magazine, found that 63 percent of French Muslims described themselves as 'croyant et pratiquant' (believers and practicing); 34 percent said they were believers but not practicing; and only two percent described themselves as nonbelievers.[22]

Gilles Kepel also studied religious observance among French Muslims, but used a different method and reached yet a third conclusion about the extent of religiosity. He interviewed fifty-eight Muslims about their personal commitment to Islamic law and dietary rules, and their willingness to sacrifice rules in order to interact with non-Muslims. The group was selected to approximate roughly the French Muslim population's key demographic characteristics. One-third were French citizens and the main countries of origin were represented. Kepel concluded that 24 percent were too orthodox to interact with French society.[23] The orthodox would not eat with a non-Muslim, for example, and insisted on following strict dietary restrictions. Kepel concluded that the strictures associated with adhering to Islamic religious rules represented debilitating obstacles to integration.

A comprehensive Dutch study of Moroccan- and Turkish-origin Muslims living in the Netherlands was published in 2004. It was based upon survey data from 1999 and 2002, and found that about one-third of second-generation Muslims visit the mosque weekly but found no evidence of increasing religiosity. 88 percent of Turkish-origin and 98 percent of Moroccan-origin Muslims consider themselves believers.[24] One-quarter of the former and half of the latter also thought that Muslims should try to spread Islam in the Netherlands, but less than ten percent of either group belonged to a Muslim or Islamic organization.

It is difficult to interpret these numbers. One problem is that surveys based upon self-reported church/mosque attendance often exaggerate actual attendance. That said, it is clear that European mosques are well-attended and that many Muslims observe some but rarely all of the rules of their faith. It is also the case that few translate faith into civic action. The Moroccan- and Turkish-origin Dutch Muslims differed little in their commitments to their faith—very high ratios in both populations declared themselves to be believers and very few joined organizations—but they did differ in the lessons that they drew with respect to public action. One-quarter of those of Turkish origin thought that Muslims are obliged to spread Islam in the West, whereas about half of Moroccan-origin Muslims thought so. As for the headscarf, one-third of the Turks thought Muslim women ought to wear it, but half of the Moroccans were in favor.

If we compare and contrast Dutch Muslims to Scandinavian Protestants, the chief difference is not one of religious faith. Nine out of ten Muslims describe themselves as believers, while six to eight out of every ten Protestants do. The chief difference is how they practice their faiths. Three out of ten Muslims say they go to the mosque regularly, but only one out of twenty Protestants say they go to church regularly.

CHURCH AND STATE IN EUROPE: THE AUGSBURG LEGACY

There are historical reasons why Europeans have few preexisting templates for dealing with religious diversity. Twentieth-century political reform movements in Europe worried little about religion. Religious minorities were 'tolerated.' Existing church-state frameworks carry the imprint of the 1555 Augsburg 'Religionsfriede,' which established the *cuius regio, eius religio* principle that subjects would have the faiths of their rulers. Religious conformity—to Protestantism or Catholicism—has been a vehicle of societal integration and assimilation ever since.[25] The Augsburg Treaty ratified the institutional and sociological imprint of the religious map created by the Reformation and divided Europe into a Protestant north and a Catholic south.

One can argue about the degree of path-dependency. The 1949 German republic recognized both Protestantism and Catholicism as national religions, and Judaism was later included as well. Nonetheless, until the arrival of Muslim immigrants the largest minority religions in Western Europe were Catholics in the north and Protestants in the south. Amish, Anabaptists, Mennonites, Brethrens and other Pietists, and Moravians are some of the small religious groups that emigrated, mostly to the USA but also to Africa or Canada. The Jewish minority suffered devastating losses as a result of the Holocaust, and after the Second World War many European Jews emigrated to the USA and Israel. European democracy evolved in concert with strong pressures of homogenization, in which the rights of minority religions and languages were sacrificed in the pursuit of social integration.[26]

Among the countries that have both constitutionally established confessions *and* publicly subsidized faiths are Austria, Denmark, Norway, Finland, Greece, and Italy. France, Italy, Germany, the Netherlands, and Sweden are constitutionally secular states but they all provide direct or indirect subsidies for institutions associated with *recognized* faiths, for example, religious schools or social and health services. In Sweden, Belgium, and the Netherlands, funding opportunities are *de jure* available to all religions, but state neutrality remains an elusive and not fully accepted goal. In Germany, the Protestant and Roman Catholic churches, as well as Judaism, but not Islam, the third largest faith, are entitled to federally-collected church taxes and the right to run state-subsidized religious social services and hospitals.

An anomaly is the Anglican Church in England, which is an established faith but receives no direct subsidies from the government. The Church of England is formally linked to the British Crown and as such it is an established religion. Fewer than half of all Britons belong to it, and it baptizes only about 25 percent of all newborn. The government provides no direct subsidy, except for 70 percent of the funds for the Church of England's fund for the maintenance of churches.

Religious schools are more controversial. In Britain there are state-funded Roman Catholic, Muslim, Jewish, Sikh, and Greek Orthodox schools. Referred to as 'voluntary-aided schools,' the schools are established by religious denominations—often a parish or a mosque—but financed by local government. Britain started funding Muslim public schools—or state schools as they are called in Britain—only recently, but in addition to the religiously managed state schools, there exists a large number of independent—or private— religious schools. Public funding covers 85 percent of voluntary-aided schools' costs, soon to be set at ten percent based upon a new government proposal.[27] The independent schools are not government funded but must teach to a national curriculum. By 2004, five Muslim public schools had been established and over eighty independent private schools accredited. In comparison, there are over 2,000 Roman Catholic voluntary (public) and 160 independent (private but publicly supported) schools in England and Wales. A quarter of all government schools are managed by the Church of England.

However, it is the Queen's role as head of state and governor of the Anglican Church of England that raises the most sensitive questions about reform of state–Church relations. The Church continues to enjoy certain constitutional privileges, including the automatic seating in the House of Lords of twenty-five bishops and archbishops. The 1999 reform of the House of Lords that led to the departure of most of the hereditary peers also proposed to allow representation for non-Christian and Christian denominations other than the Church of England. The Church of England supported the proposal but conservative Lords and the Blair government were opposed.[28] A new Joint Committee on House of Lords Reform was created in 2002, and proposals for the representation of other faith communities are likely to reemerge.

The 1949 German constitution says that the state must be *neutral* in matters of religion but the stipulation does not preclude close cooperation between church and state, an arrangement that Josef Joffe has aptly called 'a peculiar cohabitation of throne and altar.'[29] In Germany funding is available to Catholics, Protestants, and Jews, but not to Muslims. Faith groups can incorporate as public law corporations, and the federal authorities collect a nine percent church tax, which is redistributed to the recognized religions in proportion to their membership in return for a collection fee paid to the state. Taxpayers are required to indicate their faith on tax returns, although non-believers may elect to contribute to a charity in place of a religious denomination. The recognized faiths are also awarded representation on various national boards, ranging from public radio and TV to government commissions. Church-run charitable organizations—the Catholic 'Caritas,' the Protestant 'Diakonisches Werk,' and the Jewish welfare organization—receive public funding for the provision of services from hospitals to day care centers and retirement homes. The federal government also places conscientious objectors who choose social service instead of serving in the Bundeswehr (the German army) in the quasi-religious organizations.

Almost eighty percent of France's population is Roman Catholic. Islam is the second largest religion. Other religious groups include Lutherans and Calvinists, as well as a growing Jewish population. The 1905 Law of Separation eliminated the Catholic Church's special privileges and guaranteed freedom of religion, except for restrictions imposed 'in the interest of public policy.' Article 2 of the law prohibited public funding for any religion, and declared that 'all expenses concerning the practice of religions shall be eliminated from the budgets of the state, departements and townships' (translation by the French Ministry of Justice).[30] In practice, however, the government assumed responsibility for all houses of worship built before 1905, which continue to this day to be state property. They are maintained by municipalities and are used free of charge by the clergy. Since 1959, the state also pays the salaries of teachers in religious schools. About twenty percent of French students go to religious schools, mostly Catholic schools. The schools receive about eighty percent of their budgets (teachers' salaries and some operating costs) from the government. In the case of special contract schools, those on a 'contract d'association,' public funding is set at 105 percent of the cost per student in public schools. The government has yet to fund a Muslim school. An independent Muslim girls school was created in Lyon to teach girls who had been withdrawn from area high schools for wearing the headscarf, but the school is borrowing rooms from a mosque and might be considered an experiment in home-schooling.

The 1901 Law of Associations guaranteed freedom of association (undoing a ban on private association in effect throughout the nineteenth century) and allowed religious groups to pursue activities unrelated to worship and to acquire tax-exempt status. Ironically, Muslim associations have been able to obtain municipal subsidies for the creation of cultural centers and cultural activities. Until 1981, noncitizens were prohibited from creating associations and migrant groups were legally unable to form associations until the prohibition was lifted.

Special rules apply in the Alsace and Moselle areas, which were restored to France only after the First World War and are exempt from the 1905 law. The Catholic Church, the Lutheran Church, the Calvinist Church, and the Jewish community receive public funding and priests, rabbis, and pastors paid by the state. (It was nevertheless determined that the headscarf ban would also apply to Alsace and Moselle.)

Both France and Germany have strict rules against 'sects,' which disallow particular religious groups. Scientology is a well-known example. As a result, the governments are free to eject nonnational preachers whose presence is considered undesirable. The French government maintains a legal distinction between approved religious associations entitled to tax-exempt status under the 1905 law and 'sects,' and maintains a list of sects that are subject to supervision and in some cases accused of criminal behavior. Since June 2001, France has banned 'dangerous' religious sects, specifically Scientology. The law is assumed also to provide legal basis for the government's decision to expel Islamist imams.[31] Clearly, the principle of the separation of church and state is sufficiently flexible to allow for government support for faith-based public activities in some areas, and is far from being as absolute as it is sometimes presented.

In the Netherlands, the Calvinist Reformed Church was disestablished in 1796 after the Batavian Revolution. Roman Catholics, Jews, and other Protestants were given equal civil rights, but disestablishment did not mean the separation of church and state. Following a 1917 law, the government continued to pay for religious schools and religious institutions, contributing in equal measure to each of the religious 'pillars.' Between 1961 and 1975, the Dutch government subsidized the construction of churches with a total of 112 million Guilders, with the consequence that there was a church for every thirty families. Attempts were made in 1970–81 to create a Muslim 'pillar,' parallel to the Catholic and Protestant 'pillars', with public funding for Muslim TV and radio stations and for some measure of Muslim self-government. One mosque was built with government money before the 1983 amendment. The Dutch government privatized the clergy's salaries and pensions in a large buy-out in 1981 in preparation for a constitutional amendment that went into effect in 1983, after which the government ceased paying for the construction of houses of worship. After 1983, the official

N.B.

rhetoric changed to stress the 'separation' of church and state. 'The shift to state neutrality,' says Jan Rath, a Dutch sociologist, 'was like drawing up the bridge in front of the newcomers.'[32] The creation of Muslim schools under the generous Dutch rules for public funding for private religious schools has caused a great deal of controversy, to the point where many Dutch now think religious schools should be forced to 'diversify' their student populations.[33]

Belgian public policy on Islam exemplifies how difficult it can be to close the gap between constitutional commitments to state neutrality and implementation, even when the political will to do so exists. The 1830 Belgian constitution described the state as 'neutral' in matters of religion, but the state also assumed responsibility for clerical salaries and subsidized the construction and maintenance of places of worship. Religious communities were set up as national public corporations and given royal 'recognition.' Belgium recognized Islam in 1974, shortly before a state visit from King Faisal from Saudi Arabia, in the hope that the gesture would help relations with the oil-producing countries. A second measure was announced days before a second royal visit from Saudi Arabia in 1978. These initiatives had the unfortunate consequence of granting official recognition to the Saudi version of Islam, although 85 percent of Belgian Muslims are Moroccans or Turks.[34] Twenty years later, Belgium set up an elected 'high council,' the Representative Council of the Belgian Muslim Communities, but elections to the council were only held in 2004, the same year a new Royal Decree changed the funding for the six recognized religions to grant Muslims a significant increase in funding. (Islam now receives about 3.5 percent of the total funding provided for the recognized faiths and a seventh 'laic' council for associational activities for nonbelievers.) Currently, the government funds the salaries of about a hundred imams. Since January 2002, the Flemish region has additionally also provided funding for the construction of mosques. Significant practical obstacles remain to the development of a 'Muslim pillar' parallel to those in existence for other faiths. Formal theological training for imams and the imams' lack of competence in French or Flemish are particularly difficult problems that still have to be resolved.

Norway and Denmark still have state churches. Article 4 of the Danish constitution stipulates that: 'The Evangelical Lutheran Church shall be the Established Church of Denmark, and as such shall be supported by the state.' The national church is commonly referred to as the 'People's Church' (*Folkekirken*), a terminology that sustains a common belief that Denmark does not have a state church. The national tax authorities collect a special church tax for the Lutherans but not for other denominations and faiths. In addition, bishops' salaries, pensions, and a range of institutional costs are funded by way of general taxes. The clergy are civil servants and educated at public universities. The Minister of Church Affairs is the official head of the church and the Ministry its governing body.

Paragraph 68 of the Danish constitution prohibits making anyone pay dues to faiths other than their own. Residents may be exempt from paying church tax if they provide the tax authorities with proof of nonmembership of the Lutheran Church. Until such proof is provided, everybody–Catholic, Baptist, or Muslim—pays. The minority religions put the creation of a check-off system whereby taxpayers could choose which religion they would like to support at the top of their list of desired reforms.

On January 1, 2000, Sweden became the first Nordic country to disestablish the state church. The Swedish Lutheran Church—referred to as the Swedish Church, 'Svenska Kyrkan'—was previously organized on much the same lines as the Danish People's Church. However, many members of the clergy resented the constraints imposed by the Church's affiliation with the state.[35] The public was more exercised by the practice of signing all newborns up, non-Christian or Christian, as members of the state church. The practice apparently dated from the days when winter travel was difficult, and it was considered necessary to baptize children *in absentia* in the event of death in infancy. But the practice was continued long after winter travel was no longer a problem and infant death no longer a common occurrence.

Although the parishes and church associations of the Church of Sweden no longer have public status, the government continues to collect income-graduated church fees from members of the church together with taxes. The Church of Sweden continues to be responsible for the provision of cemetery plots for all Swedish residents, but the costs of funeral activities are kept separate from other church activities. And the government has issued detailed directives for how public cemeteries must accommodate various religious burial practices in collaboration with local faith leaders. Sweden has also found ways to subsidize the construction of mosques, and four have been built in recent years with the assistance of public funds. In a separate act, the Swedish Religious Communities Act, which went into effect January 1, 2000, granted other religions eligibility for state grants, albeit funding has by no means been equalized between religions. As in the case of the French 1905 ecclesiastical reform, the state assumed responsibility for the costs of main-taining church real estate. This was justified on the grounds that these buildings were part of Sweden's national heritage.

In Norway, concerns about the ability of the state church to compete with 'charismatic' churches and new faiths led the Norwegian Lutheran Church to unveil a proposal in 2002 that would have allowed for a separate constitution for the church and legislative changes that would have enabled the govern-ment to subsidize other religions.[36] In the end, however, the church decided not to ask for constitutional changes and focused rather on reforms that do not affect its official status.

APPROACHING ISLAM: PROSELYTIZING OR INTERFAITH DIALOGUE

The Christian churches have had difficulties agreeing on how to approach the 'Muslim question.' One argument is that Islam should be respected as one of the three monotheistic world religions, an 'Abrahamic' religion. However, some Christians invoke the 'clash of civilizations' thesis, and argue that Muslims cannot be trusted because they do not abide by the rules of human rights and Islam is an intolerant religion.

Speaking at the Tenth Assembly of the Lutheran World Federation (the LWF meets every six years) in July 2003, the President, Bishop emeritus Dr Christian Krause, invoked the Abrahamic triad to argue for interreligious rapprochement. Noting that while all recent terrorists had been Muslims, Krause said:

Fundamentalism can be found equally in other religions, including Christianity and Judaism. All three Abrahamic religions have the potential, on the one hand for violent fanaticism and, on the other, for enlightenment and tolerance or, politically speaking, for the rule of law and separation between church and state. The struggle against terrorism must embrace all the countries of the world as far as possible, also and especially those with a predominantly Muslim population. But it must never become a clash of civilizations or even of religions.[37]

He remarked that dialogue between Jews and Lutherans evolved only under the heavy weight of guilt from the Holocaust, and asked 'must there first be a similar catastrophe before Christians and Muslims begin a dialogue with one another?' He then proceeded to propose that the 'leadership of Christian churches' should try to enter into dialogue with 'leading representatives of Islam,' and that the theological faculties start a dialogue with Islamic scholars. Unusually candid, he acknowledged that the first step might be that they 'begin to read the Koran.' Dialogue had to begin with the realization that 'in Islam as a whole, and not just on its terrorist fringes, a tremendous amount of anger and often also of hatred has accumulated against the West and its way of life.'

Bishop Krause proposed extending to Islam the formula that Lutherans have applied to other Christian churches: 'Should we not work for the same goal of "reconciled diversity" in relations between Christianity and Islam?'

There must be no crusade against Islam, but dialogue. However, his proposal was accompanied by an exhortation to religious revival among Lutherans: 'If you do not show your colors, your color cannot be recognized.'

Scandinavian Lutherans have found the Abrahamic approach difficult to accept. Many think that proselytizing and the revival of mission at home is the proper answer to the growing presence of Islam in Christian countries. Discomfort with Islam is often tied up with a general unease about the religious practices of immigrants, who frequently challenge the austere forms of worship that characterize the Protestant state churches.[38] The established church feels that it too must change to prevent the spread of alternative faith movements and 'charismatic churches,' a term used in Protestant Europe to describe what in the USA are called evangelical churches. The first response to religious diversity is not to accept sectarian diversity. Rather, the feeling is that competing religious movements must be co-opted and constrained.

An article in a Christian Danish newspaper, *Kristelig Dagblad*, described in detail the kinds of adjustments that the Danish national church should accept in order to accommodate immigrants. A Copenhagen parish near the airport on the outskirts of the city caters to a community that is about ten percent immigrant, including some Muslims. The pastor happily reported that about a hundred people routinely turn up for services on Sunday. The parish is run by the pastor, Jesper Oehlenschläger, and an Indian-origin assistant, Rajesh David. The pastor described the sermon and the psalms as particularly difficult to absorb for the new parishioners. As for why they choose to come, he said that many immigrants from Orthodox or Catholic backgrounds choose to belong to the People's Church parishes because they think it is a better path to social and cultural integration into Danish society. 'They think that now this is where they live and then they have better be part of the national church.' They also think, he added, it is a way to get into contact with Danes.

Rajesh David acknowledged that many immigrants find the rituals boring and miss more expressive services. They still come, he said, because they get in contact with the church when they have to go and register their address. (In Denmark, the national church is in charge of the administration of the civil registry.) At the same time they ask for addresses for church communities and are often sent to the pastor. In order to accommodate the new parishioners, the parish has added genuflection and prayers for peace to the services. 'It is very positive,' the pastor concluded. He admitted that the People's Church is often regarded as being hostile to immigrants, but pointed out that the parish's summer camp included some Muslims and everybody had a good time. He concluded that the more the Church returns to its roots, by which he meant its spiritual roots rather than the official business of being a state church, the more religious, cultural, and social differences become irrelevant.[39]

Theologians do not generally share the sanguine view of spiritual revival. Speaking on the occasion of the opening of a new center for multireligious studies at the theological faculty of University of Århus, a public university, Viggo Mortensen, the center director and a professor of theology, argued that the Danish church must meet the challenge posed by Islam by strengthening itself. 'When Sulejma says "no thank you" to the good Danish chopped liver in the kindergarten a religious dialogue takes place at the next parents' meeting.' In that situation, Mortensen continued, 'the Church must be ready and assist its members in the reconstruction of a healthy Christian identity that can stand up to the spiritual struggle that we are facing.'[40]

Remarkably, this discussion of how to beat back Islam in Denmark took place on the occasion of a celebration of the opening of a publicly financed new center dedicated to the study of interreligious relations at a public university. The unabashed defense of Lutheranism as the Danish national faith was illustrated by the university provost's remarks. 'The fact that it is the People's Church that takes custody of the dialogue with Islam as its business and that it is precisely our theological Faculty that hosts this debate, this time around, sends an important signal to society, namely that Islam's presence in the Danish society cannot be seen simply as matters of culture and lifestyles, habits and dress, language and tradition.'

The Lutheran World Federation's commitment to an Abrahamic view of Islam as a partner religion is far removed from the theological practices of state-sponsored Protestantism. Often, as the Danish discussion shows, the theological faculties mostly think of themselves as representing official Christendom. Theologians and university administrators perceive Islam as a 'problem,' and they rarely approach it neutrally or with a commitment to religious pluralism. As long as this is the case, the prospects for the integration of Islamic religious scholarship and the education of Islamic teachers and scholars into public universities remain poor.

Pope John Paul II used the term 'brothers in Abraham' to describe the relationship between Christianity, Islam, and Judaism. The message of interfaith reconciliation was most clearly put in a December 2000 pontifical message for the end of Ramadan, in which the Pope said 'we can see humanity as a single family in both its diversity and its common aspirations. This is education in the fundamental values of human dignity, peace, freedom and solidarity.'[41] The Vatican's effort to reach out to Islam culminated in a March 2001 visit to Damascus, where John Paul spoke about the neighborly relations over the centuries between Christianity and Islam and delivered a message of interfaith peace.

But even before the 9/11 attacks many Catholic bishops opposed the Vatican's rapprochement with Islam. At the 1999 synod, some bishops took a dark view of Islam's growing presence in Europe. Archbishop Giuseppe Bernardini, who heads the Izmir archdiocese in Turkey, spoke of a new Islamic 'program of expansion and reconquest' in Europe through immigration and funded by 'petrodollars.' He compared Muslim–Christian dialogue to a dialogue of the deaf. 'It is a fact that terms such as "dialogue," "justice," "reciprocity," or concepts such as "rights of man," "democracy," have a completely different meaning for the Muslim than for us.'[42] Alain Besançon, a French Catholic scholar, challenged the use of the term 'Abrahamic' because it implied that the three religions were equals, and warned that Catholics had to strengthen their resolve in the confrontation with Islam, and to fight conversions.[43]

Disagreements over how to characterize Islam obscured the context for Pope John Paul II's message to the synod. He stressed the urgent need to combat religious indifference and voiced concern over the 'widening separation between private conscience and public values.' He warned that a 'consumer approach to religious experience is being propagated,' and urged Europeans to reexamine and rediscover their faith. 'Europe is more and more in need of a renewed evangelization and a new missionary effort. In some cases, it is a matter of preaching the Gospel of Christ to those who still do not know it; in others, to mend the fabric of Christian communities.'[44]

Proponents of intercultural dialogue in general and dialogue with Muslims in particular took heart from Pope John Paul II's vision of an alliance of all religions against the erosion of faith by global commercialization and state-promoted secularization. Thomas Michel, SJ, the Secretary for Interreligious Dialogue at the Jesuit Curia in Rome, writes in defense of Christian–Muslim dialogue:

To Muslims, these are not the values [profit-oriented modernism and consumerism] by which God intends that people live. Islam, like Christian faith, teaches that the purpose of human life is to know, worship, and obey God, to love and serve others, and to hope for the day when those who remain faithful to God will be rewarded with eternal life in God's presence. Thus, the values which should characterize human societies are solidarity, mutual assistance, concern for the poor, and constant recollection of God's greatness, gentleness and compassion. The God-centered society they seek to build should be one of peace: peace with God by living in accord with God's will, peace in fellowship among the various sectors of society, and peace among nations.[45]

The German Cardinal Joseph Ratzinger, now Pope Benedict XVI, has expressed admiration for religious Muslims on the grounds of their piety and commitment to marital fidelity, and he did so in order to make a contrast to

Western decadence. He voiced the view that interreligious dialogue must proceed from the mutual recognition of such fundamental values and, in effect, made Christian moral restoration a precondition for dialogue with Islam. On another occasion, Ratzinger was reported by the Vatican Radio as saying that Turkey 'in the balance of history' has been opposed to Europe and should not join 'the predominantly Christian European Union' but properly belonged in an association of Islamic states.[46] The unavoidable conclusion is that the Roman Catholic Church is as divided about how to approach Islam as are European Protestant churches and European governments.

The German headscarf ban revealed deep divisions among the Catholic and the Protestant bishops and between the supporters of interreligious dialogue and those who believe that Islam is a threat rather than an Abrahamic partner religion. The conference of Catholic bishops failed to reach an agreement before the two bishops of Baden-Württemberg endorsed the proposed head-scarf ban in their state.[47]

Testifying before the legislative committee in charge of the headscarf legislation, Michael Trensky, who as *Oberkirchenrat* (a civil service position) represented the views of both the Protestant and the Catholic bishops, explained that all four bishops—two Protestant and two Catholic—supported the ban on the grounds that, first, equality between man and women is a fundamental value that overrides religious rights, and second, there is no obligation under the Basic Law's Article 3 to treat all religions equally. Teachers are obliged to observe the neutrality requirement, but Article 15 of the Baden-Württemberg constitution states clearly that education and public values must reflect the Christian tradition.[48]

Dr Trensky relied on a particular formulation that has subsequently been used repeatedly in Germany to define the limits of religious toleration. In Baden-Württemberg, the bishops' statement said that the obligation to value neutrality implies espousing values that are colored—'christlich geprägt'—by Christian philosophy and tradition. Therefore you can, at the same time, ban the headscarves, and observe the constitutional requirements with respect to public value neutrality, religious freedom, and equality between men and women. In fact, respect for those fundamental values *requires* you to ban the headscarf.

The German Lutheran bishops were as divided as their Catholic counterparts. In the Council of the Evangelical Church in Germany (EKD), the national association of various Protestant churches, bishops from Rhineland-Westphalia, Hamburg, and Lübeck opposed the ban, because they considered it counterproductive or a violation of religious freedom. Several of the dissenters, among both Protestants and Catholics, opposed the ban because they shared the concerns expressed by the departing federal president Johannes Rau that 'banning the headscarf is the first step toward the creation of a secular state that bans religious signs and symbols from public life.'[49]

Despite the endorsement by Bishop Gebhard Fürst of the headscarf ban, the Catholic Rottenburg-Stuttgart diocese is deeply engaged in Christian–Muslim dialogue. In 2004, the diocese hosted several joint Muslim–Christian conferences and sponsored initiatives intended to help Muslims organize and present themselves to governments and policymakers. It put together one of only two seminars designed to coach imams in German expectations with respect to pastoral activities. The workshop was part of a pilot project to create an imam education project initiated by the Fedral Agency for Civic Education, a semi-independent government agency. Speaking to the thirty imams who participated, Bishop Fürst quoted Jürgen Habermas and spoke about how, rather than increased secularism, the creation of a Christian–Muslim community of interreligious learning—'christlich-muslimische Lerngemeinschaft'—is the key to toleration in a pluralist society.

The diocese also hosted a workshop organized by an advocacy group for interreligious dialogue, the KCID, which I attended. This brought together activists and theologians to discuss experiences with Muslim–Christian collaboration in public and religious life. The workshop dramatized the differences between the advocates of the 'Abrahamic' approach to interreligious affairs and those who oppose rapprochement. Martin Affolderbach, a pastor who is responsible in the EKD for relations with Islam, spoke of the disagreements over what interreligious dialogue means. The EKD regards dialogue as a goal-oriented and structured conversation between official representatives of the participating churches. An example is cooperation on particular projects, which the EKD has undertaken in the past together with the Jewish and Muslim councils. Affolderbach noted that extended dialogue with Islam is not possible at present, and would be impossible until Islam in Germany became organized in a unified structure so that church representatives could be confident that their interlocutors speak on behalf of the faith, with the backing of every Muslim household in the country. As an example, he mentioned that the EKD's invitation to the Muslim council (ZMD) to discuss its new *Islamische Charta* remained unanswered eighteen moths later. (The ZMD is one of several major Muslim associations, and it is not clear why it was selected over the others as dialogue 'partner.')

Affolderbach listed three kinds of criticism of interreligious dialogue with Muslims that are made within the church. First, Muslims are not serious about it, because they have hidden radical and unconstitutional goals, and their real purpose is to establish Islam in Germany and in the future to introduce Islamic religious law. Second, Muslims regard Jews and Christians as infidels, and are not ready to accept pluralism. They deny women's rights. Third, Christians should concentrate on strengthening the faith and address the ignorance about their own faith among Christians.[50]

The counter-argument was articulated by Abdul Hadi Christian Hoffmann, a foundation member of the Muslim Academy in Berlin. He argued that dialogue was communication. It should not be reduced to negotiation between the official churches. The precondition for communication was the ability to listen. Such communication had been possible earlier. Now that the highest representative from the EKD stated that the headscarf was political, one had to question whether he ever listened to anything that was said. (Hoffmann ignored the Catholic bishops' role.)

N.B.

Hoffman objected that Muslims are always faced with conditions when they try to engage in dialogue. They have to state that, yes, they are ready to be integrated and to demonstrate they are sincere—that they do not have hidden agendas—and are asked, first, second, and third, to reiterate their commitment to human rights and to reject terrorism. Unless you, as a Muslim, criticize Islam, you are regarded as a fanatic, an apologist, and a proselytizer. And if you protest, you are claiming victimization. He invoked the Abrahamic approach as a solution that recognizes the equal worth of the three religions and their historic presence on European territory. His personal goal, he concluded, was to make interreligious collaboration and dialogue a 'Lebenpraxis,' a lifestyle.[51]

The creation of a common interreligious prayer day, on October 3, the day of German unification, developed in response to the 9/11 attacks and has become an occasion of interfaith practice. Interfaith groups such as the KCID try to develop templates for interfaith services. At the meeting with the confrontation described above, the Abrahamic approach was put to work in an interfaith service. A Jew, a Christian, and a Muslim read passages from the Old Testament and the Koran about Abraham and Sarah, or Ibrahim and Sarah. The service had Muslims singing psalms, Jews and Christians listening to a reading from the Koran in Arabic, and Christians and Muslims listening to a reading from the Bible in Hebrew. A Muslim participant read a story about the loss of homeland comparing her own migration experience to that of the Israelites.

The shared contact point in the story of Abraham proved a thin source for the building of a shared ritual. The abstraction of the story from the normal context of the three religions was instructive, but inadvertently the experiment also revealed the lack of liturgical practices capable of sustaining interreligious worship. Theologians who are opposed to the 'Abrahamic' approach think it leads to 'religious blending,' and ultimately value relativism and a dilution of faith.

One participant, a Muslim, described to me how his own understanding of his faith had changed as he began to participate in events like that service. He had started to ask questions about interpretation of the Koran, but he also worried about the pressures on Muslims to develop 'a Christianized version' of Islam. What did he think of the confrontation between Affolderbach and Hoffmann, I asked? He was worried, he answered, about the lack of Islamic scholars who could be worthy counterparts to the Christian theologians. 'We are all engineers, accountants, or professional people,' he said, describing himself and the other Muslims engaged in interfaith dialogue and leading the mosque communities in Stuttgart. 'We cannot really speak to these issues.'[52]

EVANGELIZING VERSUS INTERFAITH TOLERATION

Europeans are generally willing to grant people the right to practice religion in private but are less comfortable with public displays of faith. However, the issues are complicated, not easily subsumed in the conventional distinctions between private and public, or ritual and belief. Ritual slaughter, prayer schedules, special holidays, etc., are essential aspects of religious exercise for Muslims. For most Muslims, religious practices are derived from the shariah, as are aspects of personal conduct. The emphasis upon ritual is at variance with Christian assumptions that faith is a matter of 'belief' and therefore about 'thought.' In this respect, Islam is more like Orthodox Judaism. In both creeds, the observance of rituals is essential. Even more fundamentally, the requirements placed upon the faithful derive from a large body of religious law. Religious scholars have responsibility for interpreting a system of laws, and for determining the relevance of various aspects of religious law for particular problems. For Jews the primary sources are the Torah and the Talmud. For Muslims they are the Koran and the hadith, which is made up of accounts of the works of the Prophet and of sayings of his followers, sometimes centuries after his death. The ahadith (*plu.*) are textual sources used by religious scholars to determine the content of the sunnah, the Prophet's divine meaning. The law itself is the shariah.

Dawah means 'the call to Islam,' and has traditionally implied the obligation to do mission and seek conversions. Today, some European Muslims treat it as a call to social activism and translate the term to imply an obligation 'to work for the common good.' Mohamed Alibhai, an American Muslim and religious scholar, thinks that all monotheistic faiths find religious pluralism difficult because, as he explained to me, 'if you think you have been chosen by God, it predisposes you to expect other cultures to give up their beliefs and values.... Christian evangelicals are the mirror image of Muslim evangelicals in this regard; they want to unify humankind under one banner and one God.'[53] Like many Muslims I met, Alibhai has come to the conclusion that 'Muslims must rethink the idea that Islam is the final revelation from God and therefore destined to spread to all peoples of the world.' I found very little support for missionary action among the Muslim leaders in my study. A large majority supported the notion that 'it is best if the different religions leave each other alone.'

The idea that Muslims think they should spread Islam is nevertheless alarming to many Christian Europeans. Proselytizing, in particular, is widely regarded as indicative of religious zealotry. Protestants have a complicated history of either embracing zealous missionary work or abandoning it completely. But the impulse to evangelize derives from basic theological propositions about belief and unbelief. It is worth noting also that some members of the Christian clergy think it is their obligation to convert Muslims, particularly in cases of intermarriage between Christians and Muslims. The difficulty is that in religiously pluralist countries, where faith is a matter of personal choice, conversion and religious 'switching' invariably becomes more common. It is striking that support for a 'free to choose' position was much stronger among French and British Muslim leaders, the two countries where the legacy of the Augsburg 'Religionsfriede' is much diminished and the state publicly assumes a neutral position, even if more in words than in practice. Danish, Swedish, Dutch, and German Muslims, in contrast, strongly supported a 'mutual respect' position. They shared in this regard a strongly articulated national taboo against interreligious 'poaching.'

HERMENEUTICS OR FATWAS?

An increasing number of European Muslims actively debate how important the apparatus of religious law is for Islamic spirituality. The new Islamic hermeneutics for reinterpreting the Koran proposed by some Muslim scholars bring Islam closer to the dominant European epistemologies of faith. It is, in a small way, a counter-movement to the neo-orthodox movements in both Christianity and Islam.

European Muslims are pulled between two poles. One is represented by the theologies of Mohammed Arkoun and Tariq Ramadan, which albeit very different, both stress historicity and contextual interpretation. The other tendency insists upon traditionalist interpretations. This view is most stridently expressed in fatwas beamed in on satellite TV and websites from Saudi

Table 5.1. Support for right to evangelize and convert

Country of residence	Denmark (%)	Sweden (%)	UK (%)	Netherlands (%)	Germany (%)	France (%)	Total (%)
Yes, conversion should be allowed	18.2	23.8	51.6	26.1	19.6	68.4	31.8
No, it is better for faiths to respect each other	75.8	66.7	41.9	73.9	78.3	31.6	64.2
Christians should be prohibited from converting Muslims	6.1	0.0	6.5	0.0	2.2	0.0	2.9
Own answer	0.0	9.5	0.0	0.0	0.0	0.0	1.2

Arabia and the Gulf states. Squeezed between these poles are exponents of a commonsensical approach that employs selective historical revisionism and a fair amount of denial to construct a 'workable' Islam. The impetus is clear. Tariq Modood and Fauzia Ahmad, who have conducted interviews with British Muslim public intellectuals, write that '[the term] "Moderate Muslim" is, at least sociologically, more like a "hyphenated identity" than an interpretation of the Qur'an, though of course the motive for it may come from the Qur'an and it may have to be justified by an appeal to Islamic texts and precedents.'[54]

Mohamed Alibhai, writing for American Muslims, is more direct in his description of the triangulation required by educated Western Muslims to keep hold of their faith. Alibhai argues that today, as has always been the case, it is the imams—like a priest or any other clergyman—who are 'the adaptive center of a religious tradition.' Unfortunately, because of the absence of educational opportunities for Western imams, and because of the prevalence of dogma at the educational institutions of the Islamic world, imams are not equipped to play this role. 'The vast majority of the imams in the Muslim world are completely sealed off from the currents of modern thought.' He contrasts the current stasis to the historical models set by the 'founding imams' of the four schools of Islamic jurisprudence, the imams Malik, Shafi'i, Abu Hanifa, and Ibn Hanbal, who each charted new courses. Educated Muslims drift away from the simply pieties of the neighborhood mosque, and turn away from the imams and the masses who follow them.[55]

The dilemma of Western Muslims is apparent. One common response takes the form of selective historical revisionism. I often heard that the effort to recast Muslim religious identity to fit national contexts is a process no different from the way Islam has always adjusted to local conditions. Some cited the peaceful coexistence of Islam and Christianity on the European continent prior to Pope Urban II's call for a Christian crusade to recapture Jerusalem in 1095. Medina, Córdoba, and Constantinople are other commonly mentioned precedents. The problem with these examples is, of course, that the systems in question are all medieval or premedieval societies lacking the elaborate state systems of contemporary societies and, perhaps most importantly, lacking the mobility and individualism that today compel individuals to challenge charismatic leadership and paternalist rule.

A new group of Western scholars of Islam and Islamic scholars—only the latter may accurately be regarded as theologians—reject the historicist parallelism, and argue instead that the Muslim melting pot in Europe is an opportunity to redefine and clarify Islam. They see democracy and scholarly inquiry as providing the opportunity for an Islamic revival movement that focuses on ijtihad—the individual believer's effort to master scriptural reading and reinterpretation—and aims to redefine all core Islamic concepts, in particular the balance between religious law and individual spiritualism. The focus on personal interpretation has radical consequences. It allows men and women equal status as interpreters of the text, and it undercuts clerical authority.

The movement has brought about a subtle shift in emphasis in some circles of Western Muslims activism. Ritualistic observance is deemphasized in favor of a focus on an ethics of faith. *Dawah* is used in novel ways to suggest a social responsibility. Occasionally I came across efforts to rehabilitate *jihad*, the obligation to wage war on behalf of Islam invoked by Islamists, but more people thought it was not a project worth pursuing. Some argued that the word has irredeemably been corrupted by the Taliban and other fanatics, but others suggested that like the Koran's instructions to cut off the hands of thieves, this was a commandment that was best ignored.

Theological reinterpretation often has large-scale political consequences, and in this case the consequence is to focus on deeds rather than rituals as the key expression of faith. A second shift regards the relative status of the Koran vis-à-vis secondary sources for the interpretation of the sunnah and the elaboration of religious law. It follows logically from the rejection of the ahistorical shariah propagated by Islamic clerics and authoritarian rulers in the Islamic world that the development of a new theology is focused on the Koran and textual reinterpretation.

With a new theology come new styles of religious observance. In some case, not so subtle shifts take place from ethnic practices, for example, the custom of animal sacrifice at Eid al-Kabir (the festival of sacrifice), which is celebrated by each family butchering a sheep, to more acceptable practices of symbolic sacrifice. In France, an estimated 300,000 animals are butchered at home or in provisional abattoirs, and the Muslim associations are trying to persuade people to replace the animal sacrifice with a symbolic donation of money to charities.[56] But in many cases the reaffirmation of faith has steered Western Muslims towards a new emphasis upon fasting during Ramadan, the introduction of small interreligious ceremonies at the breaking of the fast, particularly during the last ten days of Ramadan, and the observance of some food restrictions (but if halal foods are not available, a vegetarian meal does fine), and some dress conventions, including but not limited to a headscarf.

In other cases, the importance of ritual is deemphasized to reflect the axiom that deeds matter more than ritualistic displays of faith. Tariq Ramadan writes on this issue, in *Western Muslims and the Future of Islam* (2004), that 'practice may become a mechanical ritual, lifeless and without spirituality.' Pointing to the crimes of multinational companies and arms industries, he adds that spirituality and ethics must 'marry in action.'[57] European Muslims are on the one hand eager to free themselves from the restraint of routine and 'tribalized' versions of Islam, and on the other hand resistant to the imposition of proto-Christian norms for acceptable religious observance and behavior. But Ramadan is careful not to say that rituals do not matter. He is one of many who argue that the shariah provides guidance on all aspects of human existence. Unlike the dogmatic clerics who favor fatwas as the principal tool of guidance, Ramadan wants to make the issue of exactly what guidance can be found a matter of ijtihad.

At the risk of simplification, three positions can be defined on the status of Islamic religious law. One is that the shariah is a fixed body of law, and to second-guess the shariah is tantamount to apostasy. The second position is that religious law is essential to being a Muslim, and the shariah contains guidance on all aspects of life but is not fixed. The exact meaning of the Prophet's saying must be interpreted in ways that are sensitive to context. 'In fact, it is virtually impossible to conduct a debate about how Muslims should live in any given environment without at least partly conducting it in shariah terms,' according to Jørgen Nielsen, an Islamic Studies professor at the University of Birmingham. 'The point is that this can just as well be used to justify a modernist, pluralist and flexible approach to being a Muslim as it can an obscurantist, backward-looking and violent approach.'[58] The third position is that, if the Koran tells you to accept something that is unacceptable in today's liberal societies—that a woman's testimony counts for half of a man's in court, for example—then you must read it within what Amina Wadud refers to as 'the context of Qur'anic Weltanshauung.'[59] Wadud goes as far as to say that in such case Muslims need to 'second-guess' the Koran.

But for every Muslim leader who worries about the role and interpretation of religious law, there are many more who take a pragmatic view of things. They either put the emphasis upon the individual's direct experience of 'the book,' the Koran, or they regard the shariah as dogma in serious need of reformulation. Some go further and say that religious law is 'optional,' or they agree with the British parliamentarian who snorted, 'outmoded nonsense.' Even some imams have revisionist ideas about the role of religious law. 'The Islamic world has to accept that we are different,' several imams told me. But this position is not without its risks. One imam told me that, 'I have to be careful with what I say so I do not attract the attention of Al-Azhar.' Al-Azhar is a prestigious Islamic university in Cairo. It has educated imams and religious scholars since the tenth century and advocates a scientific approach to religious scholarship. My informant was worried that he could have his degree revoked if he was found to err.[60]

The doctrinaire view is associated with the theology of Islamism, a political movement that seeks to curtail the spread of Western secularism. Islamists regard the shariah as a constitutional principle and the source of all law. Not all Islamists are revolutionaries, like Osama Bin Laden, and advocate the use of terrorism and extra-parliamentary politics at the service of jihad, the global struggle between Islam and its enemies. But even in its nonviolent forms the Islamist position is a source of marginalization and separatism among Muslim immigrants to the West. Emigration poses both a problem and an opportunity for religious fundamentalists. The loss of control associated with exit from the realm of Islamic states makes defection possible, but Muslim emigration is also an opportunity to expand the community of the faithful beyond the old territorial boundaries of the Muslim ummah.[61] Islamism is a strategic narrative of expansion and domination. Olivier Roy describes the political outlook and strategies of contemporary Islamism as a blend of strategic realism and Salafist and Wahhabist theologies.[62]

Muslim leaders in Europe worry about the ability of Islamist clerics to mobilize European Muslims, particularly among the native-born generation, and many are prepared to take risks in order to shut their operations down. Self-designated moderate leaders often complained that they feel 'marginalized in the middle,' in the sense that they lack the resources and the institutional support to develop an alternative narrative of Muslim democratic political engagement. Ironically, the emergence of Islamist extremism can be interpreted as a product of globalism, as their evangelists prey on the need for certainty among uprooted and displaced men with a diffuse but oppositional Muslim allegiance.

Aziz Al-Azmeh, a professor of Islamic Studies at the Central European University in Budapest, writes penetratingly about the Islamist utopia. It is, he argues, a response to the failure of Arabic nationalism and is principally characterized by its romantic appropriation of a nonexistent Islamic authenticity. The Islamists reconceptualize the ummah—the pan-Islamic community of Muslims—which hitherto has been an abstract concept of the believers as 'the people,' the body politic which the Islamists represent. They imagine the nation of Islam as a dormant international revolutionary force, which must be reawakened to piety and to its purpose.

Al-Azmeh compares the ideology of Islamism to European national romanticism from Herder to the Italian Risorgimento. That, he says, is why we are faced with the effort to define a new Islamic self, through the invention of traditions, 'such as "Islamic" dress, an "Islamic" way of life, "Islamic" positions on various political matters, simulacra all of them of the invariant essence of Islam, a name which is posited as the final explanatory principle,'[63] Al-Azmeh attributes the reinvention of things 'Islamic' to the ideologies of the Taliban and the Iranian revolution, but the phenomenon he describes has obviously spread far beyond the confines of revolutionary compounds to most European cities. His critique eloquently articulates the discomfort that many secular Muslim leaders, particularly on the left, feel when faced with the invention of a Muslim identity—a 'Muslim culture,' While this is a source of tension and division, it is at the same time a resource for Muslim political activism.

Mohammed Arkoun, a retired professor of history at the Sorbonne in Paris and one of the members of the commission that proposed the headscarf ban (which Arkoun voted for), has developed a line of inquiry that aims to undo what he calls the 'dogmatic closure' of Islam. It is a project that he describes as the construction of 'a historical and epistemological critique of the principles, postulates, definitions, conceptual tools, and discourse procedures of logical reasoning used in the Islamic context.' It may be summarized as the development of a new Islamic hermeneutics based upon textual reading and interpretation combined with archeological and historical research into the origins and contexts of text and doctrine. Islam is, in Arkoun's hands, a historical project subject to the manipulation of rulers and adapted to the lives of Muslims. 'Islam as a religion should be liberated,' he says, 'from problems and responsibilities that are the exclusive province of social actors, not of God.'[64]

Arkoun's discussion of revelation and the shift in Islamic discourse perpetuated by the establishment of scriptural authority and the professionalization of interpretation through the creation of an ulama—the cadre of religious scholars—draws parallels with both the Old and the New Testaments. In an essay titled 'Who Wrote the Koran?', he discusses other ancient literature, from the Gilgamesh to the Gospels. His approach to the essential questions about the nature and origins of Islam are framed within a positivist hermeneutics in place of the traditional theology of revelation. (It is a break that to this day also arouses anger among Christians and Jews when applied to the Bible.)

Arkoun is not primarily concerned with theology, but he argues that the development of a new Islamic theology has to have roots in scholarly concerns. 'I am not proposing a mere comparison of Judaism, Christianity, and Islam as religious traditions,' he writes. 'Theological and philosophical thought developed with respect to these traditions must also become the object of modern, critical investigation.'[65]

Some of the people I interwieved, who were engaged in Koran study groups and lay Islamic academies, intuitively seized upon the ideas articulated in the scholarship of Arkoun and Al-Azmeh. (No one ever referred to the two scholars, but many people mentioned Tariq Ramadan as their source of inspiration.) They spoke of Islam as a faith rather than a religion and rejected the need for an ulema (religions authorities). I encountered multiple Koran translation projects. In Sweden alone, several groups are engaged in the enormous task of issuing a Swedish Koran. In Denmark, an imam involved in a collective translation project candidly admitted that he was an auto-didact, and that his purpose was to provide for a translation of the Koran that made sense to Danes.[66] The argument for why new translations were needed ranged from the desire to eliminate the fundamentalist mistranslations to facilitation of the use of vernacular language in religious rituals.

Tariq Ramadan is by no means alone in advocating theological renewal and an independent voice for European Muslims, but he has done more than anyone else to bring it about. Ramadan was named a 'spiritual innovator' by *Time* and listed as one of '100: The Next Wave,' in the magazine's millennium edition. Ramadan spoke in terms that were eerily reminiscent of another generation of Black civil rights leaders. 'What I'm saying is, be proud of who you are,' the magazine quotes Ramadan as saying. 'We've got to get away from the idea that scholars in the Islamic world can do our thinking for us.' *Time* gushed, 'Thanks partly to Ramadan, Islam is on its way to becoming an integral part of Europe's religious landscape.'[67]

However, post-9/11 coverage has been less positive. Ramadan is now often accused of treachery, of trying to make Islam sound acceptable while really aiming at conquest. In France, where Ramadan has a big following among Muslims, he has been accused of anti-Semitism and of being 'a dangerous man.'[68] When he was offered a professorship at the University of Notre Dame, a Catholic university, the US Department of State refused to give Ramadan a visa.

The radicalism of Ramadan's theology contradicts the accusation that it is a disguise for a more fundamental orthodoxy. If his ideas were acted upon, no return to the controlled orthodoxy of the Islamic world would be possible. Ramadan argues that European Muslims have a unique opportunity to develop a purer version of Islam, one that is 'cleansed' of the accretions that are culturally based, and have little to do with the faith. In his view, there are not many Islams, as social scientists like to say, but rather only one faith.[69]

If Arkoun and Ramadan represent different tendencies on the modernist pole of European Islam, the traditionalist end is above all represented by religious communities that are deeply rooted in the traditions of the countries of origin. In many cases, they import not only their imams but also the curricula taught at Koran schools and in the weekend madrassas organized by the local mosque communities.

The axiom of the unity of Islam—tawhid—is an important first principle and Muslim leaders often express their unwillingness to distinguish between different Muslims and regard sectarian conflict as unacceptable and even un-Islamic. In reality, the theological differences are significant and practical dialogue is contingent on recognition of the diversity of faith and practices. Most European Muslims are Sunnis, although large groups of other branches of Islam are also represented—Alevites, Ishmailis, Ahmadiyas, Deobandies, and Sufis are the largest such minorities in Europe. Among the Arab-Origin Muslims, there are also the Wahhabis, and other Salafist groups.

The Shiah–Sunni split is often described as a schism in Islam comparable to that between Protestants and Catholics. Shiah Muslims are a minority among European Muslims, and the Shiah–Sunni divide in Europe has not assumed the importance often attributed to it by the daily stream of news about wars between Shiite and Sunni clerics in Iraq or elsewhere.

The split regards a family feud that took place after the death of the Prophet over who should be regarded as the proper spiritual leader of Islam. Shiah Muslims regard Imam Ali, who was a cousin of the Prophet and married his daughter, Fatima, as the first imam and the divinely appointed authority on interpreting the Koran. The term Shiah (or Shi'ite) derives from a shortening of Shiat Ali or partisans of Ali. Shiahs think Imam Ali should properly have been the first Caliph. After Ali, spiritual leadership passed to his sons, Hasan and Husain, and to their descendents. Among Shiahs the title 'Imam' is only used to refer to these first twelve imams. Subsequently, leadership went to a council of scholars, who elected a supreme leader. The late Iranian Ayatollah Khomeni was the first contemporary cleric to use the title.

Given these complexities, Christian churches should be careful about demanding 'representative' interlocutors from European Muslims. These efforts to organize Islam run the danger of short-circuiting its ongoing reform. In one sense, that is the desired outcome. Governments want institutionalization in order to prevent political radicals from utilizing Islam for purposes of anti-Western mobilization. The churches favor clerical control as a means to avoid the diffusion of religious movements, particularly the emergence of religious entrepreneurship with supply-side diversification or 'consumerist' demand-side changes to rituals and liturgy. They fear, above all, the development of sectarianism. The problem is that if governments and churches approach the issue by working with traditionalist or ethnic leaderships, the moderates and modernists may be the first victims of institutionalization.

A promising example of how a workable accommodation may be accomplished by way of Muslim initiatives comes from Hamburg. A position paper issued in April 2004 by thirty-six mosque communities and associations in Hamburg, which joined together to found a 'Schura,' a council of Islamic communities, begins by stating unambiguously that irrespective of legal status, Muslims are not 'foreigners.' While half a million Muslims now have German passports and more are getting one every day, those without passports no longer see themselves as foreigners but as Germans entitled to claim their rights and assume the responsibilities this entails.[70]

Equal treatment in matters of faith is, according to Ronald Dworkin, the 'constitutive morality of liberalism.' The idea that 'governments should remain neutral on the question of conceptions of the good life, or what gives value to life' is the one central principle of liberal thought that has remained constant over time.[71]

In my interviews, people circled between arguing for 'equal opportunity' and 'equal protection.' The equal opportunity principle builds upon a European debate that begins with John Stuart Mill, became central to discussions of the constitution of the welfare state in the twentieth-century, and is once again at the heart of current debates about the European constitution. However, the principle sets an unrealistically high threshold for public policy. Advocates want government action to create what is often referred to in social contexts as 'a level playing field.' This might be taken to mean, for example, that Muslims and Christians should have equal opportunities to worship. The equal protection argument is perhaps the more realistic goal, and it is also a principle that would allow for a greater measure of self-government on the part of minority religions.

The principle of equal protection is not well-developed in Europe, but a considerable body of jurisprudence exists in the USA, from which we can elaborate some basic principles for what it means to treat faiths 'neutrally' or 'equitably.' The Equal Protection Clause of the Fourteenth Amendment of the US Constitution prohibits states from denying any person within its jurisdiction the equal protection of the laws. In other words, laws and the application of law must treat an individual in the same manner as others in similar conditions and circumstances.

In US law, the principle applies to race and religion. The equal protection principle is an addition to the First Amendment, for which there is no precedent in European thought or law.[72] In other words, the application of the 'equal protection' principle is independent of the First Amendment's rules about the free exercise of religion. The First Amendment contains a far-reaching understanding of the separation of church and state that is unlikely to appeal to Europeans. Indeed, it is probably impractical for European purposes, and in terms of constitutional tradition a foreign principle. It would, for example, pose legal barriers to the education of clergy at the theological faculties at public universities, something that few Europeans think should be changed. (In any case, Muslims want the system expanded to include the training of Islamic religious scholars and imams.)

The equal protection clause is not intended to provide 'equality' among individuals or classes but only 'equal application' of the laws. The consequences of a law are not relevant so long as there is no discrimination in its application. However, this principle would not allow governments to give legal protection to Christian ministers in exercising pastoral duties while denying the same protection to imams, provided imams were properly trained and certified to exercise pastoral care.

The purpose of the liberal commitment to state neutrality is to respect and tolerate, and arguably even to encourage, diverse expressions of faith, culture, opinion, and art among the citizens. It is the essence of liberalism to encourage freedom and pluralism. The obligation to be neutral falls on the state and not the citizens. It can be argued that citizens, in turn, have a duty to tolerate difference and that pluralism, in that sense, implies a reciprocal obligation. It is by no means easy to figure out what neutrality entails, however, and different governments will undoubtedly arrive at different conclusions.

Giving serious thought to the implications of 'equal protection' and 'neutrality' for government policy with respect to religion and the treatment of individuals irrespective of their faith does not mean adopting US-style policies. The USA has taken a very broad view of what constitutes a religion, for example. Europeans are unlikely to follow this path. France and Germany restrict sects, Scientology among them, and insist that religious groups must be legally organized as public corporations in order to receive public recognition. Both principles are compatible with the neutrality requirement as long as the right to recognition and incorporation is also extended to all religions. The Swedish law on religious freedom from 1951 defines religions as faiths that have regular services, a definition that would exclude the Santeria, a group of Haitians whose reliance on animal sacrifice the US Supreme Court decided to protect under the Free Exercise Clause.

We can return to Dworkin for assistance on what 'equal treatment' might mean if applied to Europe's new post-Christian reality. He writes that 'it is conceded by everyone that the government cannot make everyone equal in every respect.'[73] 'Political decisions must be, as far as it is possible, independent of any particular conception of the good life, or of what gives value to life.' This implies that you have apply the law equally to Muslims and Christians, but governments need not worry about substantive 'equality.' Therefore, there is no implied obligation to construct a Grand Mosque in every city that has a Cathedral or to admit an Islamic theology student for every Christian student admitted. However, it does follow that if Lutherans get scholarships to study theology at public universities, Muslim and Baptist students are entitled to the same support and the same access to study their religions at public schools.

The difficulty is that the recognition and equal treatment implies equal constraints for all religions. The equal treatment principle is a tough prescription for integration.

NOTES

1. *The Spiritual and Cultural Dimension of Europe*, Reflection group initiated by the President of the European Commission and Coordinated by the Institute for Human Sciences. Vienna/Brussels (October 12, 2004), 9.
2. Marianne Gullestad, 'Invisible Fences: Egalitarianism, Nationalism, and Racism,' *Journal of the Royal Anthropological Institute*, 8 (2002) 1: 45–63.
3. Joel S. Fetzer and J. Christopher Soper, 'The Roots of Public Attitudes Towards State Accommodation of European Muslims' Religious Practices Before and After September 11,' *Journal for the Scientific Study of Religion*, 42 (2003) 2: 247–88.
4. *Berlinske Tidende* (September 6, 2000); *Morgenavisen Jyllandsposten* (November 28, 2000).
5. 'Britain's Catholics at a Crossroads,' *BBC News (April 18, 2005);* http://news.bbc.co.uk/1/hi/magazine/4456105.stm.
6. 'Revealed: Tony Blair's Catholic secret,' *Daily Telegraph* (April 9, 2005).
7. 'Cardinal Sodano Puts Buttiglione Case in Perspective,' *Catholic News*, Rome (October 17, 2004).
8. Terrence Murray, 'Europe Debates God's Place in New Constitution,' *Christian Science Monitor* (April 10, 2003); http://www.csmonitor.com/2003/0410/p07s01-woeu.html.
9. http://www.ibka.org/en/articles/ag03/euconst.html; http://www.humanism.org.uk/site/cms/contentPrintArticle.asp?article = 1398.
10. Larry Seidentop, *Democracy in Europe* (New York: Columbia University Press, 2001), 191.
11. Tim King, 'Secular France takes on Islam,' *Prospect* (July 2003); http://www.prospect-magazine.co.uk/ArticleView.asp?P_Article = 12003.

12. Based upon the 1990–1 World Values Survey, Mattei Dogan pronounced victory for the nonbelievers in Europe; see 'Accelerated Decline of Religious Belief in Europe,' *Comparative Sociology*, 1 (2002) 2: 127–49. Nonetheless, even in this survey 62 percent of the French said that they believed in God. The 1999 World Values Survey revealed a significant increase in believers, even in the more secular countries; see Yves Lambert, 'A Turning Point in Religious Evolution in Europe,' *Journal of Contemporary Religion*, 19 (2004) 1: 29–45.

Table. Utilization ratios for services provided by Svenska Kyrkan and Folkekirken, 2000–1. (Percent of total population cohorts)

	Sweden	Denmark
Church membership	82.9	84.3
Christenings	72.6	77.2
Confirmations	43.2	80.0
Weddings	61.2	42.6
Funerals	87.8	92.2

13. Eurobarometer 47.1, ICPSR 2089, v463.
14. www.gallup-international.com/ContentFiles?millennium15.asp.
15. *Statistisk Årbog 2002*, Denmark; *Stiftslista 2000*, www.svenskakyrkan.se.
16. Jeff Chu, 'O Father. Where Art Thou?' Special report, *Time* (June 8, 2003).
17. Interview 16, (September 12, 2003).
18. http://www.mori.com/mrr/2001/c011116.shtml.
19. Martin Sauer and Andreas Goldberg, *Die Lebenssituation und Partizipation tür-hischer Migranten in Nordrhein-Westfalen* (Hamburg: Zentrum für Türkeistudien, Lit Verlag, 2001), 35.
20. 'L'Argent de l'Islam' by Besma Lahouri and Boris Thiolay, *L'Express* (November 21, 2002).
21. Michèle Tribalat, *De l'Immigration à l'Assimilation: Enquête sur les Populations d'Origine Étrangère en France* (Paris: Editions La Découverte: INED, 1996). The citations are from Michèle Tribalat, 'Cutural Integration of the Immigrants and Societal Integration in France'; http://www.socialcapital-foundation.org/journal/volume%202002/issue%207/pdf/15Tribalat.pdf.
22. *Les Musulmans en France*. Released January 17, 1998. Available at: http://www. ipso.fr/Canalipsos/poll/6400.asp?rubId= 26&print= 1
23. Gilles Kepel, *Les Banlieues de l'Islam: Naissance d'une Religion en France* (Paris: Seuil, 1987).
24. *Moslim in Nederland. Een onderzoek naar de religieuze betrokkenheid van Turken en Marokkanen*. Samenvatting SCP-onderzoeksrapport 2004/9.
25. Aage B. Sørensen, 'On Kings, Pietism and Rent-Seeking in Scandinavian Welfare States,' *Acta Sociologica*, 41 (1998) 2: 363–75.
26. A map of stateless minorities is available at http://www.eurominority.org/version/cartes/carte-minorites.asp. The forcible assimilation of religious minorities is the

topic of Heather Rae, *State Identities and the Homogenization of Peoples* (New York: Cambridge University Press, 2002).

27. The so-called 'voluntary Church-aided' schools are public schools managed by the church. 'Church foundation' schools are owned by the Church but public education authorities pay teacher salaries and other operating expenses. Another way of describing the difference is to say that the first category are religious public schools and the second publicly-funded private religious schools.

28. 'The practical difficulties are simply too great,' was the conclusion of White Paper, *The House of Lords: Completing the Reform.* Cmnd. 5291 (November 2001). Paragraphs 83.

29. 'Germany vs. the Scientologists,' *New York Review of Books* (April 24, 1997), 16–21.

30. http://www.justice.gouv.fr/anglais/textfond/cure.html.

31. *New York Times* (September 20, 2003), A4. The government found itself in the uncomfortable position of having its expulsion decisions undone by the courts, which allowed some of the clerics to return to France.

32. Interview 75, Amsterdam (November 28, 2003).

33. Jaw Rath et al., *Western Europe and Its Islam* (Leiden: Brill, 2001), 183.

34. Lionel Panafit, 'First for Islam in Belgium,' *Le Monde Diplomatique* (June 2000).

35. Göran Gustafsson, 'Church-State Separation Swedish-Style,' John T. S. Madeley and Zsolt Enyedi (eds.), *Special Issue on Church and State in Contemporary Europe. The Chimera of Neutrality, West European Politics*, 26 (2003) 1: 51–72.

36. *Samme kirke, ny ordning* (transl. Same church, new order), Innstillingen fra Kirkerådets kirke/stat-utvalg. Sammenfatning av høringsmaterialet (October 2002).

37. Bishop emeritus Dr. Christian Krause, *Address,* Lutheran World Federation tenth Assembly, Winnipeg, Canada (July 22, 2003); http://www.lwf-assembly.org/PDFs/President_Address-EN.pdf.

38. 'Hedningene er forsvundet!' Udgivelser om troens eksklusivitet i en multireligiøs omverden; http://www.aarhus.stift.dk.

39. 'Globalisering i folkekirken,' Elisabeth Assing Hvid, *Kristeligt Dagblad* (September 29, 2004).

40. The Danish term was 'åndskamp,' which literally means a struggle for the spirit. Viggo Mortensen, 'Den danske Folkekirke og Islam,' *Aktuelle skrifter*, vol. 3, 2001. Center for Multirelgious Studies, University of Aarhus. Available at: www.teo.au.dk/cms/fagomraader/relationer_krist_islam/kdkronik.pdf.

41. *L'Osservatore Romano,* weekly Edition in English (December 20–7, 2000), 9. *L'Osservatore Romano* is the newspaper of the Holy See.

42. The bishop made his remarks available in full to *Zenit,* a Catholic news agency, which posted them at its webpage, http://www.zenit.org/english/europe/script.html. They were also published in the December 1999 issue of *The Middle East Forum,* a US-based journal edited by Daniel Pipes; http://www.meforum.org/article/448. The editors explained their reason for publishing the bishop's remarks

and not other remarks made at the synod by saying, 'This statement raised eyebrows because it so starkly contradicts the official church position.'

43. John L. Allen Jr., 'Europe's Muslims Worry Bishops,' *National Catholic Reporter* (October 22, 1999), vol. 36, no. 1.
44. John Paul II, *Instrumentum Laboris*. Synod of Europe II. 1999. Available at: http://www.vatican.va/roman_curia/synod/documents/rc_synod_doc_19071999_europe-instrlabor_en.html
45. Thomas Michel, S. J., 'Developments in Interreligious Dialogue with Muslims,' paper, Creighton University, Omaha, Nebraska. Available at: http://puffin.creighton.edu/jesuit/dialogue/documents/documents.html.
46. *Newsletter*, Radio Vatican (August 18, 2004).
47. 'German Churches Disagree on Headscarf Ban for Muslim Teachers,' *Lutheran World Federation* (March 3, 2004); http://www.lutheranworld.org/news.
48. Ausschuss für Schule, Jugend und Sport. Ständiger Ausschuss (März 12, 2004). Stuttgart. Haus des Landtags. Drucksache 13/2793, 110–118.
49. Religionsfreiheit heute—zum Verhältnis von Staat und Religion in Deutschland. Rede von Bundespräsident Johannes Rau zum 275 Geburtstag von Gotthold Ephraim Lessing, University of Kassel. Available at: http://www.uni-kassel.de/fb10/frieden/themen/Rassismus/rau.html.
50. Martin Affolderbach, 'Erfahrungen mit Dialogkritik in den Kirchen,' *Christlich-islamischer Dialog in der Kritik. Erfahrungen, Strategien, gesellschaftliche Präsenz.* Akademie der Diözese Rottenburg-Stuttgart, Stuttgart-Hohenheim (October 8–10, 2004).
51. Abdul Hadi Christian H. Hoffmann, 'Dialogkritik. Beobachtungen und Analysen,' Ibid. Akademie der Diözese Rottenburg-Stuttgart, Stuttgart-Hohenheim (October 8–10, 2004).
52. Interview 102, Stuttgart (October 9, 2004).
53. Personal communication.
54. Tariq Modood and Fauzia Ahmad, 'British Muslim Perspective on Multiculturalism,' in *Theory, Culture, and Society*, forthcoming 2005.
55. Mohamed Alibhai, 'Islam: Faith or Religion? The Re-Education of the Modern Imam,' *Minaret*, 24 (2002) 9: 24–32.
56. Hakim El Ghissassi, 'L'Aid el Kebir Entre la Clandestinité et la Redéfinition du Sens', http://www.sesame.info (January 3, 2005).
57. Ramadan, *To Be a European Muslim*, 120–4.
58. Personal conversation (July 23, 2004), Oxford.
59. Amina Wadud, *Qur'an and Woman. Rereading the Sacred Text from a Woman's Perspective* (New York: Oxford University Press, 1999), 5.
60. Interview 36, London (March 3, 2004).
61. Sami A. Aldeeb Abu-Sahlieh, 'The Islamic Conception of Migration,' *International Migration Review* 30 (Spring 1996) 1: 37–57.
62. Roy, op.cit. (2005), 23.
63. Aziz Al-Azmed, *Islam and Modernities* (London: Verso, 1993), 21.

64. Mohammed Arkoun, *Rethinking Islam. Common Questions. Uncommon Answers* (Boulder, CO: Westeview Press, 1994), 17.
65. Ibid., 126.
66. Interview 20, Copenhagen (September 15, 2003).
67. http://www.time.com/time/innovators/spirituality/profile_ramadan2.html.
68. *Nouvelle Observateur* (October 9, 2003); http://www.nouvelobs.com/articles/p2031/a218643.htm.
69. Ramadan, *Western Muslims*, 17–80
70. 'Grundsatzpapier: Muslime in einer pluralistischen Gesellschaft,' SCHURA-Rat der islamischen Gemeinschaften in Hamburg e.V. (no date)
71. Ronald Dworkin, *A Matter of Principle* (Cambridge, MA: Harvard University Press, 1985), 191, 205.
72. The First Amendment states that 'Congress shall make no law respecting an establishment of religion, or prohibiting the free exercise thereof.' The prohibition on established religions contained in the first part is known as the Establishment Clause. The second part is the Free Exercise Clause, and imposes a duty on government not to hinder religious practices. Conflict arises because the Establishment Clause prohibits the government from favoring any religion while the Free Exercise Clause also imposes a duty to allow religion freely to develop and has been interpreted to recognize implicitly the public nature of religious exercise.
73. Dworkin, op. cit., 190.

6

Sexual Politics and Multiculturalism

The status of the Muslim headscarf—the hijab—has provoked more debate about Islam in Europe than any other issue. This is because it seems to sum up so many of the concerns that trouble Europeans when they consider the Islamic minority in their midst. These range from the status of Muslim women to wider questions of religious freedom and even national identity. And the controversy has created odd bedfellows, feminists and conservatives joining in an unlikely alliance, ostensibly in order to protect women's right to choose.

In 2004 the French government and five German state governments (Baden-Württemberg, Saarland, Hesse, Lower Saxony, and Bavaria) passed legislation to prohibit the wearing of the Muslim headscarf. Berlin passed a ban in February 2005. In Germany, the laws affect teachers in public schools, and sometimes public employees generally, but not students. In France, only the students are affected.

Feminist supporters of the scarf bans argue that it is demeaning to women to have to cover up their hair and bodies. The practice is presented as an emblem of the repression of women in Islam. Women would not subjugate themselves if they were free to choose, they argue, and therefore a ban is needed to protect women's rights.[1] However, it would be unusual for a government to force women to be 'free' by prohibiting them from a specific action, such as wearing a headscarf. Gender equality enforcement was a prominent issue in the debates but was in no case the reason given by legislators to pass the legislation.

The ostensible reason for banning the scarf in both Germany and France was the need to protect fundamental public values, but the endangered values apparently at stake were different, and the prohibitions were differently tailored. France and Germany are the only countries to have taken legislative action to date, but headscarf controversies are everywhere. Banks, cleaning companies, department stores and food chains, day care centers, and hospitals all over Europe have refused to hire women who wear headscarves. New EU employment law prohibits refusals to hire on religious grounds, but the religious status of the headscarf is contested and court challenges are, in any case, time-consuming, and the outcome uncertain.

What do Muslim leaders think of these issues? Are patriarchal men and conservative clerics pitched against moderates and modernizers who support women's equality? What are the views of Muslim women who occupy positions of political leadership? And is the headscarf a symbol of a larger problem inherent to Islam: a disregard for women's rights, even denigration of women, exemplified more painfully in forced marriages and polygamy?

COUNTING HEADSCARVES

The headscarf is now part of the European streetscape. In France, the headscarf is referred to as 'the veil'—'le voile islamique'—and women who wear it are described as being 'veiled.' However, this terminology gives the wrong impression in most cases. The contested piece of clothing may be made of a flimsy chiffon or expensive silk, or it may be a heavy, folded, black scarf made of thick fabric. One of the difficulties with enforcement turns out to be how to determine exactly which types of head coverings are prohibited. How does a principal or an employer distinguish between a headscarf worn for religious reasons and one worn for other reasons? Is a flimsy scarf a missionary statement for Islam? Is a Chanel scarf banned? Is a bandana?

Although the word 'hijab' is used in English simply to refer to the headscarf, properly speaking it refers to the general obligation to dress modestly.[2] A more rigid interpretation of Islamic dress codes involves wearing the headscarf with a tight tube sock or hood pulled over the hair and a jilbab, a floor-length dress coat. However, most women who wear a scarf otherwise dress in conventional western clothes, and for many covering-up is something you do in the mosque and on other special occasions.

I counted headscarves on my trolley rides from the immigrant neighborhood in Oost Amsterdam, where I was staying, to the city center. On average one-fifth of the women, who were mostly young and smartly dressed, wore them. The older women tended to wear more severe versions with long dress coats in dark colors. On occasion, you would come across someone wearing niqab, a piece of thin cloth that is worn to cover the face but leave the eyes uncovered.

Headscarf fashions and conventions vary from country to country in Europe, and in part reflect the varying ethnic origins of Muslims. Pakistani and Indian Muslim women usually wear a thin scarf with the colorful salwar kameez, a tunic with pajama-style pants. Many women color-coordinate their scarf with jeans or smart suits. And women wear the headscarf for many different reasons: tradition, choice, and, yes, sometimes because they are told to do so by fathers or husbands, imams or sheiks. Young women who wear the scarf generally tend to stress choice and self-discovery as their reason for doing so.[3] They experience the headscarf bans as a penalty on their personal quest for identity, a very Western project.

In Denmark and Sweden, I listened to young Muslim women joke about how people berate them for being 'suppressed' and 'throwing away their freedom.' They find it amusing that in Scandinavia it is OK to be naked but to wear a headscarf is not. At a party in the Stockholm mosque, a group of young women training to become teachers and nurses, and in one case a psychologist—all wearing headscarves—explained to me how they could never get jobs in pediatric wards but the geriatric wards were happy to take them, because Swedes did not want to work there. 'We Muslims,' they said, 'we value the old people and they quickly take to us.'[4] Discrimination rather than coercion seemed to be the primary issue in their case.

It was difficult to believe that Iram, a beautiful and bright law school student I met in the offices of an antidiscrimination watchdog organization in London, who was wearing an expensive scarf pulled over her forehead and tightly knotted under her chin, was coerced. Or whoever could force Sadia, the 'sister' chair of the Young Muslims' Association in the Stockholm mosque, to do anything she did not choose to do? Sadia adjusted her colorful scarf while telling me about how strange Swedes are because they think religion should be invisible. 'But what good is faith,' she said smiling, 'if you cannot see it?' She also confided that she would probably never marry because she was too busy with her education and political activism to think about romance.

Only a few of the women leaders I met wore headscarves, but many of the young activists did. When I asked if their mothers wore the scarf, in most cases I was told that the mothers did not wear a scarf. In contrast, several parliamentarians and prominent women leaders who do not wear the scarf said that their mothers did. It would seem that among the politically active women the headscarf is not worn out of tradition but by choice, and to make a statement about their faith and identity. All thought that women who wear the scarf pay a heavy penalty.

BANNING THE HEADSCARF: FRANCE

The French ban took effect with the start of the 2004–5 school year. The law prohibits students from wearing 'ostentatious' religious symbols. The Jewish kippa (yarmulke) as well as 'oversize' crosses are prohibited together with the Muslim headscarf. The Sikh turban was inadvertently included and France's

6,000 Sikhs tried subsequently but unsuccessfully to negotiate an exemption based upon the claim their turban is 'ethnic' dress rather than a religious symbol. Since the ban primarily affects teenage girls, one problem arising from the ban is how to educate the girls who are staying away or have been sent home from school for violating the ban.

The scarf only gradually became a charged political symbol of the presence of Islam in France. It first became a political issue in October 1989, when a principal of a secondary school in Creil, a Paris suburb, expelled three girls for wearing the scarf. In November that year the Conseil d'Etat, the highest administrative court, issued a ruling that the wearing of headscarves for religious purposes in public schools did not violate the principle of *laïcité* or other French law. In December that year, the socialist prime minister, Lionel Jospin, issued the first of a series of government rules that gave principals the authority to make decisions about the permissibility of the headscarf. Controversy broke out again one month later when teachers went on strike in support of a principal who had expelled girls for wearing the headscarf. Officials, teachers' unions, and various public figures became involved. A second 'circulaire' was issued, once again stressing the principals' rights to decide, but the controversy did not go away. In the Fall of 1994, more girls were expelled from school for refusing to take off the headscarf and further government regulations were issued. In 1999, seventy teachers of a middle school in Normandy went on strike on a Friday during Ramadan, in protest against girls wearing the hijab.

Also in 1999, the Conseil d'Etat ruled that school principals had the authority to set dress codes 'compatible with the proper functioning of the class, notably in gymnastics and science.' This decision undid a decision by a lower court from 1996 that held in favor of a girl who had been expelled from school for wearing the hijab. The lower court had given priority to freedom of expression and freedom of religious belief, but the court held that neither prevented school principals from setting dress rules. It was nevertheless a balanced decision, because the court also held that the school had not provided sufficient evidence that the headscarf was a danger to the girl and prevented her from participating in gym and science classes. From 1989, when the high court first ruled on the headscarf, until the 2004 legislation, the legal status of the headscarf remained the same: the scarf did not pose a problem for French principles of secularism, but principals could set dress codes which disallowed wearing the scarf during certain activities if well-founded and specific reasons were given.

As a result of the decision, the then socialist government headed by Lionel Jospin hired a 'scarf-mediator,' whose task it was to mediate between girls and the schools when conflicts arose. In effect, principals were free to set their own rules and the mediator, Hanifa Chérifi, the government official in charge of mediating headscarf conflicts, was only moderately busy.

Controversy erupted again with the start of the school year in 2003, when two girls, Alma and Lila Lévy, were thrown out of school for wearing the headscarf. The girls had a Jewish father and a mother who, albeit Muslim, did not wear the scarf. Alma and Lila quickly became celebrities, appearing in tabloids and women's magazines explaining how they color-coordinated their headscarf with their outfits, while their father threatened a lawsuit. This time, the president, Jacques Chirac, a conservative, declared that the headscarf breached the separation of church and state. and was a source of social disorder.

French newspapers regularly reported that fundamentalist clerics force young women to wear the headscarf and prominent feminists criticized Islam and Muslims, and headscarf wearing, as demeaning and repressive of women. In April 2003, Nicolas Sarkozy, who had been negotiating with various Muslim associations to create the CFCM, the French Muslim council (see Chapter 1), surprised his audience at a meeting of all the main associations by reverting to a 'tough on Muslims' stance and announced that henceforth all women would be required to remove their headscarf for picture-taking for ID cards and drivers' licenses.[5]

In July, Chirac created a presidential commission to 'update' the French law of 1905 on the separation of church and state, which is regarded as establishing the principles associated with 'laïcité.' Reexamination was needed, he argued, in view of the multireligious nature of contemporary French society and with particular reference to the question of 'the veil.' Members of the commission subsequently denied that it had been charged with the task of 'reexamining' secularist principles and the law of 1905, yet the title of the commission and the official announcement of its creation mentioned both and suggested that this was precisely their task.[6] The committee members rewrote the committee's change in the course of their work.

In December 2003, a group of French feminists, actors, designers, and intellectuals took out an advertisement for a petition in the fashion magazine, *Elle*, which was also published in *Le Monde*, which argued that Muslim women are suppressed by the headscarf and in need of the legal protection provided by a law that would forbid them to wear it.[7] The Chirac government agreed. Hitherto unknown for his support for feminist issues, Chirac expressed his concern in terms of the rights of women. At an early stage of the commission's deliberations, the commission president, Bernard Stasi, also expressed the view that the Muslim headscarf is 'objectively' a sign of the suppression of women. Young girls wore it only because they were forced to do so by parents, grandparents, older brothers, or religious groups.[8] Hanifa Chérifi, the headscarf 'mediator,' testified to the French National Assembly that since a majority of Muslims do not wear the headscarf, it is the symbol of

Islamic fundamentalism.[9] When asked if girls might freely choose to wear the headscarf, she responded that choice is meaningless among fundamentalists.

The Stasi commission issued its report on December 11, 2003, and recommended banning all clothing or jewelry displaying 'ostentatious' religious symbols.[10] But now the rights of women had dropped out as a primary concern. Presenting the new law to the National Assembly, the prime minister, Jean-Pierre Raffarin, stressed the importance of protecting the French way of life. 'Integration is a process that presupposes a mutual wish [to integrate], a shift towards certain values, a choice of a way of life, a commitment to a certain view of the world proper for France.'[11]

On February 10, 2004, the National Assembly voted 494 to 36 in favor of the legislation.[12] The dissenting votes came from members of the center-right UDF and the Communist Party. Edouard Balladur, a former prime minister from the RPR, now part of the UMP, Chirac's coalition, voiced concerns about the constitutionality of the bill. In his view, Article 10 of the Declaration of the Rights of Man and Article 9(1) of the European Convention on Human Rights allowed for restriction of religious freedom only if this is justified by the need to protect social and legal order.[13]

The Stasi commission had anticipated such concerns, and probably shared them. Article 9 of European Convention on Human Rights grants everyone 'the right to freedom of thought, conscience and religion; this right includes freedom to change his religion or belief, and freedom, either alone or in community with others and in public or private, to manifest his religion or belief, in worship, teaching, practice and observance.' Yet the convention also leaves the door wide open for governments to legislate on religious matters. Article 9(2) allows governments to limit 'manifestations' of religion or belief, albeit 'only to such limitations as are prescribed by law and are necessary in a democratic society in the interests of public safety, for the protection of public order, health or morals, or the protection of the rights and freedoms of others.' 'The headscarf bans exploit this exemption, Patrick Weil, a political science professor and one of the members of Stasi commission, subsequently explained, 'the Convention authorizes the limitation of the expression of religious faith in the case of problems of public order or attacks on the freedom of conscience of others.'[14]

Weil and his colleagues had expert advice on how to devise a headscarf ban that could withstand the court's scrutiny. Jean-Paul Costa, one of the vice presidents of the Human Rights Court, went before the Stasi Commission, in secret session, to advise the Commission on the court's views of what were acceptable exemptions under Article 9.[15] Judges do not usually advise governments on how to design a bill to pass the scrutiny of their own court, and Costa's appearance before the Commission was controversial among his colleagues on the court.

BANNING THE HEADSCARF: GERMANY

The headscarf is seen in a different light in Germany. The German bans were a matter of state law, and what exactly is prohibited varies from state to state. In Berlin, the legislation included all civil servants and all signs of faith, encompassing crucifixes and yarmulkes together with the Muslim headscarf. In other states, only the headscarf is affected. And in Bavaria, a ban on headscarves was accompanied by a law that required the placing of crucifixes in public schools. The problem, it is argued, is that women who wear the scarf are acting as missionaries for their faith, and proselytize in the classroom for values that are incompatible with fundamental German values.

The controversy began in July 1998 when the Stuttgart school system refused to hire a German-Afghani woman, Ferestha Ludin, as a teacher, because she wore the headscarf. She had come to Germany as a political refugee from the Taliban, and had started wearing the headscarf later. She took her case to court and, in September 2003, the German Constitutional Court reached an ambiguously worded decision that held that her rights had been violated and yet gave local governments the authority to legislate against the headscarf. Ms Ludin's rights were violated, the court said, because no law existed that prohibited teachers from wearing the headscarf.[16] The decision thus set off the rush to pass state laws banning the headscarf.

The court did not reach its decision, as one might have expected, on the grounds that religious freedom is guaranteed by Article 4 of the German Constitution. The refusal to hire Ms Ludin was unlawful simply because no prior law existed in the state of Baden-Württemberg (where Stuttgart is the state capital) saying that teachers could not wear a headscarf. The Stuttgart school system had argued that the schools were obliged by the Basic Law's Articles 6 and 7 to remain neutral in religious questions, and that the headscarf constituted proselytizing. The Court did not directly address the neutrality argument but declared that competence to regulate the meaning of neutrality rested not with the federal government but with the states (which in what follows will be referred to by the German term, 'Länder,' in order to avoid confusion.)

The decision, together with a 1995 ruling in which the Constitutional Court struck down a Bavarian law school mandating the placement of a crucifix in every classroom, can be seen as the beginning of a muddled dialogue between the Länder governments and the Court on the meaning of the constitution's provisions with respect to religion.[17] The Bavarian legislature reacted to the 1995 decision by passing a new law that once more mandated the placing of crucifixes in classrooms, and referred to Christianity as the Bavarian cultural inheritance. The new law bypassed the court's objections to the previous law by creating a procedure for complaints. Students (or parents) may demand that the crucifix be removed from the classroom, if they can demonstrate 'serious and consequential reasons' ('ernsthaften und nachvollziehbaren Gründen') for removing it. School principals are charged with the responsibility of reviewing complaints and must, in doing so, also be sensitive to the concerns of the religious majority of the community.

Following the Ludin decision, on April 1, 2004, Baden-Württemberg passed a law prohibiting teachers from wearing the headscarf in the classroom. The prohibition of religious symbolism was justified on the argument that the headscarf is a threat to core 'Western' norms and constitutes a challenge to the fundamental values of the state. The crucifix was not banned from the classroom, however, on the argument that universal human rights and democracy derive from Christian norms. The legislators accepted that the state must be neutral in religious matters, but they denied that this means it should be neutral with respect to fundamental values. On the contrary, public schools are charged with the task of educating children in the values on which the republic is based. The Christian Democratic culture minister, Annette Schavan, who pushed the bill through with great speed, gave as the reason for the apparent inequity in the treatment of Christianity and Islam that Christianity is an essential part of the value systems of the 'occident.' It is therefore a matter of public ethics to keep Christianity in the classroom. 'We cannot allow a spiritual vacuum to emerge that would leave our society without guidance,' the Minister warned. 'We must stand by our cultural and religious traditions as they are expressed in our Constitution.'[18] The constitution in question is that of the state of Baden-Württemberg, but it should be noted that the Länder are also obliged to observe the values and rights expressed in the federal constitution as well as the international conventions on human rights to which Germany is a signatory.

Cultural policy is subject to devolution to the Länder. Religious freedom is a federal matter. After the Ludin decision, the Constitutional Court was criticized for bucking its obligations by defining the headscarf as a cultural matter rather than an issue of religious freedom. One of those critics was Johannes Rau, the departing Federal President, who pointed out that if Germans wanted to ban the Muslim headscarf in schools, they would also have to ban Catholic nuns' wimples or priests' habits.[19] The states count on the Constitutional Court's reluctance to assert federal power over the Länder. But the argument that the crucifix is 'value-neutral' and the Muslim headscarf is 'religious proselytizing' because the former is part of the value heritage of occidental nations and the latter not clearly engages the constitution's definition of religion, and will likely wind its way back to the Constitutional Court.

A member of the German Bundestag told me that, in her view, when the history of how Muslims changed Europe will be written, the conclusion will be that they promoted secularism and the separation of church and state. 'Because of this decision by the constitutianal court (the Ludin decision), we are having a discussion about secularism,' she remarked. 'I do not say that things will change in two months, but we are looking for a new parity of state and secularism and religion in Germany. It is very interesting that Islam has brought a new dimension to the discussion in this country. It is a very big difference, and when you look in five years, in ten years, things will have changed as a result of this decision.'[20]

In the Ludin decision, the Constitutional Court dodged engagement with two articles in the German Constitution, Article 3, which stipulates that 'All persons shall be equal before the law' (section 1) and that 'No person shall be favored or disfavored because of sex, parentage, race, language, homeland and origin, faith, or religious or political opinions . . .' (section 3), and Article 4, which says that 'Freedom of faith and of conscience, and freedom to profess a religious or philosophical creed, shall be inviolable' (section 1). It does not seem possible any longer to postpone a legal interpretation of the application of these articles for German Muslims.

EUROPEAN HUMAN RIGHTS LAW

Headscarf controversies have ended up in courts across Europe, and the bans have mostly been deemed legally acceptable. Human rights enforcement is now entrusted to two European courts, the European Human Rights Court, which was created under the European Convention of Human Rights (ECHR), and the ECJ, which interprets EU law. Confusion arises because the courts have different jurisdictions—different countries are signatories to the treaties enforced by the two courts—and the ECJ has so far ruled only on employment law and EU citizenship issues. In the recent treaty expansion, parts of the ECHR have been incorporated into EU law and the ECJ will in the future be able to apply some of the same rights paragraphs that in the past have only applied under the Convention. It typically takes ten years for a case to wind its way through the court to a decision, which means we will have to wait a while to see what role the court will play.

The Consolidated EC Treaty (Amsterdam plus Nice) restates the prohibition in Article 13(5) to include discrimination based on sex, racial or ethnic origin, religion or belief, disability, and age or sexual orientation, and empowers the commission to 'take action.' This means that the Commission can

take the initiative and issue directives.[21] The difference is that antidiscrimination rules have now moved from the realm of international law to directly
applicable community law. It is probable that in the medium-term the
Commission may assume the more important role as arbitrator of the diffusion of convention norms into domestic law and policymaking.

The human rights court has been cautious in its interpretations of the
Convention on matters of religious rights, and has mostly held with governments. It has had several opportunities to define the limits of the exemption
under Article 9(2). A recent case decided by the human rights court, *Sahin v.
Turkey*, is relevant to the French and German headscarf bans. It concerned a
fifth year medical student, Leyla Sahin, who was refused admission to training
in various medical specialties at the University of Istanbul in 1998 after the
university passed a dress code. She subsequently enrolled at the University of
Vienna. Sahin's lawyers argued that the university's headscarf ban forced
students to choose between education and religion, and therefore discriminated between believers and nonbelievers. They further argued that the headscarf does not pose a threat to public order, and is therefore permissible under
Article 9(2). The Turkish government responded that the ban was justified
under section 2, because the 'Islamic-style headscarf is a symbol against the
principles of the Republic. Such a situation can lead to chaos in the country. It
also contradicts with [*sic*] the principle of secular education.'[22] The court held
with the Turkish government.

In an earlier and similar case, involving a nursery school teacher, the court
held with the Swiss government that the obligation not to proselytize in
public schools could be used to justify a headscarf ban.[23] Likewise, the
court upheld a requirement by the Turkish government that women remove
their headscarves for ID card pictures.[24] The cases show that the court is
inclined to grant governments a great deal of freedom to exploit the exemption in Article 9(2). The test for permissible bans on religious expression—as
in the case of the headscarf bans—is that restrictions otherwise covered by the
freedom of religion clause contained in Article 9(1) must be based on
evidence that public order is threatened by the behavior that is to be
restricted. A second requirement is that restrictions on religious expression
can be imposed only by legislation—they must be 'democratic'—and not
simply derived from administrative rules. A third requirement is that the
legislation must be 'proportionate' and 'necessary', and must regard religious
exercise that constitutes a manifest threat to public order.

If the French government takes heart from the Sahin decision, the German
'Länder' governments expect that the decision regarding the Swiss nursery
school teacher will provide support for their argument that protecting the
integrity of public education requires the removal of the headscarf from

teachers' heads. Neither decision, of course, can be interpreted as supporting the permissibility of crucifixes in the classroom, and the end result of the Länder's haste to prohibit the headscarf may still have unanticipated consequences for the place for Christianity in public schools.

In Britain, the courts have taken a very different view of Article 9, as became clear in the Shabina Begum case, which I will discuss in detail below. The British government intervened 'by proxy,' in the sense that a well-known QC, Cherie Booth, Tony Blair's wife, acted as counsel for Shabina when the case went to the Appeals Court. It is, as far as I know, the first time the right to wear religious dress has been upheld by a high court in Europe and with implicit support from the government.

The US Justice Department intervened in the trial regarding an eleven-year-old girl, Nashala Hearn, who was sent home from school twice for wearing a headscarf. The Muskogee Public School District in Oklahoma argued that the girl's headscarf violated school dress codes. The Department of Justice took the girl's side, arguing that the dress code violated her constitutional rights, specifically Title IX of the Civil Rights Act of 1964. Outgunned, the school district entered a consent agreement on May 19, 2004, in the US District Court, allowing the girl to wear the scarf and agreed to revise school dress codes.[25]

Interestingly, the consent agreement established quite cumbersome procedures for obtaining a religious exemption from dress codes. The agreement allowed the school district to forbid headgear, 'Head coverings of any sort whatsoever will not be worn by students to class or within school buildings.' But it also established that, 'Any student who requests permission to wear any head covering for religious reasons will submit a written application on the form provided by the School District for such purpose,' and enumerated a multistep procedure for granting the exemption. Even in the USA, you need certification to receive an exemption from rules that stipulate allowable dress styles before you can claim a right to break such rules.

The US government appealed to the right to religious expression, well-established in the USA but still not entrenched in most European legal systems. Nonetheless, in practice the difference between European and US rules are smaller than first principles suggest. There is no right in Europe to wear the headscarf, but outside the French and German bans—which may yet be modified further—governments and courts have applied a reasonableness test and set limits for dress codes, for instance by allowing employers to make assistants in perfume departments wear fashionable clothes, or to ban headscarves in occupations where uniforms are worn. On the other hand, courts have generally disallowed headscarf bans for clerical workers in back offices, and for janitorial staff. The unanticipated consequence of European legal reasoning is to banish headscarves to low-skilled jobs and close off access to professional occupations for Muslim women who wear the headscarf.

BANNING THE JILBAB: WHERE IS THE LIMIT?

N.B.

Within certain boundaries, the collective and individual levels of tolerance prevailing in society are subject to constant negotiation and adjustment. The headscarf issue is an interesting example of the negotiation of boundaries. Most European Muslim leaders think that women should be free to choose to wear the headscarf or not, but they also draw the line at the niqab and the burqha, the tent-like head to toe cover that the Taliban and other radical Islamic groups require women to wear. It is regarded as an ethnic custom that is debilitating for routine social intercourse and detrimental to pluralist coexistence.

The headscarf bans, in contrast, are seen as an invasion of the freedom to choose, and an attempt to legislate religious expression that is demeaning to Muslims as a group and contrary to Western values. My informants often remarked that it is just as unacceptable to prevent a woman from wearing a headscarf as it is to force her to wear one. One Danish city councilor, who spoke laughingly of a relative who had decided to 'become religious' and now looks like 'Bin Laden's wife,' still thought that it was 'her choice' and not something a democratic government should get involved with.[26]

Most Western European countries have gone through one or more episodes of public controversy and legal challenges on the issue of the right of Muslim women to wear the headscarf at work or in public settings. In the Netherlands and Britain, the headscarf is widely tolerated by private and public employers, although the Amsterdam police chief was forced to withdraw a proposal to allow policewomen and meter maids to wear headscarves with their uniforms. In Britain, policewomen and parking officers have been issued uniforms with headscarves, if they request them. British doctors and nurses can freely wear the headscarf, as do many other professional women and students.

In other countries headscarf conflicts led to lower-level arbitration and have not been a matter of national lawmaking. In some instances, laws have been proposed and failed. Adjudication of employment law issues in Europe typically goes to tribunals or administrative agencies rather than proper courts. The reasons for firing women wearing the headscarf have ranged from 'occupational hazard' grounds to uniform requirements and other dress codes. A Danish case from the early 1990s concerned a Muslim doctor who was barred from working at a hospital because she insisted on wearing a headscarf. The hospital management argued that the headscarf was disallowed for 'practical and hygienic' reasons but also that, 'neither patients nor other employees can accept that doctors wear headscarves because they diverge from the hospital's normal standards for attire.' Upon appeal, the case went to three different ministries and all three upheld the hospital's decision.[27]

Supermarkets have been involved in many cases across Europe. In 1999, a Danish supermarket chain fired a cashier for wearing a scarf to work on the argument that it might get stuck in the cash register. The court held with the chain, and rejected the defense's argument that if baseball caps and Santa Claus hats—'nissehuer'—were permissible at work, the Muslim headscarf should be too. A large Swiss supermarket chain issued a prohibition on headscarves in November 2004, but rescinded it a few weeks later in response to criticism. In Sweden, cashiers and stockers are allowed to wear the scarf.

Dress codes that prohibit the more restrictive styles of Islamic dress have been less controversial, in part because they affect few women and in part because the majority view among Muslims is that no religious grounds can be invoked in their defense. Many Muslims therefore consider dress codes that disallow burqas or jilbabs in schools or at work acceptable. In Britain, the Court of Appeals, on March 2, 2005, held with a sixteen-year-old girl, Shabina Begum, against a principal, who in September 2002 sent the then thirteen-year-old student home for wearing a jilbab. She had been admitted to the school in 2000 and had not previously protested the dress code.

Shabina says that she had reached the conclusion through her own religious studies, that the Koran requires an observant Muslim woman to completely cover her body, with the exception of her face and hands. The lower court held with the school, and argued that the school had the right to set dress codes providing proper accommodation was made for religious students, which the court found the school had done. The school allowed Muslim students to wear the shalwar kameez, baggy pants and a long tunic. Local Muslim leaders and imams had approved and supported the school's rules. Muslim parents and students at the school, Denbigh High School in Luton, told the press that they supported the dress code and the principal's decision. Eighty percent of the students and the principal are Muslim.

The case acquired celebrity status when a well-known QC, Cherie Booth, decided to represent the girl in the Court of Appeal.[28] The Muslim Council of Britain at first refused involvement with the case, but then changed its mind and issued a statement in her support. Shabina became an orphan during the trial, when her mother died. When she first turned up in a jilbab her brother, Sherwas Rahman, and another unidentified man accompanied her. Throughout the case, the brother spoke on her behalf in dealings with the school and as her 'litigation friend' in court. Rahman is a supporter of the extremist Islamist group, Hizb-ut-Tahrir (HT). This became publicly known after the trial ended, when HT took credit for having 'advised' Shabina. The principal and the school's lawyer pointed out the connection to extremists in the argument before the lower court, but the issue did not receive much attention. The principal stated, 'there is a number of girls in the school which [*sic*] relies on us to help them resist the pressures from the more extreme groups. I fear that if the school uniform were to be replaced to include the jilbab.... These girls would be deprived of proper protection and would feel abandoned by those upon whom they were relying on to preserve their freedom to follow their own part of the Islamic tradition.... [S]ince this case has been given publicity, the school has been picketed by groups of mainly young men who would appear to be from the more extreme Muslim traditions.'[29]

Would the Muslim Council of Britain have stuck to its original reluctance to support Shabina Begum's lawsuit against her Luton High School for refusing to allow her to wear a jilbab to school, if it was widely known that her brother was an extremist? Would Cherie Booth have decided to represent Shabina? The political and factual aspects of the case largely confirm the French sentiment that girls are being manipulated by men and political extremists, and that it is only extremists who demand Islamic dress. The Shabina Begum case, it should be noted, was not about the headscarf—which was tolerated at Luton High—but about the more restrictive dress.

Why did the Court of Appeals reach the conclusion that the school could not prevent Shabina from wearing her jilbab? Interestingly, the justices decided for Shabina based upon their understanding of Article 9 in the European Court of Human Rights, the same Article under which the French government justifies banning the headscarf. (The European Convention on Human Rights was made directly applicable in British courts by the 1998 Human Rights Act.) The British justices argued that Shabina's right to wear religious dress was covered by Article 9(1), and the school had failed to demonstrate that it was justified in insisting on the application of its dress code as required by Article 9(2), which allows restrictions on religious rights under specific circumstances related to safety and social order.[30] The curious outcome is that, in Britain, the European Convention of Human Rights is interpreted to prohibit schools from having dress codes that disallow the jilab but allows other forms of religious dress including the headscarf, such as the one in effect at Denbigh High, whereas in France it is seen as allowing a blanket prohibition on the headscarf, the turban, and the yarmulke.

N.8

Irrespective of the discord on the legality of headscarf bans, the politicization of the headscarf has had difficult consequences for many Muslim women. A young Swedish Social Democrat said to me, 'My mother wears the headscarf; just a pretty small scarf. She is the strongest woman in the world, yet they have now made her into a victim and they do no see her for what she is.'[31] The irony is that twenty years earlier her mother had been welcomed to Sweden as a celebrated political refugee and was much admired for her courage. She wore the headscarf then, too, but once Swedes decided that the headscarf was not a quaint foreign custom one had to respect but prima facie evidence of female suppression, the woman was transformed from a freedom fighter to a victim.

Invariably, politicization works also to make the scarf a symbol of resistance. Pola Manzila Uddin, a Labour peer, described in a letter to the *Guardian* her own path to an assertive and politicized Muslim political persona.[32] She wrote to express her dismay over the lower court's decision in the Shabina Begum case, and explained how as a Muslim she had joined Labour because only the left held out the promise of social improvement for Muslims. Now, with Labour failing to deliver on its promise to help Muslims improve their status, she was disappointed. Muslims who want to keep their faith were afforded few choices about where to put their energies and votes. Baroness Uddin explained how, when she recently had occasion to put a headscarf on, it felt 'right' to keep it on for the time being. She was shocked, she wrote, that friends and colleagues interpreted her choice as a political statement. (Which, of course, she had just said it was.)

Baroness Uddin's embrace of a contested symbol as a personal statement of identity—and, one has to conclude from her own explanation, also a political statement—does not fit with any of the assumptions normally made about why women wear the scarf. It is evidently a political statement—she did not use to wear one previously and now she does because she is protesting about certain political developments. But Baroness Uddin is not a fundamentalist, and she is not repressed. She wears the headscarf by choice to show her allegiance to her faith, and for political reasons. But she does not wear it all the time, so it is not an obligation. It seems to me that to prohibit Baroness Uddin from wearing the scarf as she carries out her duties as a member of the House of Lords—which would be the case if she were a member of the French Senate—would be to violate *both* her political and her religious rights.

Muslim women who wear the headscarf argue that they are victims of discriminatory homogenization. A Stockholm city councilor, a Social Democrat, wears a headscarf. In official Sweden, she said, discrimination is not allowed but there are many problems for immigrants, and particularly for Muslims. Headscarves are a very important problem, she said, adding,

'Islamophobia is real.'[33] It is assumed, she says, that a woman who wears a headscarf is an Islamic 'fundamentalist' and that she will be trouble, and therefore should be avoided.

Headscarf bans have become a litmus test for European feminists. On one side are feminists who argue that backsliding cannot be allowed, and the force of law must be used to defend women's gains. And on the other side are feminists who say that consciousness changes slowly and that the most successful changes are voluntary.

The frequently made argument that women must cover up to prove themselves 'chaste' and 'pure' illustrates that it *is* intended as a restriction on women's sexual freedom. If women's bodies must be hidden because they are distracting to men or offensive, it *does* connote female inferiority. The misogynistic justifications for the 'veiling' requirement expressed by some imams and religious scholars are all too familiar reminders of a not so distant era when women were deemed responsible for their own victimization. Yet even if you agree that to regard women as responsible for their own purity is an inherently misogynist position, it does not follow that governments should prohibit women from covering up. It is easy to see why Muslim women regard government dictates in this matter as yet another interference with their freedom and another obstacle to their social integration.

The headscarf controversies have had perverse effects. Muslim scholars and theologians are increasingly reluctant to say that the headscarf is a matter of choice for reasons that have more to do with a desire to protect women's rights than with a wish to suppress women. The view that the headscarf is 'optional' is seen as lending credibility to the argument that the headscarf is 'political,' and therefore not covered by the European Convention of Human Rights' Article 9. The courts have stipulated that for something to be covered as a matter of religious freedom, it must be seen as unambiguous religious obligation. One unfortunate consequence is that the prohibitions may have a chilling effect on liberal interpretations of Islam's religious obligations.

A British imam explained to me, 'I used to say that there is no doctrinal basis in the Koran for the hijab, but I will not say that anymore.'[34] To say that the hijab is optional would, he continued, lend credence to the argument used in favor of headscarf bans that women 'do not have to wear' the scarf and the bans therefore do not violate any principles regarding toleration of religious expression.

Nevertheless, Muslims disagree on how to interpret the Koran's instructions. Religious scholars and feminists argue that the hijab requirement is the same for men and women. Amina Wadud, in *Qur'an and Women: Rereading the Sacred Texts from a Woman's Perspective*, argues that the Koran's prohibitions against 'wanton display' (verses 33: 33 and 24: 60) clearly applies to both men and women and that nothing specific is said about what dress to wear.[35] And then there are all those who think it does not matter what the Koran says or does not say about dress, because sleeve length and head coverings are unimportant aspects of what it means to be a Muslim.

WOMEN AND ISLAM

There are problems with the subjection of women in Islam—and among Muslims, which is a different thing. It is hardly a problem peculiar to Islam, but this is not the place for a comparative evaluation of how different faiths treat women. Women's legal equality is a more recent phenomenon in Europe than we often care to think about. In Germany, the legal subordination of wives to husbands remained a matter of law until the reform of the Civil Code in 1956, when legal patriarchy was abolished.[36] The political influence of Catholic thinking had a great deal to do with the lateness of the reform. Fifty years have passed, and it is in part the gains that European feminists have made that cause them to take a hard line on Islam. They sometimes overlook the fact that misogynist clerics do not speak for all Muslims.

'Because women are not deemed as important as men in most Muslim majority or minority communities,' writes Amina Wadud, 'Muslim women do not enjoy a status equal to men.'[37] Like many other Muslim feminists, she has chosen to address the problem by rereading the Koran. She insists that women belong in the mosque, and may even lead a congregation in prayer and preach the khutbah. A group of Canadian feminists, the Canadian Council of Muslim Women in Ontario, entered into a heated debate with local religious leaders on the question of women's imamate after a woman gave a sermon in a local mosque. 'There is no reliable hadith that prohibits women from leading men in prayers,' the Council declared in a letter to local religious leaders, and rejected the authenticity of a particular hadith which is usually regarded as an unequivocal scriptural prohibition on female prayer leaders in the mosque.[38]

Muslim politicians and activists, and many religious leaders, often point out that Islam—and Muslims—must revisit religious teachings on the position of women. Khalida Khan, a British Muslim activist, complains that things are getting worse as a new—male—Muslim political elite is emerging in Europe. 'There is an unhealthy trend towards an alliance of men in building structures of power, excluding and marginalizing the role of women.'[39]

A common complaint among Turkish-origin politicians about the Turkish communities in Europe is that they have held on to conservative values and expectations, particularly about women's roles, that are outdated in Turkey itself.[40] Forced or arranged marriages are another frequently cited example of patriarchal conservatism. Arranged marriages are not a religious but an ethnic custom, widespread both among Turks from rural areas and among British Asians. Restrictive immigration laws have had the unintended consequence of providing economic and legal incentives for the continuation of the practice. In many cases, a 'cousin marriage' is a way of helping relatives to send a young woman or man to Europe. South Asian families—Muslim and Hindu—often view marriages as a way to strengthen family networks. Bhikhu Parekh has defended consensual arranged marriages, arguing that, 'the wider society is right to ban imposed marriages or those contracted under duress as defined in a culturally sensitive manner, but to go further is to be guilty of moral dogmatism and unjustified cultural interference.'[41]

For many feminists, myself included, the difference between an arranged and a forced marriage is murky, and any defense of parental interference with sexual freedom suspect. This is not a 'feminists versus Muslims' argument. Several of the imams I interviewed advocated changing public policy so that religious marriages are made legally binding. The measure would, among other things, make polygamous marriages impossible, because the imams would be required to ascertain that the parties were legally able to agree to marriage. It might at first glance seem a simple change, but it raises complex questions about the legal status of imams who currently have neither the legal rights nor the legal obligations afforded to other clergy.

Without the right to issue legally binding marriage documents, imams cannot prevent anyone who is not freely entering into the marriage from marrying in religious ceremonies. The problem has many permutations ranging from forced marriages, under-aged marriages, and polygamous marriages. As long as religious ceremonies are not legally binding, marriage law does not apply to the union, and nor does divorce law. Women who marry in religious ceremonies have no legal claims on their husbands. The more common problem regards men who remarry after legally divorcing their first wives in civil procedures but do not seek religious divorces. The consequences for the women are at times severe. Women who have obtained civil divorces cannot remarry another Muslim, if the husband refuses a religious divorce. Moreover, some men marry different women in religious and civil ceremonies, and in effect commit polygamy.

Naser Khader, a Danish member of parliament, has called for legislation that would compel conformity between religious and secular law in this connection. The British Shariah Council issued a report on October 22, 2004, in which it estimated that as many as 4,000 men skirt the ban on polygamy by marrying second wives in religious ceremonies. 'We are concerned for the women—the second wife or subsequent wives usually find they have no rights if the relationship breaks down,' a spokesman for the council said.[42]

ISLAMIC DIVORCES AND LEGAL DUALISM

Another controversy related to the position of Muslim women and of Islam in European law and public policy has arisen over the shariah, the expressed desire on the part of some Muslims to apply Islamic religious law in Europe. Generally, Muslim leaders agree that it would be a serious mistake to grant statutory status to Islamic religious law, and admit that this would be particularly bad for women. The common accusation that Muslims want to make religious law binding for everybody is absurd. For one thing, Muslims are a minority and cannot impose any law on Western democracies. Nor would they want to. Most Muslims do not follow shariah. Many Muslims say, as did one parliamentarian, 'shariah! What nonsense.'[43] It is only fringe groups like Hizb-ut-Tahrir that argue for the generalized imposition of Islamic religious law on everybody.

Religious people may argue that Muslims are obliged to follow shariah in their personal life, but that this is a matter of personal choice, and that they are constrained by secular law. The argument goes that the Koran may be read to mandate stoning as a punishment for certain crime, for instance, but that stoning is illegal everywhere in Europe. Therefore no European Muslim can endorse stoning. This is a pragmatic way for Muslims who are disinclined to engage in theology to neutralize parts of Islam with which they do not agree and still keep the faith. However, it does not satisfy religious people who take a literal approach to the interpretation of religious law. It also leaves believers who want to follow the shariah but do not know how to do so in a vacuum. And if no reliable authorities exist capable of interpreting religious law and no courts are willing to apply it, the void will be filled one way or another. Self-help is readily available on the Internet. A large number of online advice columnists dispense advise about how to follow the righteous path in the land of disbelief.

Technically speaking, the shariah is a code of law derived from the Koran and from the teachings and example of Mohammed. It is the task of Islamic religious scholars, organized in shariah councils, to arbitrate disputes where interpretations of religious law are involved. Fatwas are not declarations of war, as many Europeans think, but pronouncements of the application of shariah to particular moral or public issues, where interpretations of religious law are involved.

In contrast to the Muslim states in Asia, the Middle East, and now even Africa, there are no state-mandated shariah councils and no shariah courts upholding religious law in Europe, and here Muslims are free to make their own decisions about which law they will follow. However, for those who care about observing shariah, there may already be too many experts. Multiple Islamic law bodies are uneasily competing to develop authoritative statements of Islamic law for European Muslims. One is the Dublin-based European Council for Fatwa and Research discussed earlier. One highly regarded French imam and rector pointed out that this too was a consequence of freedom. 'They [the fatwa council] take advantage of the freedom in Europe to do what they couldn't do at home.'[44]

The imams I interviewed generally regarded the fatwa council and al-Qaradawi unfavorably. Outside Britain, I found little support for the ideas that shariah councils were needed. As a young Danish woman put it, 'the imams have already lost their power.'[45] In Britain, however, the Muslim Law (Shariah) Council associated with the Muslim College in Ealing, London, takes a very different view of its role and a different approach to the elaboration of religious law. The Council oversees a network of regional shariah councils. The purpose is to provide expert opinion in family disputes and to advise civil courts on Islamic law issues involved in court cases. A number of civilly educated lawyers associated with the Council have specialized in the application of religious law in secular courts. As one person associated with the council explained to me, 'you can find many different opinions about the meaning of shariah, and our task is to find the basis for helping British Muslims get on with their lives here.' He stressed that the council was particularly concerned about helping women, and finding legal interpretations that protected women's status.[46]

Abduljalil Sajid is a British Islamic religious leader of Pakistani descent. He is imam of the Brighton Islamic Mission and a Muslim chaplain for the National Health Service. He is engaged in interfaith organizations and was for five years chair of the MCB's social policy subcommittee. He is also a Muslim judge in the Muslim Family Court in Brighton. Imam Sajid writes and talks widely on Islam and preaches integration and coexistence. He is also a conservative Muslim, whose views articulate the reformist neo-orthodox position of many establishment Muslims in Britain. His views on the role of shariah in Britain are suggestive of how conservatives bridge the gap between liberalism and secularism on the one hand, and religious neo-orthodoxy on the other.

Shariah is not a divine law, he says, but a human interpretation of the sacred text made by religious scholars since the days of the Prophet. Muslims living in Britain must first observe British law and then Islamic religious law. Islam contains rules for human conduct in all aspects of life, but since it is man-made law people have the right to make objections against some of its provisions and to change the law, Imam Sajid says. The Koran is revealed divine truth but truth is subject to context and interpretation is important. He points out that his view of shariah as man-made and historically contingent sets Muslims like himself off from the literalists (or fundamentalists) who reject such relativism. He supports reforms that will allow the codification of Islamic religious law and its application in secular courts for Muslims. His views of the Koran allow for a generous interpretation on the question of the treatment of women. 'Qur'anic revelation raised the status of women in marriage, divorce and inheritance,' he says and cites in support a passage in the Koran: 'Men and women are equal in the eyes of God; man and woman were created to be equal parts of a pair (51:49).'[47]

N. B.

Imam Sajid's moderate conservatism does not have many supporters among European Muslim leaders outside Britain. I asked the leaders who completed the survey that I used in all six countries if they supported the application of Islamic religious law in civil law and what special legal exemptions were needed to accommodate the application of Islamic religious law in Europe. The majority responded that no laws had to be changed to accommodate Islam, and that Islamic religious law should remain a private matter.

One question elicited strikingly different responses from Muslim leaders in the different countries. The question was, 'Should secular civil law respect religious law and allow imams and Islamic legal scholars to decide on legally binding decisions for Muslims living in country X?' This question was specifically designed to test the support for allowing Islamic religious law to become legally binding for European Muslims. In my phrasing of the question, I allowed for 'choice,' that is, the question suggested that Muslims themselves could choose between getting a divorce, for example, under religious personal law or secular civil law. The question mentioned divorce, which is one of the most controversial issues because it involves women's rights under Islamic law, but Islamic personal law covers a range of issues, of which divorce is only one of the more contentious matters. Table 6.1 shows the distribution of support for the application of Islamic religious law as binding law—by choice or for all Muslims—in each of the countries in the study.

Four out of five of the British participants in the study supported the proposition that the state should allow the application of shariah law in some cases. In Scandinavia, respondents were emphatically opposed. The majority of the Dutch Muslims rejected the possibility that religious law should have legal status but allowed that perhaps some choice in the matter should be permitted. The ambiguity about choice may reflect some lingering affinity for earlier (but now discontinued) Dutch experiments with

Table 6.1. Question: Should secular civil law respect religious law and allow imams and Islamic legal scholars to decide on legally binding decisions for Muslims living in country X?

	Denmark (%)	Sweden (%)	France (%)	Germany (%)	Netherlands (%)	UK (%)	Total (%)
No	81.3	85.7	83.3	74.4	60.9	20.0	65.6
Maybe	9.4	0.0	8.3	15.4	26.1	10.0	12.1
Yes	9.4	14.3	8.3	10.3	13.0	70.0	22.3
Total	100.0	100.0	100.0	100.0	100.0	100.0	100.0

$n = 157$

'multiculturalism,' which involved the recognition of an independent 'Muslim pillar.'

One out of ten Dutch Muslim leaders was in favor, and three out ten were inclined to support the proposal with reservations. The lack of support for traditionalist measures reflected in part value judgments and in part a realistic assessment of the Dutch political context.

The reasons for the difference between British Muslims and Muslims elsewhere in Western Europe are almost certainly related to ethnic origin, but that may not be the whole story. In personal conversations, British Muslim leaders alluded to 'the Indian solution' as a possible template for how British law could be changed. The reference here is to the Indian constitution's support for partial devolution of legal power on cultural questions to religious and ethnic authorities in a system of legal pluralism or, as it is sometimes termed, legal federalism. The difficulties of making such provisions in European legal systems may not be well understood. It should be noted also that British Muslim parliamentarians, from both the House of Commons and the Lords, had little sympathy for allowing legal dualism.

Religious law is well entrenched, in different ways, it should be noted, in Pakistan and India but has not been accepted in Turkey since the Kemalist revolution in 1923. The different legacy of the usage of Islamic religious law in these countries may to some extent explain the cross-national difference observed here. British Muslims come primarily from South Asia. Muslims elsewhere in Europe are primarily of North African or Turkish background, and draw on a different history.

The different recruitment patterns for political elites in the six countries may also play a role. Generally speaking, parliamentarians and, in some cases, city councilors were more supportive of integrationist and secular values and policy choices than the leaders who were associated with national and regional Muslim associations. The political parties act as filters, and we therefore tend to find that individuals who subscribe to the neo-orthodox and more conservative views of Islam are excluded from the political elite. This is not the case in Great Britain, however. Recruitment to the House of Commons is highly centralized but local governance structures are highly decentralized, which helps explain, in part, why we find higher rates of support for the integration of shariah in Britain than in other countries.

British Muslims are also consistently more inclined towards a conservative theology. Ethnic origin and the different approaches to religious exercise associated with various ethnic and national histories are part of the explanation. None of this should be taken to mean that Pakistani-origin Muslims are conservative and Turkish-origin Muslims are not. That would be a gross simplification. The differences reflect patterns of demographic variation and theological propensities as well as elite recruitment that require more sophisticated analysis than is possible in the context of this study.

BALANCING RELIGIOUS AND CIVIL LAW

Giving Muslims a choice between which personal law they want to rely on poses many practical problems, but it would in effect allow people who are pious to rely on religious law to regulate family affairs. Orthodox Jews have been able to do this for some time. New York state amended the 1980 Domestic Relations Act in 1992 to allow civil courts to fine husbands who use the refusal of a religious divorce—a *get*—to extract concessions from their wives in divorce proceedings or otherwise to punish their former wives. The amendment was a reaction to what was seen as a growing problem with Orthodox Jewish women trapped in 'Agunah,' the so-called 'chained women,' who are unable to remarry in religious ceremonies because their husbands refuse them religious divorces after divorce has been obtained in civil courts. The issue arises because, within Orthodox Judaism, rabbinic courts grant divorces only upon the husband's request. Rabbis have complained that the 1992 amendment unfairly coerces husbands, who feel compelled to grant a *get* for financial reasons.

The 'choice' option implied in my question may appear to provide an attractive way of balancing secular and religious law, but it does not. The New York controversy illustrates how difficult it is to achieve such a balance without sacrificing either religious freedom or civil rights. It also illustrates some of the problems that Muslim women experience. Orthodox Jewish women have the option of ignoring the rabbinic courts and remarrying in civil ceremonies, but they may face opposition from their families, suffer loss of status, and be obliged to marry a partner who does not share their faith. Children from that union would be regarded as illegitimate.

Implementation raises complicated questions about the circumstances in which individuals should be allowed to choose not to exercise their rights under secular law—and again, this is an issue mostly for women. It is arguable that 'choice' in this matter violates principles about the equal application of the law. If religious law is incorporated into civil law, secular courts, lawyers, and solicitors will have to familiarize themselves with religious law. A practical solution discussed in Britain is to have a special corps of Muslim lawyers available to adjudicate such cases.

Any attempt to institutionalize shariah in Great Britain will probably produce a split between traditionalist and modernist Muslim leaders. In Canada, controversy has erupted over the efforts of a Muslim group—the Islamic Institute for Civil Justice—to create a shariah court for family law and inheritance disputes under Ontario's 1991 Arbitration Act. The Arbitration Act created a legal basis for a 'multicultural' approach to family law. The Ontario government recently commissioned a report to defuse 'the confusion' over the proposal to create the shariah court. (It supports the initiative.) The report, written by Marion Boyd, who was responsible in 1991 for the passage of the Arbitration Act, states that 'Canada is a multicultural society and the fundamental tension that must be addressed is between respect for the minority group and protection of a person's individual rights within that minority.' Submitting to religious arbitration is a voluntary act, the report noted.[48]

The Canadian Council of Muslim Women attacked the report, as did other Muslim groups in the province. The Council accused Boyd of being 'naive' and demanded that Muslim women and children be given the same legal safeguards that others enjoy. Demonstrating once again the infinite elasticity of the human rights rhetoric, the Council cited the Canadian Charter of Rights and Freedoms in their support, the very same act that, according to Boyd, imposes an obligation on Canadians to respect the rights of religious groups, and so requires Canada to embrace legal multiculturalism.[49]

GENDER AND SUPPORT FOR SHARIAH

The women in my study were notably less supportive of legal pluralism and multicultural devolution of authority to Islamic scholars and imams than were the male leaders. They overwhelmingly supported freedom of choice to embrace religious law—but without the possibility of legal sanctions in matters of behavior—or secular circumscription of the institutions of faith. Gender differences were particular salient in matters of personal law, with women generally disinclined to accept religious exemptions (Table 6.2).

Only one woman participant in the study agreed that secular law should be changed to devolve authority to imams in divorce cases and other personal law matters. Half of the men in the study outright rejected the idea but three-quarters of the women did. As for the opposite proposition that imams should be bound by law to grant religious divorces in cases where civil divorces had been obtained—an issue that has some importance because of the women's inability to remarry in the absence of a religious divorce—three-quarters of the women agreed but only three in five men did.

Overall, although there are women leaders who support the traditionalist perspective on the institutionalization of Islam, most female leaders are generally more inclined than their male counterparts to support the more secular or integrationist models. Even women who otherwise expressed traditionalist views prefer to see an accommodation between Islam and European legal norms that protect women's rights. These views were consistent also with women's strong support for the right to wear the headscarf, which Muslim female civic and political leaders generally regard as a women's rights issue.

A young British lawyer objected strenuously when I retold the 'Shariah! What nonsense!' remark: 'I love the shariah!' she exclaimed. I told her that as far as my research suggested, most women did not share her view on this question. I explained that I had found next to no support, even among women who described themselves as 'very religious,' for allowing imams and shariah councils to issue binding decisions following religious law on issues related to marriage and divorce. 'But oh no,' she said, 'they are right. You cannot trust these matters to imams. That would be terrible for women. We must have professionals make those decisions.'[50] I finally understood that for her shariah meant a codified body of law, developed and managed by professional lawyers like herself. It is not clear, however, that this is practical. A Canadian law scholar, Natasha Bakht, who has studied the operation of the Canadian Arbitration Act, concludes that decisions taken by Arbitration tribunals cannot stand up on appeal to the courts because there is no standard

Table 6.2. Support for application of Islamic law by gender.

	No (%)	Maybe (%)	Yes (%)	Total (%)
Female	76.7	6.7	16.7	100.0
Male	62.0	13.2	24.8	100.0
Total	64.9	11.9	23.2	100.0

interpretation of religious law.[51] From a legal perspective, this poses big problems, as there is no guarantee of equal application of the law.

MULTICULTURALISM AND THE SHARIAH

Multiculturalists argue that Western states must grant self-governance to minority groups in certain areas of law and policy directly related to cultural differences. The application of different culturally contingent laws—for example, the shariah—to minority population groups is a core feature of the multicultural program. Typically, family practices and language are among the first on the list for legal pluralism. Critics argue that these arrangements violate Western societies' cultural preferences for cohesive national communities based on entrenched—and often hard-fought for—value systems and value-affirmative policies.

Critics who belong to the affected minorities point out that the more serious issue is that members of minority groups are deprived of their right to equal protection under the law and that, while self-government may appear to give the group special privileges, individuals who belong to the group are potentially deprived of certain rights. Women's rights are the most contested. In one view, legal pluralism is inherently conservative because it empowers unelected traditional elites and, in the case of gender relations, disadvantages women.[52]

One of the difficulties with multiculturalism is how to decide whose rights come first, a question that also plagues the Ontario debate over religious rights versus women's rights. Sikhs and other minorities subjected to Francophile assimilation in Quebec have complained that their minority protection is more extensive in Anglophone Canada. Jewish women, who oppose the orthodox rabbis' control over Israeli family law, object that their rights have been sacrificed to those of the Orthodox Jews.[53]

Will Kymlicka, a proponent of multiculturalism, acknowledged 'the possibility of tragic conflict, the possibility that no conception of justice may prove adequate even in principle to eliminate the experience of imposition and injustice in social life,' but he did not suggest how the conflict might be resolved.[54] French Canadian claims for cultural and political self-government have inspired much of the multicultural theorizing in Canada but, paradoxically, as the conflicts between non-French minorities and the province of Quebec have shown, primacy for one exposed culture—in this case the Quebecois versus Anglo-Canadians—inevitably means less tolerance for other differences. One of the difficulties of the multiculturalist project has been to come up with institutional solutions that provide fair solutions to the problem of how to balance the need for solidarity—for example, an equal right to social protection—against the need for self-government and cultural and political autonomy for communities that claim to have distinct identities which set them apart from the majority.

Multiculturalists argue that uniform legal codes may be unjust in societies characterized by cultural pluralism because they invariably assert a particular set of values at the expense of others. They recognize that uniform codes may be appropriate in certain contexts, defense or taxation, for example, but not in matters related to core cultural or religious values.[55] Family law and educational policy are typical examples of areas where some measure of legal pluralism and devolution are in place from this perspective.

Examples of institutional arrangements of this sort include the Dutch 'pillared' system and the so-called 'Indian model.' Both types of arrangements are also sometimes referred to as 'internal' federalism. Not only is it right, it also works, says Will Kymlicka, a proponent of such arrangements, who evaluated the institutions of minority self-government used by French-speaking Quebec and Swiss and Dutch ethno-linguistic groups. He concluded they have 'worked well' and are 'a cause for optimism.'[56]

The Indian constitution devolves legal authority on certain issues to substate actors. Article 29 guarantees religious groups the right to maintain different cultures, and Article 30 bars the state from interfering with the ability of religious communities to establish separate educational institutions with public funding and prohibits discrimination.[57] This arrangement is also sometimes called 'internal federalism,' because self-government is devolved to nonterritorial groups defined by social, religious, or ethno-linguistic characteristics. In India, Hindus and Muslims were allowed culturally specific personal law traditions that accommodate religious laws and practices. European precedents for devolution of circumscribed legal authority to nonterritorial groups defined by religion or language are found in the Netherlands, Belgium, and Switzerland.

Some multiculturalists push the boundaries of minority rights further to include affirmative action and broad delegation of rights to self-government on many areas of policymaking. Iris Marion Young thinks that self-government is insufficient; minorities are entitled to preferential treatment because they are disadvantaged simply because they are a numerical minority.[58] The separatist implications of such arrangements worry critics. Bhikhu Parekh proposed instead that legal exemptions given to particular minority groups have to be negotiated in reiterated rounds of democratic conversations between minorities and majorities. Special rights must be subjected to democratic scrutiny rather than exempt from it, as suggested by Young and Kymlicka.

N.B.

The institutional arrangements proposed by multiculturalists suffer from inherent tensions between collective and individual rights. The entitlement of a religious or ethnic minority group to use legal sanctions to protect their traditions often clash with individual wishes for mobility and equal protection under the law. Critics of the Indian system point out, for example, that political tension over how to balance uniformity of rights within the state has deteriorated into competition for 'special privileges' between groups and become a cause of separatist nationalist mobilization. In judicial terms, legal pluralism is often exceedingly difficult to manage, and appears invariably to lead to a codification of minority cultural practices that is detrimental to the objectives of enhanced pluralism and flexible adjustment.[59]

Dutch multiculturalism collapsed for similar reasons. It is not possible to maintain group-based self-government in societies with a high degree of social and geographic mobility. While immigrant groups—exemplified by Pakistanis and Bangladeshis in England—may at this point in time exhibit sufficient internal cohesion to make religious or cultural self-government reasonably workable, it is unlikely that future generations will feel comfortable with such arrangements.

The Dutch system of political and social organization based upon religious 'pillars' emerged as a uniquely Dutch version of national liberalism between 1870 and 1920, and served as a vehicle for the emancipation of the lower middle classes. The system bridged religious and linguistic cleavages by allowing each group—Protestants and Catholics, liberals and socialists, farmers and workers—to develop separate but parallel social and political institutions.[60]

'Generally speaking,' write Ruben Gowricharn and Pim Mungra describing the system, 'each "pillar" had its own schools, shops, youth organizations, recreation facilities, churches, radio and television broadcasting corporations, newspapers, literature, trade unions, employer organizations, political parties, even universities.'[61] The norm was that nobody mixed and everybody respected each other. Government funding was evenly allocated between the pillars, and the rules of coordination within national organization allowed each group a right to self-determination in appointments and political representation. Dutch 'pillarization' began to break down in the 1960s in response to increased geographical and social mobility that gave people incentives to defect from their assigned pillars. A brief attempt to revive the pillared system for immigrants was made in the 1980s, but today Dutch political leaders are disenchanted with the attempts to promote Muslim integration by means of separate but equal institutions. Muslims are disenchanted, too, and often note that the institutions were only separate and never equal.

HUMAN RIGHTS AND EUROPE'S MUSLIMS

The gender issues are indicative of the disagreements concerning the limits for Islamic autonomy in Europe. In general, European Muslim leaders want parity and respect for Islam, but they want to edit which aspects of Islam they choose to put into practice. And they want the full protection of the law that is afforded other faiths and other citizens. They want equal rights, not different rights. This is the reason why there is so little support for multiculturalist solutions outside Britain. Multiculturalism has been tried and failed, say Dutch and German Muslims. Swedish and Danish Muslims insist first and foremost upon equal treatment. Only British Muslims—and not all—support limited derogation (and with opt-out options in place) from civil law to empower religious law with statutory status on occasional issues.

The power of appeals to human rights rests primarily upon the ability of groups and individuals to point to national violations and to base appeals for change on moral grounds or on apparent instances of conflict between international norms and national policies. A recent study of the socialization of international human rights norms into national politics, edited by Thomas Risse, Stephen C. Ropp, and Kathryn Sikkink, concluded that 'lesson number one' is that transnational networks and human rights advocacy groups are essential for the dissemination of human rights into domestic politics.[62] Unfortunately, there are no significant 'external actors'—no think tanks, no Ford foundation researchers, and no UN support groups—who have made the difficulties that religious Muslims experience in secular and Christian Europe their particular concern. The exception is some of Europe's Green parties, which have increasingly asserted a new European liberalism based upon a human rights discourse sensitized to cultural and religious pluralism.

The development of European Islam will, for most Muslims, proceed within a conception of rights that stresses individual freedom and choice. The collective identity as Muslims derives from personal affinity with a faith, spirituality, and has little to do with the traditionalist collectivism of immobile societies or the coerced Islamization of the Islamic countries. It implies a radically new approach to Islam and Islamic religious laws, which are likely to be seen as 'suggestions' or, in the case of the neo-orthodox, self-imposed obligations.

NOTES

1. Sixty French and North African intellectuals, writers, and professors signed a manifesto declaring themselves 'pro-Islam' but opposed to the misogyny, homophobia, and anti-semitism that they argue characterize the Islamic 'revival' in France. 'Manifeste. Être de Culture Musulmane . . . et contre la Misogynie, l'Homophobie, l'Antisémitisme et l'Islam Politique,' *Prochoix. La revue du droit de choisir*, 28 (spring 2004), 69–72.
2. 'The word 'hijab' comes from the Arabic word 'hajaba' meaning to hide from view or conceal.' According to the Institute, 'a woman should not show her beauty or adornments except what appears by uncontrolled factors such as the wind blowing her clothes, and the head covers should be drawn so as to cover the hair, the neck and the bosom;' http://www.usc.edu/dept/MSA/humanrelations/womeninislam/whatishijab.html.
3. Françoise Gaspard and Farhad Khosrokhavar, *Le Foulard et la République* (Paris: Découverte, 1995).
4. Group interview, Stockholm (November 4, 2003).
5. John R. Bowen, 'Muslims and Citizens. France's Headscarf Controversy,' *Boston Review* (February–March 2004), 31–5.
6. 'M. Chirac Crée la "Commission Stasi" pour Redéfinir la Laïcité,' *Le Monde* (July 2, 2003).
7. *Le Monde* (December 9, 2003), 23.
8. *Le Monde*, 'Laïcité: le Voile Islamique est "Objectivement un Signe d'Aliénation de la Femme" ' (November 2, 2003).
9. Assemblée Nationale, *Rapport Fait sur la Question du Port des Signes Religieux à l'Ecole*. Tome II, 1ère partie. Auditions (June 11, 2003), 26.
10. Commission de Réflexion sur l'Application du Principe de Laïcité dans la République. Rapport au Président de la République (December 11, 2003).
11. Jean-Pierre Raffarin, Project de Loi Relatif à l'Application du Principe de Laïcité dans les Ecoles, Colleges et Lycées Publics, Assemble Nationale (February 3, 2004); http://www.diplomatie.gouv.fr/actu/print_bul.asp?liste=20040204.html.
12. The popularity of the measure was conspicuously present in the National Assembly's debates. A spokesperson for the prime minister noted that 72 percent, in effect 'the whole world,' supported the bill; http://www.assemblee-nationale.fr/12/cra/2003–2004/153.asp.
13. Ibid.
14. Patrick Weil, 'Lifting the Veil of Ignorance,' *Progressive Politics*, 3 (March 1, 2004). Presented as a talk at the Center for European Studies, Harvard University (May 10, 2004).
15. Costa's appearance was confirmed by three independent sources. A clerk at the court told me about it when I called to ask when the Sahin decision was scheduled to be released. Another witness who testified told me about it, when we met in Paris. And another judge on the court confirmed that discussions had taken place

among other judges about a censure motion for what some members of the Court considered a breach of judicial ethics. No motion was passed, apparently because current ethic rules do not preclude such actions.

16. BVerfG, 2 BvR 1436/02 vom 3.6.2003, Absatz-Nr. (1–140). Available at: http://www.bverfg.de/entscheidungen/rs20030603_2bvr143602.html.

17. BVerfGE 93, 1 (May 16, 1995). See par. 112, BVerfG, 2 BvR 1436/02 (September 24, 2003); (http://www.bverfg.de/entscheidungen/rs20030603_2bvr143602.html)

18. Land Baden-Württemberg, Meldung vom 01.04.2004. See also *Financial Times Deutschland* (November 11, 2003).

19. http://www.heute.t-online.de/ZDFheute/artikel/9/0,1367,POL-0–2095209,00.html.

20. Interview 110 Berlin (November 8, 2004).

21. The language repeats Article 14 in the European Convention on Human Rights, which states, 'The enjoyment of the rights and freedoms set forth in this Convention shall be secured without discrimination on any ground such as sex, race, colour, language, religion, political or other opinion, national or social origin, association with a national minority, property, birth or other status.'

22. *Leyla Sahin v. Turkey* (no. 44774/98) (November 19, 2002), and *Tekin v. Turkey* (no. 41556/98) (withdrawn).

23. *Dahlab v. Switzerland* (42393/98) (February 15, 2001), concerned a primary school teacher who was prohibited from wearing the headscarf. The court said that the authorities were allowed to determine that teachers cannot wear the headscarf while teaching in order to ensure 'the neutrality of the state primary education system.'

24. *Sen and Others v. Turkey* (45824/99) (July 8, 2003). The court spoke at length about the importance of Article 9 and religious pluralism but upheld the government's requirement that women remove their headscarves for ID card photos.

25. US District Court for the Eastern District of Oklahoma, Eyvine Hearn et al. Plaintiffs, *USA-Intervenor v. Muskogee Public School District.* CA No.: CIV 03–598-S.

26. Interview 12, Copenhagen (September 10, 2003).

27. *Diskrimination på arbejdsmarkedet. Sager siden 1996.* Published by Dokumentations- og rådgivningscenteret om racediskrimination (Copenhagen, 2003).

28. *The Times* (June 16, 2004).

29. *The Queen* (on the application of Shabina Begum through her litigation friend Mr. Sherwas Rahman) *v. Headteacher and Govenors of Denbigh High School,* 2004, EWHC 1389 (Admin), par. 82.

30. EWCA Civ 199 (March 2, 2005).

31. Interview 60, Stockholm (November 7, 2003).

32. Pola Manzila Uddin, 'Once, Muslims and Labour Were Natural Allies. Not Now,' *Guardian* (June 19, 2004). Available at: http://www.guardian.co.uk/comment/story/0,3604,1242461,00.html.

33. Interview 45, Stockholm (November 3, 2003).

34. Interview 36, London (March 3, 2004).

35. Wadud, op.cit., 98. The sura reads, 'Say to the believing man that they should lower their gaze and guard their modesty; that will make for greater purity for them; and Allah is well acquainted with all that they do. And say to the believing women that they should lower their gaze and guard their modesty; and that they should not display their beauty and ornaments except what must ordinarily appear thereof; that they should draw their veils over their bosoms and not display their beauty except to their husbands...' (Qur'an 24: 30–1.)

36. Jutta Limbach and Marion Eckertz-Höfer (eds.), *Frauenrechte im Grundgesetz des geeinten Deutschland* (Baden-Baden: Nomos, 1993).

37. Wadud, op.cit, ix.

38. From 'A letter to the Imams/Shayks. Participation of Women in the Eid Sermon.' Available at: http://www.ccmw.com/. The Council goes as far as to say that the doctrine that women cannot lead men in prayer derives from a forged interpretation. 'As for the *hadith* "Verily! The woman is not an Imam over men," it has been addressed by scholars before and refuted. The chain of transmission contains Abdullah ibn Muhammad al-Tamimi, who is considered unreliable and a forger of hadith. (Banna, al-Fath al-Rabbani, vol.5, 3:1375, 234.) This is why Muslims do not generally accept it.' The conclusion is doubtful, as it is widely accepted that a prohibition against female imams exist.

39. *Q-News* (June 2004, 19).

40. Interview 12, Copenhagen (September 10, 2003).

41. Bhikhu Parekh, *Rethinking Multiculturalism. Cultural Diversity and Political Theory* (Cambridge, MA: Harvard University Press, 2000), 275.

42. Associated Press, *International Herald Tribune* (October 23–4, 2004), 4.

43. Interview 30, London (October 15, 2003).

44. Interview 83, Lyon (May 24, 2004).

45. Interview 2, Copenhagen (September 4, 2003).

46. Interview 36, London (March 3, 2004).

47. Dr Abduljalil Sajid, 'Basic Information about Islam and Muslims,' Muslim Council for Religious and Racial Harmony.

48. *Dispute Resolution in Family Law: Protecting Choice, Promoting Inclusion.* December 2004. Executive Summary. Report prepared by Marion Boyd. I am grateful to Mohamed Alibhaim for bringing the controversy over the Arbitration Act to my attention. Available at: http://www.attorneygeneral.jus.gov.on.ca/english/about/pubs/boyd.

49. Initial Response to Marion Boyd's Report on the Arbitration Act. Canadian Council of Muslim Women. Available at: http://www.ccmw.com.

50. Personal conversation (July 23, 2004), Oxford.

51. Natasha Bakht, 'Family Arbitration Using Sharia Law: Examining Ontario's Arbitration Act and its Impact on Women,' *Muslim World Journal of Human Rights*, 1, 1 (2004), 15.

52. Susan Moeller Okin, in Joshua Cohen, Matthew Howard, and Martha C. Nussbaum (eds.), *Is Multiculturalism Bad for Women?* (Princeton, NJ: Princeton University Press, 1999).

53. In 1981, the Quebec government issued a position paper that clearly stated that cultural pluralism was acceptable only within the context of French-speaking society and the adoption of measures strengthening the French language—indeed, establishing its domination. The report, *Autant de Façons d'Être Québécois*, established the domination of the Québécois by distinguishing between French-Canadians, who were referred to as the members of the 'Québécois nation,' and other 'cultural communities.' The latter included the British-speaking residents, Greeks, Italians, etc., who were not defined as *Québécois*, even though they also are residents of Quebec. Cited from Danielle Juteau, Marie McAndrew, Linda Pietrantonio, 'Multiculturalism à la Canadian and Intégration à la Québécoise. Transcending their Limits,' in Rainer Bauböck and John Rundell (eds.), *Blurred Boundaries: Migration, Ethnicity, Citizenship* (Aldershot: Ashgate, 1998), 99

54. Will Kymlicka, *Liberalism, Community, and Culture* (Oxford: Clarendon Press, 1991), 182–205.

55. Important discussions of multicultural principles are Parekh, op.cit., and in addition to his previously cited book also Kymlicka, *Multicultural Citizenship: A Liberal Theory of Minority Rights* (Oxford: Oxford University Press, 1995) and *Politics in the Vernacular. Nationalism, Multiculturalism, and Citizenship* (Oxford: Oxford University Press, 2001).

56. Kymlicka, *Politics in the Vernacular*, 3.

57. http://www.constitution.org/cons/india/const.html.

58. Iris Marion Young, *Justice and the Politics of Difference* (Princeton, NJ: Princeton University Press, 1990).

59. Susanne Hoeber Rudolph and Lloyd I. Rudolph, 'Living With Difference in India,' in David Marquand and Ronald L. Nettler (eds.), *Religion and Democracy. The Political Quarterly* (Oxford: Blackwell, 2000), 20–38.

60. Arend Lijphart, a Dutch-American political scientist, has done much to popularize the system as a prescription for multicultural accommodation by developing a theory of what he calls 'consociationalism'. Arend Lijphart, *The Politics of Accommodation. Pluralism and Democracy in the Netherlands* (Berkeley: University of California Press, 1968).

61. Ruben Gowricharn and Pim Mungra, 'The Politics of Integration in the Netherlands,' in W. A. R. Shadid and P. S. van Koningsveld (eds.), *Muslims in the Margin. Political Responses to the Presence of Islam in Western Europe* (Kampen: Kok Pharos Publishing House, 1996), 116.

62. Thomas Risse, Stepehn C. Ropp, and Kathryn Sikkink (eds.), *The Power of Human Rights. International Norms and Domestic Change* (Cambridge: Cambridge University Press, 1999).

Conclusion: Liberal Muslims and the Emergence of European Islam

How committed are Europe's Muslim leaders to liberal values? At one level the answer is simple. Europe's Muslim leaders have embraced liberalism by engaging with the institutions of democracy. They invoke human rights to claim equality, or they appeal to the principles of humanist universalism to argue for the 'equal worth' of Christianity and Islam. Either way, they draw on varieties of liberalism.

Experts on Islam, from Mohammed Arkoun and Olivier Roy to Gilles Kepel, nevertheless warn that Islam's embrace of liberalism is insincere. The charge poses a challenge to the argument of this book. How can democracy seek accommodation with political or theological movements that do not genuinely believe in the rights and freedoms associated with liberal individualism? It is a familiar problem, which in the past has been posed in connection with the rights of communist and neo-Nazi parties and groups.

Olivier Roy is critical of Huntington's thesis because, he says, it conflates religion and culture. Roy argues that a 'post-Islamist' transformation is taking place, which has led to the development of a 'global Islam' focused on a new Muslim identity, an imagined de-territorialized pan-Islamic community, the ummah. The 'neo-fundamentalists' feign acculturation but in reality no serious reconsideration of basic doctrines has taken place. He describes the new groups as 'neo-brotherhoods' to underline the continuity between past and present Muslim associations, and concludes that a new sectarian discourse has emerged, which he likens to 'new age religiosity.' It adopts the language of multiculturalism, but exploits it to reject integration. He notes the possibility of an alliance between religious Christians and Muslims, but argues that it foreshadows the 'recommunitarianization' and disintegration of secular society. (Roy writes about 'Europe' but his arguments and evidence focus on France.) I have identified similar trends, but I suggest that the weakening of ancestral ethnic ties facilitates integration and that alliances with Christian churches are a path to the normalization of conflicts over Islam.

I have more fundamental disagreements with Roy. He sees no evidence of any serious rethinking of religious dogma among European Muslims. I am convinced, on the contrary, that a 'European Islam' is emerging based upon a new epistemology of faith and a new hermeneutics of textual interpretation. Roy identifies as the defining vision of the new Muslim associations the mythology of the ummah as the victim of Western aggression. Very few people whom I interviewed ever used the term, and those who did were primarily focused on building solidarity with the Palestinians. Muslims of Turkish origin never used it, nor did any of the Muslim parliamentarians and city councilors, or the imams and mosque council leaders I spoke with. Roy is right that the term has become a catch-word used for political purposes, but it is not the ubiquitous phenomenon he describes. His conclusions are based upon extensive reading of Islamic websites, mostly originating in the Gulf states, Saudi Arabia, and Pakistan. But as he notes, we have no information about who and how many people read those websites, nor how they are used.[1]

The Muslim leaders with whom I met expressed a variety of views on the proper relationship between Islam and the state, but with a few exceptions all were realists. Their common premise is that Islam is minority religion in Europe, and that Muslims must find their place within the framework of liberal democracy. However, it has to be said that Roy's description does fit a handful of leaders, whose expressed commitment to liberal values is a prag-matic, even a tactical choice. Among my informants, an imam in Denmark, a British association leader, a Swedish and a German mosque leader, all men and none associated with established political parties, saw free speech as an opportunity to pursue Islamic solidarity and, in one case, even as a means to bring about an Islamist transformation in Arab countries. But for the over-whelming majority of Muslim leaders, democracy was not a means but an end. Their views and policy preferences do not derive from faith or theology. They are the product of individual negotiation, choice, and contextual adaptation.

French criticisms of the deficient liberalism of Muslim leaders and intellectuals often boil down to accusations of 'communitarianism.' If I had asked the leaders in my study to choose their favorite political philosopher, which I did not, and if the leaders were inclined to political theory, which some were but most were not, I suspect that Michael Walzer would have received more votes than John Rawls. Rawls is often described as a 'contractarian liberal.' In *A Theory of Justice* (1971), his main book, he argued that individual rights are 'inviolable' in liberal democracies, and that no concessions can be made to accommodate group interests or the welfare of society in general. Walzer's argument for 'complex equality,' which he articulated in detail in *Spheres of Justice* (1983), is regarded as friendly to religious and other identity commu-nities. Walzer supports a degree of value relativism between communities but within a minimalist framework of value commitments. The latter he describes as a 'shared meaning,' but he also requires equality before the law.[2] Walzer's theory of 'complex justice' leaves room for some measure of 'multiculturalism,' and he is therefore often criticized for being insufficiently attuned to the value premises of French Republicanism and German constitutional 'patriotism.' But is Walzer less of a liberal than Rawls? I do not think so. Their differences are similar to those that divide French 'universalism' and Anglo-American 'small platoons' liberalism, but this is an argument that long predates controversies over the integration of Islam in the West.

The argument that the state must recognize the equal worth of different religions, and so must accept Muslims' right to respect and representation, engages Walzer's concept of 'complex equality.' It is based upon the view that government cannot, or should not, impose equality in all matters, but that all citizens in liberal societies are entitled to be treated with dignity and to be granted equal worth. In my conversations with Muslim leaders, the equal worth argument was often enunciated on transcendental grounds. Human beings therefore have equal rights 'under God.' Arkoun—and many other contemporary philosophers—regard this position as unsophisticated and insufficiently modernist, but it is a point of view that Muslims share with many Christians.

The divine origin of human rights was an eighteenth-century idea. It inspired the US Declaration of Independence and influenced the French Declaration of the Rights of Man. The revolutionary ancestor to today's French National Assembly 'recognized' and 'proclaimed' the rights of man and the citizen, 'in the presence and under the auspices of the Supreme Being.'[3] There are, to be sure, secular justifications of equal rights, but many people continue to think that Caesar cannot take away what God has given, and that is why states and public policy must observe certain values. The case against the death penalty, which many Europeans identify as a distinguishing feature that sets European 'civilization' apart from that of the USA, is invariably phrased as a question of 'higher' values.

It should therefore not be a surprise that some Muslim leaders support the insertion of references to 'fundamental values,' and even the explicit mentioning of 'Christian' values, in the EU's new constitution. They support it for the same reason that, under certain circumstances, they support the Christian Democratic parties, on the grounds that secularism alone cannot provide for moral government. Like many Christians, they argue that human rights and the right to dignity derive from the sacred nature of human beings.

Social Democrats and supporters of the Green parties were disinclined to base their argument for equality on the divine origins of mankind and spoke instead about legal and constitutional principles deriving from human rights. These arguments are, logically speaking, no less unsatisfactory than the equal worth argument based upon a view of a divine master plan.

Human rights are not self-executing legal norms. The translation of international human rights conventions into national law and practical policy invariably involves the negotiation of conflicting principles. The right to free religious expression, for example, comes into conflict with the right to express your sexual orientation without discrimination. If Muslims claim equal rights on the basis that all citizens are equal, irrespective of religion and any other cultural, demographic, or social characteristics, they will be required to tolerate homosexuality and treat women as the equals of men.

Kenan Malik, a British Muslim intellectual, argues that Muslims want nothing short of equality, 'not because it is a concept that "we Western liberals believe in," but because it is at the heart of any form of emancipatory politics.' Malik knows his principle cuts deep. 'Equality cannot be relative, with different meanings for different social, cultural or sexual groups.'[4] Many Muslim intellectuals and political leaders agree that the claim to equality necessarily implies that there must be changes also to European Islam and to Muslim lifestyles and family practices. They insist that change does not have to be legislated, and that it does not have to happen overnight, but they embrace the emancipatory process that Malik describes as representing a desirable and inevitable future. The transformation of European Islam may be a radical project in which religious practices and theological thinking adapt to reflect the changed sociological and legal circumstance of European Muslim lives.

European Muslim leaders are overwhelmingly secular in outlook and supportive of core liberal values about individual choice and the separation of religion and politics. Precisely because they hold to these beliefs they are angered and alienated when they conclude that European governments are not allowing Muslims the right to choose, a right that in other contexts these governments define as an essential democratic value.

What if the adoption of a rhetoric of equal rights or 'Abrahamic' interreligious cooperation are purely tactical moves? According to Gilles Kepel, organizations like the French UOIF signal a new and subversive strategy on the part of the Muslim Brotherhood, which he traces to its decision in 1989 to seek influence through a 'Trojan horse' tactic. Unlike the Wahhabis and other salafists, who remain dedicated to the dissemination of orthodox religious dogma, the Brotherhood saw the collapse of communism as an opportunity to mobilize Europe's underclass, now heavily Muslim, by rooting itself in civil society.

Keppel believes that the creation of Muslim associations that seek accommodation between Islam and the West through moderation is comparable to the Euro-communist strategy in the 1980s, when Europe's large communist parties sought power by renouncing Leninism and discarding ties to the Soviet Union.[5] Keppel claims that the new associations play the same role as the 'village headman' assumed for the British Raj, or the dupes whom the communist parties used to describe as 'the useful idiots,' or the 'front' organizations that were used to build up support for the Soviet Union.[6] He suggests that Tariq Ramadan exemplifies this strategy. 'There is the Ikhwan [the Muslim Brotherhood] represented through its various fronts, such as the UOIF,' explained Kepel in an interview with *Q-News*, a British Muslim magazine. 'Then there is the Tariq Ramadan phenomenon. Ramadan tried to create alliances with what remains of the extreme left and the antiglobalization movement, through the European Social Forum process. His ultimate aim was still a Muslim-Brotherhood-type ideology.'

Ramadan has been a popular speaker at the Forum, but it is difficult to imagine how he could possibly harness this unruly movement to a masterplan made up by the Brotherhood. The European Social Forum is an international traveling political circus that attracted over 20,000 participants to its 2004 meeting in the Millennium Dome in London. London's mayor, Ken Livingstone, who contributed £500,000 to the London Forum, was pressed to explain both why the meeting was too 'corporate' and 'mainstream,' and why it had been 'swamped' by the Socialist Workers' Party. The 'hosts' for the London meeting were the clerical workers union, UNISON, and four other unions, including the fire fighters' union.

Nevertheless, the analogy to Euro-communism is appropriate. The UOIF's various subsidiary organizations—the women's association (LFFM) and the student's association (EMF)—can fittingly be described as 'front organizations.' Their aim is to boost the organization's reach, and they have no real independent life outside the highly centralized UOIF leadership. But is the UOIF a creature of the Muslim Brotherhood? I doubt it.

Euro-communism was a generalized phenomenon, which affected the Italian, French, and Spanish communist parties. The UOIF and its subsidiary associations have no parallel in other European countries. If it does indeed reflect a Muslim Brotherhood masterplan, the plan has failed everywhere except, perhaps, in France. The UOIF's format resembles the 'popular front' models of political mobilization used in the past by the French Socialist and Communist parties and their associations, but it also takes advantage of the procedures established by the French government to obtain influence on the CFCM, the council established by the government.

The parallel with Euro-communism suggests other reflections. Euro-communism was a response to the growing alienation on the part of European communists from the Soviet Union. The Soviet leadership condemned Euro-communism as a defection, but the movement inspired Soviet dissidents and eventually paved the way for *glasnost*, Mikhail Gorbachev's reform initiative in 1985.

N.B.

A realist would argue that it does not matter *why* a group is accepting the rules of the game and asking for recognition and responsibilities. In politics, process matters more than motives. The fear of 'insincere' integration is misplaced. Integration is a social and not a moral fact. When Ramadan propagates a new Islamic theology it does not matter if his personal ambition is to strengthen Islam and to extend its reach. What matters is that European Islam is adapting to the values of individual liberalism and a democratic society. In politics, it is the consequences of and not the motives for action that matter. From the German Social Democrats in the 1880s to the Euro-communists in the 1980s, the decision to participate in democratic politics has always had transformative consequences for radical movements. If the Muslim Brotherhood now seeks influence through a strategy of integration into European societies, it too will be changed in the process. And the transformation of Islam in Europe may have repercussions in the Islamic countries.

According to Kepel, however, European (or rather French) Muslim associations either promote 'communalism', which undermines individual freedom, or suck young Muslims into the vortex of neo-salafist political movements in the suburbs. 'It is unsurprising,' concludes Kepel, 'that religious leaders should take advantage of their plight to advance their own agenda.'[7]

European debates revert to the same syllogism, again and again. If they have not abandoned their faith, Muslims are religious fundamentalists. Since choice is meaningless among fundamentalists, only victims or bullies are Muslim. Much of the discussion of choice focuses on coercion in the family, and of the family as the transmission belt of fundamentalism. The threat of violence in the family and in relationships is always present, but mechanisms exist to help young women and men to make meaningful choices about who they want to be. Parents no longer wield great authority in European families, and this applies also to immigrant families. Social workers are more inclined to complain about the lack of parental authority than its excess, and to note that since the children often have better language skills than their parents, the balance of power in the family is shifting in an unhealthy way. Education also breeds individualism and antiauthoritarianism. The reason that there is a demand for better educated and professionalized imams is that the imported imams are regarded with disdain and disrespect. And consequently the role of the imams has already changed from that of a charismatic interpreter or authority to a professional service provider. Forced marriages do take place, but many more marriages are love matches. And both often end in divorce. The rapid increase in one-parent families is one reason why religious leaders worry about fixing marriage practices among Muslims, and try to bridge the gap between religious and secular law. Kepel himself concludes optimistically that the next generation of European Muslims will reconcile Islam and modernity, once the doors to upward social mobility open. And indeed the European transformation of Islam is an irreversible sociological process.

Choice also has theological significance. European Muslims want a version of Islam that fits with their lifestyles. The stack of five hundred 'consumer surveys,' written in Danish, English, and Arabic, which a Danish-Moroccan imam handed me to show how he was in tune with his congregation, were a telling example of the existence of a religious market mechanism. In the case of Islam the significance of demand-side choice is reinforced by the absence of supply-side regulation. Believers go looking for a faith—or a version of their faith—that suits them. And money matters. The moderates are disadvantaged because they lack resources. The consequence is that the development of European Islam is too often in the hands of those who are willing to commit their lives to religious institution-building or who prefer to avoid public scrutiny. The development trajectory of European Islam lacks coherence because very little structure is supplied, except for what is imported from Islamic countries and political groups. There is a reason why the Internet plays such an important role in the dissemination of religious instruction. Start-up costs are low and it is a democratic means of communication. Anybody can make use of it.

But not all is as it appears. Just as the London mayor's office issued a report in January 2005 detailing the moderate qualifications of Sheikh Yousuf Al-Qaradawi, the controversial head of the European Council for Fatwa and Research declared in his Friday sermon on Qatar TV that the blame for the tsunami disaster fell on the victims for their toleration of sex tourism:

People must ask themselves why this earthquake occurred in this area and not in others. Why did it occur at this time and not another? Why? Whoever examines these areas discovers that they are tourism areas. Tourism areas are areas where the forbidden acts are widespread, as well as alcohol consumption, drug use, and acts of abomination. Whoever knows about tourism in our age knows this. These areas were notorious because of this type of modern tourism, which has become known as 'sex tourism.' [...] Don't they deserve punishment from Allah?

Al-Qaradawi is no more a moderate Muslim than Jerry Falwell is a moderate Christian. (Falwell had to retract comments he made after the 9/11 attacks, which blamed feminists, gays, and lesbians for bringing on the terrorist attacks in New York and Washington.[8]) The Qatar cleric undoubtedly has the support of many British Muslims, but many more people will defend his right to speak—and to meet with the mayor of London. The problem of interpretation arises because expressions of support for Al-Qaradawi's views are indicative of an antimodern—and arguably even antiliberal—worldview, but support for his right to speak (and for Livingstone's right to meet with him) is a quintessentially liberal free speech position. Clearly, Livingstone wanted to signal to Muslims that he 'heard their pain,' but one wishes he had been more discerning in his choice of issue. On the other hand, a pandering politician is a clear sign that Muslims are now voters like everyone else.

I have disputed the thesis that Europe is in the throes of a 'clash of civilizations.' Certainly there are strains and conflicts as states accommodate large numbers of Muslims, who are a relatively recent presence in Western Europe. However, the difficulty is not that Muslims are generally antidemocratic. The challenge is rather that they seek integration in European societies and claim a voice in European institutions, while insisting on equitable treatment for their communal organizations. This puts European governments on the spot. There can be religious pluralism only if European governments change existing church-state policies and public philosophies, and that generates controversy and political conflict. The established churches also face an unaccustomed challenge. Muslims want to include Islam under an umbrella of 'Abrahamic' faiths, and many Christians are inclined to resist.

It is misleading to see all this as a straightforward confrontation between Western governments and Muslim populations. There is a four-way conflict, with secular, and sometimes anticlerical, Christians and Muslims on the one side and, on the other side, religious Muslims and Christians. The growth of Islamic terrorism is incidental to the conflicts over the accommodation of Muslim religious practices in Europe, but it lends urgency to a problem that has been in the making for decades. European governments have the means to resolve these conflicts in a way that promotes integration, but only if they act together with a broad spectrum of Muslim representatives.

NOTES

1. Roy, op.cit., 7.
2. Michael Walzer, *Spheres of Justice* (New York: Basic Books, 1983).
3. The Declaration is available at http://www.hrcr.org/docs/frenchdec.html.
4. Kenan Malik, 'Race, Pluralism, and the Meaning of Difference,' *New Formations*, 33, Spring (1998).
5. Kepel, op.cit., 253.
6. 'The War for Muslim Minds,' interview with Giles Kepel by Abdul-Rehman Malik, *Q News* (January 2005, 42).
7. Kepel, op cit., 286.

8. According to CNN, Falwell described the attacks as God's judgment on America for 'throwing God out of the public square, out of the schools. The abortionists have got to bear some burden for this because God will not be mocked;' http://archives.cnn.com/2001/US/09/14/Falwell.apology.

Appendix: Methodology

CASE SELECTION

The majority of Europe's Muslims live in the six countries included in this study—Sweden, Denmark, the Netherlands, France, Germany, and Great Britain—but other reasons for studying these six are that they include countries with colonial ties to the resident Muslim populations (France, the Netherlands, and Britain) and countries without such ties (Germany, Sweden, and Denmark), and countries with a measure of historical religious pluralism (Britain and the Netherlands) and both Protestant and Catholic monoreligious countries (France, Sweden, and Denmark). The six also include countries with officially recognized or established religions (German, Denmark, and Britain) and countries without (Sweden, the Netherlands, and France).

The case selection does not discriminate, so to say, with respect to the system-specific variables, which loom large as potential explanations for why conflicts may arise over policy issues related to the integration of Islam and Muslims. If monoreligiosity is the cause of trouble so far as Muslims are concerned, the range of possible variation (Catholic versus Protestant domination, denominational pluralism vs. homogeneity) is represented in the case selection. If the timing of migration is critical, the cases include both recently settled communities (notably, in Sweden) as well as relatively long-established communities (as in Britain, Germany, and the Netherlands).

A study that aimed to describe the present conditions of Muslims in Europe would obviously need to include Eastern Europe, and would have to pay particular attention to Bosnian and Albanian Muslims. However, the purpose of this study is more restricted. The focus here is on the Muslim leaders who have joined mainstream Western European political organizations and institutions, and their views on the accommodation of Islam in Europe.

Italy and Spain, both large countries with substantial Muslim minorities, are not included in the study. Muslim migration to Spain and Italy is mostly recent and largely illegal. Spain has received about four million illegal immigrants in the last ten years. The government announced in February 2005 an amnesty designed to register and legalize illegal residents with steady employment. It is expected that around one million people will qualify. In Italy, the problems faced by Muslims are also closely related to the lack of legal status. For example, only an estimated 50,000 Italian Muslims can vote. These factors weighed against including the two countries in a study designed to describe the emerging Muslim elites in countries where Muslims are beginning to assert their democratic rights. Different methodologies would have been required to study the political objectives of population groups with no legal status and no formal rights.

Austria and Belgium each have about 500,000 Muslim residents, and both have set up government-recognized national councils, roughly similar to the French CFCM (although it should be noted that both countries have failed to implement fully the Council designs as planned). Norway has a small Muslim population, numbering about 100,000. The three countries would have added little to the comparative matrix of the study but weighed down the narrative structure of the book.

DEFINING 'MUSLIM'

The label 'Muslim' is used in this book to describe both demographic origin and faith. Some of the participants in the study accept the label in the former sense only, and describe themselves as 'secular Muslims.' Others see their faith as the critical source of their identity. A few of the participants in the study were converts.

A Muslim, or in the case of women, a Muslima, is a person who practices Islam. Islam is the name of the religion. Strict adherence to these definitions would make the label 'secular Muslim' a contradiction in terms. Introductions to Islam often begin by stating that the term describes only believers. 'You become a Muslim not by birth but by confession,' states one such primer.[1] Yet such are the real-life complexities of taxonomies that people readily accept that being Muslim is not just a matter of faith but also a sociological fact. We readily speak of being 'Jewish' or 'Catholic' in the same sense to connote heritage rather than belief.

Olivier Roy describes this usage of the label as the 'ethnicization' of Muslims as a social group in Western Europe. 'The term "Muslim" is often used in the West in what I call a neo-ethic sense,' writes Roy, and he gives as parallel examples the use of labels such as 'Maghrébins' in France and 'Asians' in Britain. 'Neo-ethnicity means the construction of an ethnic group, which previously did not exist as such,' he concludes.[2] The readiness of non-practicing Muslims to accept the description as 'Muslim' is, we may surmise, a reflection of the process of identity-formation described by Roy. However,

Roy's justification for adding 'neo' to 'ethnicity' is not persuasive. The constitution of a particular population group as a separate cultural group invariably takes place through a process of differentiation that is particular to a specific historical context. The sociological and cultural differentiation of European Muslims reflects the specific characteristics of both Muslim migration histories to the different countries and the European context. The script is familiar, even though the actors are new.

In practice, it proved unproblematic to use the label 'Muslim' to designate a cohort of political and civic leaders for special study. Public records, some available over the Internet, as in the case of directories of parliamentarians and city councilors, and publications by Muslim advocacy groups and councils listing their boards of directors, public spokespeople, and so on, were used to produce a comprehensive list of named individuals, who were contacted by phone, email, or fax. With the exception of British Asians, European naming conventions make it relatively easy to identify an individual's background. In the case of Muslim associations the faith identity of individuals contacted was not in question.

Biographical information is readily available for parliamentarians, and it was only in the case of local officials that doubts arose about a particular individual's faith. All participants were asked to indicate their faith, and the methodology produced less than a handful of Christians. A Palestinian and a Chilean Catholic, a Ugandan Protestant, and a Somali Coptic were all asked to participate in the study, and to comment on the situation facing Muslims as seen from their backgrounds as immigrants belonging to a minority religion. They represented, from a methodological viewpoint, control cases testing the idea that Muslims in particular are victimized. Interestingly, all thought that other immigrant religious minorities share the problems facing Muslims, while agreeing nevertheless that Muslims are particularly exposed to bias and that their problems were more intractable.

DEFINING 'ELITE'

Political elites, to use a traditional political science definition, are persons in authoritative positions. For the purpose of the present study, members of the political elite were identified as individuals in elected or appointed office in national or local governments, and in national, regional, or large city civic organizations ranging from political parties to secular councils for mosques and advocacy groups. The latter included both groups aiming to represent specific Muslim interests and groups with significant Muslim participation but aiming at more broadly defined activities. The British Muslim Council is an example of the former, while the advocacy group FAIR (Forum Against Islamophobia and Racism) is an example of the latter.

Why study the elite? Elite studies are a common theme in political science, although these often focus on established elites or, as in the case of labor unions and left parties, 'established' counter-elites.[3] However, studies of subaltern groups or minority groups rarely focus on the elite's role in shaping the claims and narratives that sustain representation. The literature on social movements has tended to focus on collective action and social change from 'below.'[4] Democratic transition is often studied through the lens of social movements, but there is no civil rights movement brewing among Europe's Muslims that we can study. There is, however, a new presence of national Muslim associations pressing for change and a small but increasing number of Muslims have joined mainstream political organizations. These leaders are shaping the strategies and perceptions of Muslim political identities. Democracies adapt in part by encapsulating and integrating new social groups and their political and civic leaders.[5] It is from this vantage point that new elites become the bridgeheads for compromise and adjustment, or alternatively for protest and confrontation.[6] The prospects for a future accommodation with Islam in Europe rest to a large extent on the ability of Muslim elites to obtain influence and to be recognized as representative voices when it comes to debates on policies having to do with the position of Islam and Muslims within national institutions.

FROM ORAL INTERVIEWS TO WRITTEN QUESTIONNAIRES

I decided to use both in-depth oral interviews following a flexible set of comparable but country-specific questions and written questionnaires with fixed and only marginally adjusted questions for all countries. The oral interviews were designed to uncover the narrative connections between basic propositions related to faith and social status as a Muslim leader—whether or not faith was personally important to the person being interviewed—and how these propositions shaped policy preferences. They also served to provide context and in-depth understanding of particular conflicts between Muslim political actors and with government policymakers.

The chief purpose of the written questionnaires was rather to establish some basic parameters for making comparisons, both across the six countries and between segments of the community of leaders and across key demographic and cultural data. One particular difficulty associated with multi-country polling is that questions that make sense in one country often make little sense in others. Comparison requires a measure of issue consistency across countries. This is not always the case. For instance, Sweden does not provide public funding for private schools, while Denmark and the Netherlands have few restrictions on such funding. In Germany, the controversy over discriminatory treatment of Muslims has focused on religious instruction in private schools, which is carried out (in most but not all German states) by local clergy from the different recognized faiths. Most questions were identical in all six countries, however, with the exception of questions related to schooling.

The quotes used in the book are from personal face-to-face interviews or excerpted from emails or other written communications received from participants in the study. The tables are based on a standard questionnaire distributed in all six countries. Oral interviews proceeded according to a script in my head but often involved large detours around issues and stories of particular interest. The written questions were phrased with fixed answer alternatives, but space was allowed for extended comments.

Oral interviews usually lasted about forty-five minutes, and some much longer. In France, the Netherlands, and Germany, I used a translator, when interviews could not be conducted in English. When the circumstances allowed it and I obtained permission, oral interviews were recorded and subsequently transcribed. A master list was maintained providing a numbered index to all interviews. Citations to oral interviews are provided giving the time and location of an interview, and a number that refers to the master list.

All questionnaires were translated into the national language and were accompanied by a cover letter describing the study and guaranteeing anonymity. They left ample room for write-in comments, and particularly in email communications many respondents added extensive personal commentaries.

The questionnaires were indexed similarly to the oral interviews, enabling cross-reference between the original address list of respondents and the assigned index number. This system of double-bookkeeping was a check against double submissions and double coding of questionnaires. The indexing protocol was also designed to comply with federal, state, and Brandeis University policies and procedures regarding research with human subjects.[7]

Response rates varied from one-third to two-thirds of all persons contacted in Sweden, Denmark, and the Netherlands, to 10–25 percent in the big countries. It is unknown how the variation in response rates affected the results, and indeed it is unknowable at this point in time because we have no basic parameters for determining the distribution of views between, say, secular and practicing Muslims, or male or female leaders. With a few exceptions, I personally met with all of the Muslim parliamentarians in the six countries in the study. I also spoke with the heads or an official spokesperson from most of the national Muslim associations.

Some essential personal statistics describing who participated in the questionnaire-based study are listed in Table A.1. The average age of the participants was forty to forty-two, except in France where I reached a much younger cohort. The ratio of women was generally low: around one-fifth of the participants were women in four of the six countries. France and Sweden were notably different from the others on this measure. In Denmark, Sweden, and Germany, one-third of the respondents were elected officials; in France, the Netherlands, and the UK there were many fewer. Aside from two recently elected Muslim senators, whom I interviewed, I identified very few French elected officials of Muslim origin in local government.

The education variables should be read with care, as I found it very difficult to define 'higher education' in a consistent fashion. There are significant national variations in the status of professional training programs for engineers, translators, and social workers. Political refugees were often put through training programs in these fields as part of their government-determined 'introduction programs.' Denmark's proclivity for retraining immigrants and political refugees in non-university degree programs may explain the curious mix of a high level of in-country retraining but comparatively low educational achievement of the leaders there.

The purpose of the present study is not to ascertain the distribution of attitudes across European Muslim leaders but rather to describe the attitudes themselves. I have tried to find out what the leaders regard as the key issues that confront Muslims in Western Europe, and what they think should be done about them. From this perspective, the methodology worked. There were, for example, a sufficient number of responses from anticlerical Muslims, a distinct minority, to allow me to describe the views of anticlericals in some detail. I am less confident that the range of opinions among women leaders

Table A.1. Characteristics of the participants in the study

	n	Women (%)	Average Age	Elected Office (%)	Higher Education (%)	Some education in country of residence (%)
Denmark	33	21.2	42	39.4	30.3	84.9
Sweden	22	31.8	40	31.8	45.5	77.2
France	19	52.6	34	5.3	68.4	78.9
Germany	47	14.9	41	29.8	63.0	78.7
Netherlands	23	17.4	40	4.3	50.0	52.1
UK	31	16.1	42	16.1	60.0	80.7

has been adequately established. All I can say is that a good number of Muslim women leaders are present at the highest rings of power but this is not the case in the community organizations and Muslim associations. It proved difficult to locate women to interview in these offices, despite extra effort.

Certain cross-national differences may reflect a change in my procedure. I asked Swedish and Danish parliamentarians to fill out the questionnaires as a supplement to my oral interviews, but I had to stop doing this, as it became clear that parliamentarians did not like to be asked to fill out forms. The collection of written data posed particular difficulties in France and Germany. In France the reluctance to participate led to a disappointingly low response rate, but not in Germany. When we engaged potential French respondents in a conversation about their disinclination to participate in the study, the arguments mostly centered on how the questionnaires might be used. Many referred to what they considered to be misrepresentation of their views by journalists or previous experiences with social scientists. But curiously the reluctance affected only the written questionnaires. It did not apply to oral interviews. There was also the problem that reporting religious affiliations is largely prohibited in France. The National Statistical Institute, INSEE, which is in charge of collecting the census, is legally prohibited from asking individuals about their religious affiliation. (Ironically, the office may ask people if they are religious, just not which religion they practice.) Nor may the government—or government funded research—ask people what their faith is. I may have skirted rules by not seeking official permission to ask questions about personal faith. The application of such rules are problematic when all the subjects of the study were, so to say, selected for inclusion because they are publicly identified as Muslims.

The national origin of the participants in the study is tabulated in Table A.2. The participants in the study were extraordinarily diverse with respect to origin.

National origin occasionally mattered in the sense that certain consistent differences of opinion correlated with the respondents' national origin. This applied to questions about the implementation of shariah law, which Turkish-origin Muslims consistently opposed but large numbers of British Muslims of Pakistani and Bangladeshi origin thought a good idea. With this exception, and a few more, the surprise was how little national origin mattered.

EXPLAINING CONFLICTS OVER ISLAM IN EUROPE

Two studies of Muslims in Europe were published just as I completed work on this book. Both focused on the countries studied here and tried to account for

The Islamic Challenge

Table A.2. National origin of respondents

	Denmark	Sweden	France	Germany	Netherlands	UK	Total
Native-born	4	1	10	12	6	5	38
Turkey	15	8	2	27	10	0	62
Bosnia	1	1	0	2	0	0	4
Morocco	3	0	5	1	4	0	13
Algeria	1	0	0	0	0	0	1
Tunisia	0	1	2	2	0	0	5
Pakistan	2	0	0	0	0	12	14
India	0	0	0	0	2	4	6
Bangladesh	0	0	0	0	0	8	8
Middle East	3	7	0	1	0	1	12
Other	3	3	0	0	0	1	7
Total	32	21	19	45	22	31	170

the resistance to the accommodation of Islam. Jocelyne Cesari argues that the legal architectures of Europe fail to live up to the standard for religious toleration and public neutrality set by the USA and calls for constitutional changes emulating the First Amendment of the US Constitution.

Joel Fetzer and Christopher Soper conclude that the French, German, and British governments have shaped policies for accommodating Muslims in the image of preexisting policies for religious accommodation. Europeans are Christians, they say, and have reacted to the introduction of Islam by assimilating Islam into existing templates for the Christian denominations.[8] The methodology and focus of the two books differ (from each other and from this book) but their explanations for current conflicts are mutually congruent, and they are generally supported by the present study. Still, my research does not fully corroborate either view.

Europeans are unlikely to embrace a strict separation of faith organizations and public policy, as proscribed by the First Amendment and advocated by Cesari. European states are deeply involved in subsidizing civil society, and a general sense that sectarianism must be curbed prevails. European Muslims are also Europeans and a majority shares these expectations. And, while preexisting institutional frameworks are obviously important in shaping the conflicts over adjustments needed to accommodate Muslims, it is nevertheless clear that striking similarities exist across the countries discussed in this book which are not immediately accounted for by what is often referred to in the political science literature as 'national incorporation' regimes.[9] The fact that Muslims who wish to be buried according to religious rules' cannot be accommodated in cemeteries in Protestant Denmark and in Catholic France for the reason that these are municipal properties administered by parish councils suggests a degree of commonality that this approach fails to capture.

NOTES

1. Ira G. Zepp, Jr., *A Muslim Primer: Beginner's Guide to Islam* (Fayettesville University of Arkansas Press, 2000), xxxv.
2. Olivier Roy, *Globalized Islam. The Search for a New Ummah* (New York: Columbia University Press, 2004), 125.
3. Examples include the Danish and Norwegian 'power reports,' which were sponsored by the national parliaments. Both 'reports' consisted of multiple but coordinated and specialized studies of elites in the media, the political parties, and business, and of the patterns of participation among women and ethnic minorities. A review of both studies can be found in *Scandinavian Political Studies*, 27 (2004) 4: 423–7. For an example of a study of working-class elite integration, see Ruth Berins Collier, *Paths Toward Democracy: The Working Class and Elites in Western Europe and South America* (New York: Cambridge University Press, 1999).
4. Doug McAdam, Sidney Tarrow, and Charles Tilly, *Dynamics of Contention* (New York: Cambridge University Press, 2001).
5. Juan J. Linz and Alfred C. Stepan, *Problems of Democratic Transition and Consolidation: Southern Europe, South America, and Post-Communist Europe* (Baltimore, MD: Johns Hopkins University Press, 1996).
6. For a survey of the literature, see John Higley and Michael G. Burton, 'The Elite Variable in Democratic Transitions and Breakdowns,' *American Sociological Review*, 54 (1989) 1: 17–32.
7. The research for this book was conducted following a protocol approved by the Brandeis University Committee for Protection of Human Subjects.
8. Jocelyne Cesari, *When Islam and Democracy Meet: Muslims in Europe and in the USA* (New York: Palgrave Macmillan, 2004); and Joel S. Fetzer and J. Christopher Soper, *Muslims and the State in Britain, France, and Germany* (New York: Cambridge University Press, 2004).
9. Adrian Favell, *Philosophies of Integration: Immigration and the Idea of Citizenship in France and Britain* (New York: Palgrave, 2001).

Bibliography

Al-Azmed, Aziz (1993). *Islam and Modernities*. London: Verso.

Aldeeb Abu-Sahlieh, Sami A. (1996). 'The Islamic Conception of Migration,' *International Migration Review*, 30(1) (Spring): 37–57.

Alesina, Alberto, and Edward L. Glaeser (2004). *Fighting Poverty in the US and Europe: A World of Difference*. Oxford: Oxford University Press.

Alibhai, Mohamed (2002). 'Islam: Faith or Religion? The Re-education of the Modern Imam,' *Minaret*, 24(9): 24–32.

Arkoun, Mohammed (1994). *Rethinking Islam. Common Questions. Uncommon Answers*. Boulder, CO: Westview Press.

Alvarez, Michael R., and Tara Butterfield (2000). 'The Resurgence of Nativism in California? The Case of Proposition 187 and Illegal Immigration,' *Social Science Quarterly*, 81(1): 167–79.

Bakht, Natasha (2004). 'Family Arbitration Using Sharia Law: Examining Ontario's Arbitration Act and its Impact on Women,' *Muslim World Journal of Human Rights*, 1:1.

Ballard, Roger (1994). *Desh Pradesh: The South Asian Presence in Britain*. London: Hurst.

Baumann, Gerd (1996). *Contesting Culture: Discourses of Identity in Multi-Ethnic London*. Cambridge: Cambridge University Press.

Bowen, John R. (2002). 'Islam in/of France: Dilemmas of Translocality.' Paper presented at the 13th International Conference of Europeanists, Chicago, March 14–16.

—— (2004). 'Does French Islam Have Borders? Dilemmas of Domestication in a Global Religious Field,' *American Anthropologist*, 106(4): 43–55.

—— (2004). 'Muslims and Citizens. France's Headscarf Controversy,' *Boston Review* (February–March): 31–5.

Brubaker, Rogers (2001). 'The Return of Assimilation? Changing Perspectives on Immigration and Its Sequels in France, Germany, and the United States,' *Ethnic and Racial Studies*, 24(4) (July): 531–48.

Cesari, Jocelyne (2004). *When Islam and Democracy Meet: Muslims in Europe and in the United States*. New York: Palgrave Macmillan.

Cohen, Stanley (1972). *Folk Devils and Moral Panics. The Creation of the Mods and Rockers*. London: McGibbon and Kee.

Collier, Ruth Berins (1999). *Paths Toward Democracy: The Working Class and Elites in Western Europe and South America*. New York: Cambridge University Press.

Dalrymple, William (2004). 'The Truth About Muslims,' *New York Review of Books* (November 4): 31–4.

Davidman, Lynn (1991). *Tradition in a Rootless World: Women Turn to Orthodox Judaism*. Berkeley University of California Press.

Diskrimination på arbejdsmarkedet. Sager siden 1996 (2003). Published by Dokumen-tations-og rådgivningscenteret om racediskrimination, Copenhagen.

Dogan, Mattei (2002). 'Accelerated Decline of Religious Belief in Europe,' *Comparative Sociology*, 1(2): 127–49.

Dokumentation. Frühjahrsumfrage: Neue Daten und Fakten über den Islam in Deutsch-land (2002). Nr. 1/ 2004 15. Zentralinstitut Islam-Archiv-Deutschald. Soest-Deir-ingsen, May.

Dworkin, Ronald (1985). *A Matter of Principle*. Cambridge, MA: Harvard University Press.

Eickelman, Dale F., and James Piscatori (1996). *Muslim Politics*. Princeton, NJ: Princeton University Press.

Fetzer, Joel S., and J. Christopher Soper (2003). 'The Roots of Public Attitudes Towards State Accommodation of European Muslims' Religious Practices Before and After September 11,' *Journal for the Scientific Study of Religion*, 42(2): 247–88.

—— —— (2004). *Muslims and the State in Britain, France, and Germany*. New York: Cambridge University Press.

Gaspard, Françoise, and Farhad Khosrokhavar (1995). *Le Foulard et la République*. Paris: Découverte.

Gerstle, Gary (1997). 'Liberty, Coercion, and the Making of Americans,' *Journal of American History*, 84(2): 524–58.

Gleason, Philip (1964). 'The Melting Pot: Symbol of Fusion or Confusion?' *American Quarterly*, 16(1): 20–46.

Glendon, Mary Ann (2001). *A World Made New: Eleanor Roosevelt and the Universal Declaration of Human Rights*. New York: Random House.

Golden, Claudia (1994). 'The Political Economy of Immigration Restriction: The United States, 1890–921,' in Claudia Goldin and Gary D. Libecap (eds.), *The Regulated Economy: A Historical Analysis of Government and the Economy*. Chicago: University of Chicago Press.

Golder, Matt (2003). 'Explaining Variation in the Success of Extreme Right Parties in Western Europe,' *Comparative Political Studies*, 36(4): 432–66.

Goldberg, Andreas, and Martina Sauer (2003). *Konstanz und Wandel der Lebensitua-tion türkishstämmiger Migranten in Nordrhein-Westfalen*. Essen: Zentrum für Tur-keistudien.

Gowricharn, Ruben, and Pim Mungra (1996). 'The Politics of Integration in the Netherlands,' in W. A. R. Shadid and P. S. van Koningsveld (eds.), *Muslims in the Margin. Political Responses to the Presence of Islam in Western Europe*. Kampen: Kok Pharos Publishing House.

Guiraudon, Virginie (2000). 'The Marshallian Triptych Reordered: The Role of Courts and Bureaucracies in Furthering Migrants' Social Rights,' in Michael Bommes and

Andrew Geddes (eds.), *Immigration and Welfare: Challenging the Borders of the Welfare State*. London: Routledge.

Gullestad, Marianne (2002). 'Invisible Fences: Egalitarianism, Nationalism, and Racism,' *Journal of the Royal Anthropological Institute*, 8(1): 45–63.

Gustafsson, Göran, (2003). 'Church-State Separation Swedish-Style,' *Special Issue on Church and State in Contemporary Europe: The Chimera of Neutrality*, John T.S. Madeley and Zsolt Enyedi (eds.), *West European Politics*, 26(1): 51–72.

Haddad, Yvonne Yazbeck (1999). 'The Globalization of Islam: The Return of Muslims to the West,' in John L. Esposito (ed.), *The Oxford History of Islam*. Oxford: Oxford University Press.

—— and John L. Esposito (eds.) (2002). *Muslims on the Americanization Path?* New York: Oxford University Press.

Hatton, Timothy J., and Jeffrey G. Williamson (1998). *The Age of Mass Migration: An Economic Analysis*. New York: Oxford University Press.

Higley, John, and Michael G. Burton (1989). 'The Elite Variable in Democratic Transitions and Breakdowns,' *American Sociological Review*, 54(1): 17–32.

Hollinger, David (1995). *Postethnic America: Beyond Multiculturalism*. New York: Basic Books.

Huntington, Samuel P. (1993). 'The Clash of Civilizations?' *Foreign Affairs*, 72(3): 22–8.

—— (1996). *The Clash of Civilizations and the Remaking of World Order*. New York: Simon and Schuster.

—— (2004). *Who Are We? The Challenges to America's National Identity*. New York: Simon and Schuster.

Jackson, Vicky C., and Mark Tushnet (1999). *Comparative Constitutional Law*. New York: Foundation Press.

Joffe, Jospeh (1997). 'Germany vs. the Scientologists,' *New York Review of Books*, April 24, 16–21.

Juteau, Danielle, Marie McAndrew, and Linda Pietrantonio (1998). 'Multiculturalism à la Canadian and Intégration à la Québécoise. Transcending their Limits,' in Rainer Bauböck and John Rundell (eds.), *Blurred Boundaries: Migration, Ethnicity, Citizenship*. Aldershot: Ashgate.

Kaya, Ayhan, and Ferhat Kentel (2004). 'Euro-Turks: A Bridge or a Breach between Turkey and the European Union?' Research Report, Center for Migration Research, Istanbul Bilgi University, September.

Kaufman, Debra R. (1991). *Rachel's Daughters: Newly Orthodox Jewish Women*. New Brunswick, NJ: Rutgers University Press.

Kepel, Gilles (1987). *Les Banlieues de l'Islam: Naissance d'une Religion en France*. Paris: Seuil.

—— (2004). *The War for Muslim Minds. Islam and the West*. Cambridge, MA: Harvard University Press.

Knigge, Pia (1998). 'The Ecological Correlates of Right-Wing Extremism in Western Europe,' *European Journal of Political Research*, 34(2): 249–79.

Kumar, Krishan (2002). 'The Nation-State, the European Union, and Transnational Identities,' in Nezar Al-Sayyad and Manuel Castells (eds.), *Muslim Europe or Euro-Islam. Politics, Culture, and Citizenship in the Age of Globalization.* Lanham, MD: Lexington Books.

Kymlicka, Will (1991). *Liberalism, Community, and Culture.* Oxford: Clarendon Press.

—— (1995). *Multicultural Citizenship: A Liberal Theory of Minority Rights.* Oxford: Oxford University Press.

—— (2001). *Politics in the Vernacular: Nationalism, Multiculturalism, and Citizenship.* Oxford: Oxford University Press.

Lambert, Yves (2004). 'A Turning Point in Religious Evolution in Europe,' *Journal of Contemporary Religion,* 19(1): 29–45.

Lamont, Michele (2000). *The Dignity of Working Men: Morality and the Boundaries of Race, Class, and Immigration.* Princeton, NJ: Princeton University Press.

Lewis, Bernard (1993). *Islam and the West.* New York: Oxford University Press.

Lijphart, Arend (1968). *The Politics of Accommodation. Pluralism and Democracy in the Netherlands.* Berkeley University of California Press.

Limbach, Jutta, and Marion Eckertz-Höfer (eds.) (1993). *Frauenrechte im Grundgesetz des geeinten Deutschland.* Baden-Baden: Nomos.

Linz, Juan J., and Alfred C. Stepan (1996). *Problems of Democratic Transition and Consolidation: Southern Europe, South America, and Post-Communist Europe.* Baltimore, MA: Johns Hopkins University Press.

Lubbers, Marcel, and Peer Scheepers (2001). 'Explaining the Trend in Extreme Right-Wing Voting: Germany 1989–98,' *European Sociological Review,* 17(4): 431–49.

Malik, Kenan (1998). 'Race, Pluralism, and the Meaning of Difference,' *New Formations,* 33 (Spring).

Mann, Michael (1988). *States, War, and Capitalism: Studies in Political Sociology.* New York and Oxford: Basil Blackwell.

McAdam, Doug, Sidney Tarrow, and Charles Tilly (2001). *Dynamics of Contention.* New York: Cambridge University Press.

Modood, Tariq and Fauzia Ahmad. 'British Muslim Perspectives on Multiculturalism,' *Theory, Culture, and Society.* Forthcoming.

Mohammad-Arif, Aminah. 'Young South Asian Muslim Identity in the US.' Unpublished paper (no date).

Morone, James A. (2003). *Hellfire Nation: The Politics of Sin in American History.* New Haven, CT: Yale University Press.

Myrdal, Alva R. (1941). *Nation and Family: The Swedish Experiment in Democratic Family and Population Policy.* New York: Harper.

Myrdal, Gunnar (1960). *Beyond the Welfare State: Economic Planning and Its International Implications.* New Haven, CT: Yale University Press.

Nieuwenhuizen, Eddie. 'Political Participation of Migrants in the Netherlands,' Research Report, Landelijk Bureau ter bestriding van Rassendscriminatie (no date.)

Nimer, Mohamed (2002). *The North American Muslim Resource Guide: Muslim Community Life in the United States and Canada.* New York: Routledge.

Okin, Susan Moeller, in Joshua Cohen, Matthew Howard, and Martha C. Nussbaum (eds.) (1999). *Is Multiculturalism Bad for Women?* Princeton, NJ: Princeton University Press.

Panafit, Lionel (2000). 'First for Islam in Belgium,' *Le Monde Diplomatique*, June.

Parekh, Bhikhu (2000). *Rethinking Multiculturalism. Cultural Diversity and Political Theory.* Cambridge, MA: Harvard University Press.

Rae, Heather (2002). *State Identities and the Homogenization of Peoples.* New York: Cambridge University Press.

Ramadan, Tariq (1998). *To Be a European Muslim.* Leicester Islamic Foundation.

—— (2004). *Western Muslims and the Future of Islam.* New York: Oxford University Press.

Rath, Jan, Rinus Pennix, Kees Groenendijk, and Astrid Meyer (2001). *Western Europe and Its Islam.* Leiden: Brill.

Rex, John, Daniele Joly, and Czarina Wilpert (1987). *Immigrant Associations in Europe.* Aldershot: Grover.

Risse, Thomas, Stephen C. Ropp, and Kathryn Sikkink (eds.) (1999). *The Power of Human Rights: International Norms and Domestic Change.* Cambridge: Cambridge University Press.

Roy, Olivier (1994). *The Failure of Political Islam.* Cambridge, MA: Harvard University Press.

—— (2005). *Globalized Islam. The Search for a New Umma.* New York: Columbia University Press.

Rudolph, Susanne Hoeber and Lloyd I. Rudolph (2000), 'Living With Difference in India,' in David Marquand and Ronald L. Nettler (eds.) (2000). *Religion and Democracy: The Political Quarterly.* Oxford: Blackwell.

Rushdie, Salman (1989). 'The Book Burning,' *New York Review of Books*, 36(3): (March 2).

Sauer, Martin, and Andreas Goldberg (2001). *Die Lebenssituation und Partizipation türkischer Migranten in Nordrhein-Westfalen.* Hamburg, Zentrum für Türkeistudien: Lit Verlag.

Seidentop, Larry (2001). *Democracy in Europe.* New York: Columbia University Press.

Sniderman, Paul M., Louk Hagendoorn, and Markus Prior (2004). 'Predisposing Factors and Situational Triggers: Exclusionary Reactions to Immigrant Minorities,' *American Political Science Review*, 98(1): 35–49.

Soysal, Yasemin Nuhoglu (1994). *Limits of Citizenship: Migrants and Postnational Membership in Europe.* Chicago, University of Chicago Press.

Spuler-Stegeman, Ursula (2002). *Muslime in Deutschland, Informationen und Klärungen.* Friburg: Herder Spectrum.

Sørensen, Aage B. (1998). 'On Kings, Pietism and Rent-Seeking in Scandinavian Welfare States,' *Acta Sociologica*, 41(2): 363–75.

Timmer, Asheley S., and Jeffrey G. Williamson (1996). 'Racism, Xenophobia, or Markets? The Political Economy of Immigration Policy Prior to the Thirties,' National Bureau of Economic Research, Working Paper 5867 (December), Cambridge, MA.

Togeby, Lise (1999). 'Migrants at the Polls: An Analysis of Immigrant and Refugee Participation in Danish Local Elections,' *Journal of Ethnic and Migration Studies*, 25(4): 665–84.

Tribalat, Michèle (1996). *De l'Immigration à l'Assimilation: Enquête sur les Populations d'Origine Étrangère en France*. Paris: Editions La Découverte: INED.

Vertovec, Steven (1999). 'Conceiving and Researching Transnationalism,' *Ethnic and Racial Studies*, 22(2): 447–62.

Wadud, Amina (1999). *Qur'an and Woman Rereading the Sacred Text from a Woman's Perspective*. New York: Oxford University Press.

Walzer, Michael (1983). *Spheres of Justice*. New York: Basic Books.

Weil, Patrick (2004). 'Lifting the Veil of Ignorance,' *Progressive Politics*, 3 (March 1).

Werbner, Pnina (2002). *Imagined Diasporas Among Manchester Muslims*. Oxford: James Currey.

Wellisch, Dietmar and Uwe Walz (1998). 'Why Do Rich Countries Prefer Free Trade Over Free Migration? The Role of the Modern Welfare State,' *European Economic Review*, 42(2): 1595–612.

Zepp, Ira G. Jr. (2000). *A Muslim Primer: Beginner's Guide to Islam*. Fayettesville: University of Arkansas Press.

Zolberg, Aristide R., and Long Litt Woon (1999). 'Why Islam Is Like Spanish: Cultural Incorporation in Europe and the United States,' *Politics and Society*, 27(1): 5–38.

Young, Iris Marion (1990). *Justice and the Politics of Difference*. Princeton, NJ: Princeton University Press.

Government Sources

European Union. *Charter of Fundamental Rights of the European Union*, Official Journal of the European Communities, 18.12.2000/En/C364/01.

European Union. *The Spiritual and Cultural Dimension of Europe*, Reflection group initiated by the President of the European Commission and Coordinated by the Institute for Human Sciences. Vienna/Brussels, October 2004.

France. Haut Conseil a L'Integration, *L'Islam dans la République* (Paris, November 2000).

France. Assemblée Nationale. *Rapport Fait sur la Question du Port des Signes Religieux à l'Ecole*. Tome II, 1ère partie. Auditions. 11 juin 2003.

France. Commission de Réflexion sur l'Application du Principe de Laïcité dans la République. *Rapport au Président de la République*. Remis le 11 décembre 2003.

Germany. Deutsche Bundestag. *Antwort der Bundesregierung auf die Grosse Anfrage der Abgeordneten Dr. Jürgen Rüttgers, Erwin Marschewski, Wolfgang Zeitlmann, weiterer Abgeordneter und der Fraktion der CDU/CSU*. Drucksache 14/2301. 08.11.2000.

Germany. Ausschuss für Schule, Jugend und Sport. Ständiger Ausschuss. Freitag, 12. März, 2004. Struttgart. Haus des Landtags. Drucksache 13/2793, 110–18.

The Netherlands. *Moslim in Nederland. Een onderzoek naar de religieuze betrokkenheid van Turken en Marokkanen.* Samenvatting SCP-onderzoeksrapport 2004/9.

United Kingdom Home Office Research Study 220. *Religious discrimination in England and Wales.* Home Office Research, Development and Statistics Directorate. February 2001.

United Kingdom. *White Paper, The House of Lords: Completing the Reform.* Cmnd. 5291. November 2001.

United Kingdom. *Focus on Religion.* Census 2001, Office for National Statistics: http://www.statistics.gov.uk/focuson/religion.

Index

Page references followed by *t* indicate a table; followed by *fig* indicate an illustrated figure.

French Declaration of the Rights of Man, 176, 206
French Muslim associations
  CCMTF (Comité de Coordination des Musulmans Turcs de France), 38
  CFCM (Conseil Français du Culte Musulman), 36, 39–40, 47–8, 116, 175
  FIOE (Federation of Islamic Organizations in Europe), 37, 38
  FNMF (La Fédération Nationale des Musulmans de France), 37, 38
  French laws governing activities of, 144–5
  Grand Mosque, 38–9
  Union des Jeunes Musulmans, 77
  UOIF (Union des Organisations Islamiques de France), 36–7, 39, 44, 207, 208
French Socialists, 25, 26–7
fundamentalism
  found in all religions, 148
  headscarf perceived as symbol of, 175–6, 186
  lack of choice under, 209
Fürst, Bishop Gebhard, 153

Gadard, Barnard, 116
Gallup International Millennium Survey, 139
gay rights, 73–4
German Basic Law
  headscarf ban arguments using the, 177, 179
  Lundin decision and, 179
  naturalization and commitment to, 21
  protection of animals under, 118–19
  regarding state-Church relations, 144
  on state religious neutrality, 31, 152
German Christian Democratic Party (CDU), 10
German Muslim associations
  DITIB of, 30, 31, 32, 33
  Hamburg Schura, 33

IFB (Islamische Föderation Berlin), 33, 44
IZA (Islamische Zentrum Aachen-Bilal Moschee), 32
Milli Görüs, 31, 32, 43–4
VIKZ (Verband Islamischer Kulturzentren) of, 32
ZMD (Zentralrat der Muslime in Deutschland) of, 31–2, 44, 118, 153
Germany
  Alevites (Turkish-origin) in, 33
  animal protection act (1972) of, 118
  anti-Muslim discrimination sources in, 58, 59*t*, 60, 63
  asylum granted by, 68
  changing naturalization rules in, 21–2
  DVU (Die Deutsche Volksunion) party of, 60, 123
  estimates of illegal population in, 6
  foreign imams regulation in, 114
  foreign worker recruitment by, 28
  Green Party of, 23, 24, 25, 123
  headscarf ban in, 152–3, 171, 177–9
  integration of Islam policy choice in, 94–6*t*, 95*t*
  Kulturkampf (culture war) [1871–1891] in, 130
  legal definition of religion in, 165
  Ludin decision on state-religion relations, 177–9
  Milli Görüs blacklisted by government of, 43–4
  mixed signals coming out of, 2
  Muslim membership in political parties of, 26
  Muslim population citizenship in, 21
  Muslim priorities and preferences for policy policies, 64, 65*t*, 66, 67*t*, 68
  Muslim religious observance study in, 140

248 *Index*